The
Saatchi & Saatchi
Story

Philip Kleinman helped to start *Campaign*, the trade journal
of the advertising industry, and won a place in the 1982
British Press Awards for his *Guardian* articles on advertising,
marketing and media. He is the author of *Advertising Inside
Out* (1977) and *Market Research – Head Counting Becomes
Big Business* (1985), and has been editor since 1983 of the
illustrated annual *World Advertising Review* and since
December 1988 of the monthly newsletter *Marketing
Advantage*.

Philip Kleinman

The Saatchi & Saatchi Story

Pan Books
London, Sydney and Auckland

First published 1987 by George Weidenfeld & Nicolson Limited
This edition published 1989 by Pan Books Limited
Cavaye Place, London SW10 9PG

9 8 7 6 5 4 3 2 1

Copyright © Philip Kleinman 1987 and 1989

ISBN 0 330 30689 8

Printed and bound in Great Britain by
Richard Clay Ltd, Bungay, Suffolk

Contents

Illustration Acknowledgements		vii
Preface		ix
1	Before the Beginning	1
2	In the Beginning	11
3	Better with the Conservatives	27
4	The Takeover Trail	36
5	Friends Fall Out	56
6	Top of the Heap	65
7	The Backlash	75
8	The Global Market	84
9	Coping with Conflict	106
10	New Horizons	114
11	Rivals and Imitators	127
12	The Collector	148
13	Money Matters	155
14	Which Way Now?	162
Epilogue		171
Select Bibliography		179
Index		181

Illustration Acknowledgements

The photographs in this book are reproduced by kind permission of the following:

Camera Press (photographer Jane Brown, *The Observer*) 3 below; Conservative Party Central Office 3 above; *The Daily Telegraph* Colour Library (photographer Terry O'Neill) 6, 7; *The Financial Times* 8 below; Image (photographer Robin Laurance) 5; The Press Association (courtesy of the Health Education Authority) 2; Rex Features 4.

Preface

The Conservative Government's victory in the British General Election of June 1987 focused attention once more on a company which in the British public mind is closely linked with that Government even though its main activities have nothing to do with politics. Saatchi & Saatchi, a name practically unknown outside the advertising profession ten years ago, became a household word as a result of the company's advertising work for the Conservatives, beginning before the 1979 election which brought Mrs Thatcher to power.

However, despite the fact that everyone has heard of the Saatchi brothers – Charles and Maurice – very few people, even in advertising, know much about them. Among the general public little is known even about what their company does other than help Mrs Thatcher win elections. It is assumed that Saatchi & Saatchi is the name of an advertising agency. Strictly speaking it is not. True, when the brothers started their company in 1970, as young men in their twenties, it was an ad agency – a small one – and Saatchi & Saatchi was its name. By the time they began work for Mrs Thatcher the name was that of a holding company, even though its main property was indeed one particular ad agency, now a large one, also known, though inaccurately and confusingly, as Saatchi & Saatchi.

In the eight years that followed Mrs Thatcher's first victory the Saatchi company also went from victory to victory, buying up advertising agencies across the world to become the biggest of its kind. It also moved into other business areas, so that the Saatchi & Saatchi name now covers not merely one ad agency or even many agencies but a business services conglomerate drawing the major part of its revenues from overseas.

The story of the company's rise from obscurity to international fame in a few short years is both complex and fascinating. It is not a story of unmixed brilliance and success. Human affairs are not like that. It does not detract from the brothers' quite remarkable achievement to point out that they have had their ups and downs, that their company has its strengths and weaknesses and that luck has played an important role in the story, as they themselves acknowledge.

There was a time when Saatchi & Saatchi was the darling of the London Stock Exchange and very little critical comment on the company's affairs ever saw the light of day. That changed in 1986 as the company grappled with the severe problems thrown up by the sheer scale of its American acquisitions and as expectations of its future financial growth were scaled down. That they should be scaled down was inevitable. No company can go on growing at a compound rate of 30% a year for ever. Financial analysts now look to Saatchi for a growth rate of between 15% and 20%.

Some of the flak came from commentators who in the past had allowed themselves to be perhaps too uncritical and were now making up for it. There was more *schadenfreude* to be had in June 1987 when reports surfaced in the press of discord in the Conservative Party camp about the effectiveness or otherwise of Saatchi election advertising, which by common consent had been less impressive than on previous occasions, though this may have had more to do with the improved advertising performance of the Labour Party and its advisers than with any decline on the Saatchi side.

Norman Tebbit, the Conservative Party chairman, defended the company and suggested that some of the rumours about its alleged failings during the election had been inspired by its competitors who were envious of its international success. Whatever really went on behind closed doors at Conservative Central Office, though, the most important thing about the 1987 election was, for Saatchi & Saatchi as for the rest of the country, that the Tories won. The company's fortunes had been identified with those of Mrs Thatcher's party for so long that an electoral failure by the latter would have been seen as a sinister omen for the Saatchis.

In the commercial world, as in the political, nothing succeeds like success. There is no evidence that the universally praised Saatchi election advertising of 1979 was what tipped the votes Mrs Thatcher's way, and the influence of advertising on the outcome of the 1987 election is equally difficult to quantify. In the end it does not matter. Ad agencies are used to sharing the credit for the marketing successes of their commercial clients even when advertising is the least important element in their marketing mix – and used also, of course, to getting the blame when the clients' brands lose market share for whatever reason.

Being the brand leader is good for business. Working for a brand leader is good for an advertising agency's business. The Conservative Party has been brand leader in the British political market for a long time now. Whatever the reasons – and they clearly have much more to do with the division of the Opposition than with any possible influence of anyone's advertising – Saatchi & Saatchi reaps the rewards of being on the winning side. Despite all the rumours, the company's share price leapt up by 30p after the announcement of the Tories' third win in a row.

But, though British General Elections are what get the Saatchi name into the British newspapers, the future of what is now a very important company has little to do with the vagaries of UK politics. Charles Saatchi speaks of building a company that will last for 100 years. It is a company present at several of the most interesting growth points of modern economic society. The story of how it got there is told in the pages that follow.

One point that must be emphasised at the outset is that this is not an official, or even tacitly approved, record. Charles Saatchi, who in the past has been fairly communicative to this book's author – or as communicative as, reticent character that he is, he ever chooses to be – declared he did not wish to see any book written about him or his company. By which he presumably meant no book that was not vetted by him.

This book has not been vetted by anyone. It attempts to be an impartial account, written without malice and without favour. Saatchi & Saatchi, a public company of which the founding brothers now own less than 3% of the equity, is big enough, important enough, unusual enough to be a legitimate object of public curiosity. The story told here is an exciting one. The chapters that remain to be written in the future, whether or not that future lasts 100 years, will probably be no less exciting.   June 1987

I

Before the Beginning

This is the story of two clever young men who made a fortune for themselves and a great noise in the world. It is also the story of an industry – advertising – which has grown, prospered and come to occupy a central and respected position, economically and culturally, instead of being sneered at as a mere 'pimple on the arse of capitalism'.

Saatchi & Saatchi, the company of which those two young men were the eponymous founders, became in 1986, after only sixteen years of existence, the biggest advertising-based group in the world. This extraordinary result was achieved through a combination of determination, talent (that of others as well as of the Saatchi brothers themselves), impudence, clever public relations and, especially in the early years, sheer luck.

The group now has extensive interests outside advertising, and they are likely to become more important as time goes on. We shall pay due attention to them, but the story began in Adland, most of its action – and certainly all the most dramatic action – has taken place there, and it is with the advertising business, rather than management consultancy, market research, sales promotion or any of the other areas in which the Saatchi empire has possessions, that this book will be principally concerned.

That the name Saatchi & Saatchi could become almost synonymous with that of the advertising industry would have seemed to any inhabitant of Adland in 1970, the year when the brothers Charles and Maurice Saatchi went into business together, a possibility so remote as to be ludicrous. In London, where they set up shop, the industry was dominated in those days by a number of American-owned international agency networks. Chief among them, in terms of UK turnover, was J. Walter Thompson. JWT was, and had been for many years, not only the biggest ad agency in Britain but also, despite its American parentage, the poshest.

JWT, which had been one of the first London agencies to make a policy of recruiting university graduates, enjoyed a reputation for both brains and gentlemanliness. Having the right kind of social contacts was a very great plus for an ad agency, for under the rules of the Institute of Practitioners in Advertising (the ad agencies' trade association) it was forbidden to make direct approaches to potential clients to solicit their business. There was no rule, however, to prevent directors of agencies from meeting directors of manufacturing companies at their clubs and cultivating their acquaintance. JWT also made good use of its own dining-room, to which captains of industry would be invited, not to be the targets of any vulgar salesmanship but to exchange views with others of similar background and interests.

The IPA was later to scrap its anti-soliciting rule. It is salutary to remember, however, how different things were such a relatively short time ago from the way they are today. It was as if the leaders of British advertising – and most of the larger agencies were members of the IPA – were ashamed of belonging to the 'persuasion industry' and were trying to prove it by abstaining from doing any overt persuasion on their own account. There was indeed a defensiveness on the part of many advertising people about their work, reflecting the greater hostility to it then than now on the right as well as the left of the political spectrum.

Notwithstanding the role of the old school tie in client-agency relationships, advertising was thought of as a predominantly American business not only because the US was where all the big worldwide agency networks had their headquarters but because the US, and especially New York, was where most of the industry's creative ideas originated. In that respect the most powerful name to conjure with in 1970 was Doyle Dane Bernbach. DDB was an agency whose London office was not then (and is not now) much of a financial success but whose New York advertising was admired and imitated all over the world. The late Bill Bernbach, of DDB, was the acknowledged leader of what was called the Creative Revolution. His agency's ads for Volkswagen and other clients had shown that imagination and self-deprecating humour could be just as effective commercially as pompous puffery.

Two other things about British Adland at the beginning of the previous decade now strike one as curious, given the subsequent history of the industry in general and the Saatchi & Saatchi company in particular. One is that party political advertising was a subject that aroused little interest and held no great commercial attraction for agencies. True, one agency had made itself famous for a time by running the Conservative Party's first professional advertising campaign in 1959, the one with the slogan 'Life's better with the Conservatives. Don't let Labour ruin it.' The agency was Colman Prentis and Varley, but the fact that CPV had subsequently gone into steep decline (for reasons unconnected with its political work) did not help to convince ambitious competitors that a political account was the key to success.

The other respect in which the ad agency scene then was very different from now was the low regard in which agencies were held by the City of London. True, some of the larger agencies obviously had plenty of money and allowed their executives to lead self-indulgent lives, but their profit margins were thought to be small, their vulnerability to account losses high and their appeal to investors minimal. Not that there was much opportunity to invest in them. Very few were publicly quoted, and the disasters that befell two that did go for a public flotation at that time were such as to frighten off most of the others.

One of the two agencies was Dorland Advertising, which in 1971 fell into the hands of young John Bentley, the precocious financier, who realised that the Dorland share price greatly undervalued its property holdings. In classic asset-stripping style he bought and sold Dorland and its subsidiary W. S. Crawford, all within three months. A larger and even more property-rich agency, S. H. Benson, finding itself similarly exposed to financial predators, took fright and sold itself to Ogilvy and Mather, the American agency founded by the British David Ogilvy.

Dorland was later to come into the possession of the Saatchi company at a time when the latter was starting to prove that being publicly quoted could be an enormous advantage, rather than a disadvantage, for an ad agency. It was also proving that political advertising could be turned to commercial account in a manner nobody had foreseen. But by then much else had happened to make people pay serious attention to a firm which, when it started, seemed just one among a shoal of minnows.

Back, however, to 1970 and the beginning. Or rather, since the beginning was, as in every story, a further event in an existing sequence, let us see who the brothers were and what they had been doing before they launched their company.

Charles and Maurice Saatchi are the middle two of four sons of an Iraqi Jewish businessman settled in North London. Their surname, which was to inspire much curiosity and some hilarity when their company became a topic of political conversation, means 'watchmaker' in Iraqi Arabic (in literary Arabic it would be Sa'ati). Charles, the elder of the two, left school in the early 1960s at the age of eighteen and started his working life by going into advertising at a very small agency, doing various jobs for two years. He graduated to copywriting at the London office of the American-owned Benton & Bowles and soon exhibited outstanding ability at the craft. At B & B he teamed up with an art director, the slightly older Ross Cramer, and the pair of them moved as a team to another agency, Collett Dickenson Pearce.

CDP was already breaking ground as one of the most creative of London ad agencies. British-owned, its chairman was John Pearce, who had broken away from Colman Prentis and Varley, taking some of its business with him. In charge of CDP's creative output was Colin Millward, an art man, whom the young Charles Saatchi greatly admired and whom he was to remember as being an advertising genius. Among the work with which CDP had made its mark was its 'gold box' campaign for Benson & Hedges Special Filter cigarettes. The agency was to go on until the present day producing memorable and distinctive advertising for B & H and other products, including Hamlet cigars and Hovis bread.

Here a word might be in order about the relationship between art directors and copywriters. An outsider might be forgiven for imagining that the way things happen in an ad agency is that copywriters think up something to say and then hand over a text for which someone else supplies the pictures. Years ago that was indeed the normal procedure. The Creative Revolution of Bill Bernbach and others put an end to that. Instead, copywriters and art directors began working together in two-person teams, with no rigid dividing line of responsibility between them. Art directors were encouraged to suggest headlines and copywriters to think in visual terms.

At one time art directors were known as visualisers, a term discarded as not being grand enough. In fact it is not a bad word to describe what both art directors and copywriters do. In modern Western advertising, so much of which is produced for television, the visual element is of prime importance. Skilful creators of advertising, whether for TV or the press, pride themselves today on their ability to integrate the visual and the verbal so as to produce a single advertising effect. Long gone are the days when a typical copywriter was a would-be novelist for whom writing ads was merely a second best.

The good modern copywriter, such as Charles Saatchi was – and still is! – is an advertising conceptualiser who may well have no desire, and possibly no ability, to do any other kind of writing. Certainly Charles has declined many invitations to write articles on the grounds that it is not his forte. He has more than one forte, as his record shows, but copywriting was the one that enabled him to climb the first rung on the ladder of success.

At CDP he and Ross Cramer together created a campaign that caused a stir in the advertising business and brought Charles his first experience of being at the centre of controversy. The campaign was for Ford cars and it broke the rules of the Institute of Practitioners in Advertising forbidding 'knocking copy' or direct comparisons between one product and another. These IPA rules, like those barring the soliciting of clients, were later changed.

Cramer and Saatchi by now had a reputation in the ad business. The normal thing for bright young copywriters and art directors, perceived to be on their way up, is to be head-hunted by other employers. That is what happened to them. At the small John Collings agency a man named Richard Cope (who today runs his own small agency) was trying to set up a division with high creative standards. He tempted Cramer and Saatchi away from CDP to work for Collings, but the pair did not get on with the company's boss, Andrew Blair, so after a brief spell they moved on to start their own creative consultancy, Cramer Saatchi. The year was 1967.

A creative consultancy differs from an agency in that, while an agency is in the business of buying advertising time and space, a consultancy is concerned only with making ads. Some creative consultancies, such as David Bernstein's well-known Creative Business, operate almost like conventional agencies, dealing direct with clients but leaving media buying to be done by another specialist company. Other consultancies work mainly for agencies, being called in by them to make up for a shortage of suitable staff or, when there are enough staffers, for a shortage of good ideas. In the UK, agencies usually keep quiet about their use of outside creative talent, though in Japan it is standard practice for a big agency such as Dentsu to put much of its creative work out to be done by small consultancies, and everyone knows it and accepts it.

Cramer Saatchi began by working only for agencies, including Collings, for which it was agreed the consultancy would do the creative work for the Israeli airline El Al, one of the accounts handled by Richard Cope. The firm opened with a staff of five, including a secretary. One of the original team, apart from Cramer and Saatchi themselves, was John Hegarty, a young art director whom the partners had first met at Benton & Bowles and who had turned up again at John Collings. Today Hegarty is a partner in his own successful ad agency, Bartle Bogle Hegarty. Another early recruit to Cramer Saatchi was Jeremy Sinclair, a copywriter who was to play an important part in the future Saatchi & Saatchi group.

The consultancy was very successful. Within a couple of years of its foundation it had been given jobs by fifteen of London's top twenty ad agencies. At first it declined to do creative work directly for client companies, fearing that to do so would jeopardise relations with the agencies on whose goodwill it depended. The first exception made to this self-denying ordinance was the Health Education Council, a name which was to bulk large in Charles Saatchi's track record.

Cramer Saatchi acquired the HEC through a happy accident. Ross Cramer met a woman whose child was at the same school as his and who also happened to work for the HEC. The Council, she told him, might be interested in the offer of some good creative work. At first the work consisted only of designing brochures and posters. Later the HEC found it could afford to spend more on advertising. Cramer Saatchi ran a striking newspaper campaign about the risks of smoking cigarettes. One ad, written by Charles, carried a picture of an oily black substance captioned 'The tar and discharge that collects in the lungs of an average smoker.'

People who knew Charles Saatchi during the early part of his consultancy career remember him as very much the typical advertising creative person, little interested in the business side, which he was content to let Cramer look after. Charles lived well on the proceeds of his professional success, driving an Aston Martin at an age when most youngsters would have been happy with an old jalopy. But, these witnesses concur, he did not appear seriously concerned with making money until a point arrived at which he suddenly changed and his commercial ambition was aroused.

Whatever the truth of this perception, it was Charles and not Ross Cramer who became intent on turning their prosperous little consultancy into a full-service ad agency, with all the risks attendant on such an enterprise. The opportunity to join the agency game arose when the Health Education Council, encouraged by the admiration and editorial attention its £100,000 anti–smoking campaign had attracted, offered to hire Cramer Saatchi as its agency. At about the same time the Citrus Marketing Board of Israel ('Jaffa' brands) offered the firm its account, also on the understanding that it would supply a full range of services.

A decision was taken to turn the consultancy into a fully fledged agency. However, the price of the decision was the loss of Ross Cramer, who wanted no part of running just another of the UK's hundreds of small ad agencies and left to embark on a career as a director of television commercials. In his place Charles brought in his brother Maurice, who by then had graduated from the London School of Economics and had been working as a junior executive at Haymarket, the magazine publishing company which owned, among other things, the advertising trade weekly *Campaign*. This paper was to play a not inconsiderable part in the fortunes of the newborn advertising agency which chose to call itself Saatchi & Saatchi.

The story of *Campaign* is itself fairly remarkable, even though the magazine, wealthy and influential as it has become, is known only to comparatively few people. It is worthwhile digressing for a moment to summarise that story.

Campaign was launched in 1968 by Haymarket, which at that time was controlled by the old (pre-Maxwell) British Printing Corporation. BPC had saved Haymarket and its chairman, Michael Heseltine MP, from financial ruin after the failure of their glossy and well-regarded, but unprofitable, magazine *Town*. Having taken a majority share in Haymarket, BPC used Heseltine's company as its periodical publishing division, shovelling into it a number of trade papers BPC had acquired. One of these was *World's Press News*, which had started life as a magazine about newspapers, as the title implied, but had drifted into becoming mainly an advertising trade paper and a feeble competitor to the old-established (founded in 1913) *Ad Weekly*.

Heseltine and his managing director, Lindsay Masters, were given *carte blanche* to keep *WPN* going, kill it, rejig it or replace it. They chose to replace it with a new paper that would give *Ad Weekly* a run for its money. An editor was hired in the person of Michael Jackson, who had the unusual distinction of having worked both as a Fleet Street journalist (on the *Daily Herald* and *Daily Sketch*) and as an ad agency (CPV) copywriter. Jackson in turn hired two other Fleet Street journalists (one of them the author of this book) to help run the about-to-be launched weekly, which they resolved would be like no other trade paper.

The aim was to make *Campaign*, as it was decided to call the new paper (against the advice of the management, which preferred *AdPress*), read like a Fleet Street pop daily. It would be brash, even sensationalist; it would ask questions and eschew the use of bland press releases; it would cut out jargon and write so as to be understood by any intelligent layman who might pick it up. The hope was to break the quasi-monopoly position of *Ad Weekly*, which held the lion's share of the market for classified ads for jobs in advertising, by making *Campaign* a much more compelling read than its richer rival.

Both the aim and the hope were triumphantly fulfilled. The new magazine was an instant editorial success; the management going along with a style which it did not much like but which it recognised to be the best way of taking readers away from the competition. Commercial success took longer to achieve, since *Ad Weekly* was able to hang on to its lead in classified for a year or two, but eventually the advertisers followed the readers. Mercury House, the publishing company that owned *Ad Weekly*, having begun by complacently ignoring the newcomer, finally responded with a series of panic editorial shake-ups, but they were too late. *Ad Weekly* (or *Adweek*, as it had by then been retitled) folded in 1975, and Mercury House itself was sold a little later.

Meanwhile *Campaign* became a hot property which within a few years of its launch was making estimated profits for Haymarket of a million pounds a year. Its success, coinciding with a cash flow problem at BPC, also helped Heseltine to get the City backing with which to buy back control of his own company instead of being pushed out of it altogether, as BPC was rumoured to be planning in 1968. Brash and breezy *Campaign*, therefore, probably helped to save Heseltine's political, as well as his business, career, since the Conservative Party, of which he was to become a leading light, has rather more respect for successful than for unsuccessful businessmen.

It is interesting, incidentally, that successive editors of *Campaign* have not shared the benefits of its commercial progress. Six of them before the recently appointed present incumbent ended by being forced out starting with the first, Michael Jackson, who was largely responsible for devising the winning editorial formula. To answer the question why that should have been so would take us too far away from our main subject. So let us go back to the late 1960s, when the magazine was getting going, making some enemies among both ad agencies and media owners because of its aggressive editorial stance, but also gaining the enthusiastic attention of many of the younger people in the advertising business.

One of the first people to see that *Campaign* not only provided a good read but could, precisely because it was read closely, be used as a valuable public relations tool was Charles Saatchi. Whether or not he was always more ambitious than some of his friends at the time took him to be, whether or not he foresaw how important a friend the magazine might be thereafter, when he came to run an agency that did not yet exist, whether or not he simply enjoyed the PR game, Charles put himself out very early on to be useful to *Campaign*. With the number of contacts he had as a creative consultant, he picked up a lot of ad industry gossip – accounts being shifted from one agency to another, executives being hired and fired – before the editorial people at the magazine did. He passed the gossip on to them by telephone and thus provided the raw material for many scoops.

It was entirely natural that the journalists to whom he was supplying an exceedingly useful – and free – news service should take a friendly interest in news of his own doings, first as a creative consultant, later as an agency boss. But he did not rely simply on their feelings of gratitude. Charles was adept at tailoring stories in such a way as to appeal to journalists. Having proved himself an excellent copywriter, he turned out to have, if anything, an even greater flair for publicity. Perhaps, at bottom, it was the same skill – that of taking a set of facts, not necessarily fascinating in themselves, and dressing them up in such a way as to rivet attention. This is what good advertising, good PR and indeed good journalism are all about.

Of course, Charles was not, and is not, the only adman with an understanding of publicity, though it is curious how many ad agencies appear to be lacking in publicity sense when it is a question of promoting themselves. Traditionally, however, ad agency publicity has tended to be linked to the cult of personality; the outstanding example being Ogilvy & Mather, built up to begin with on the basis of David Ogilvy's unblushing self-promotion. Saatchi publicity, on the other hand, has always boosted the company and its activities rather than the individuals within it.

This policy came naturally to Charles, a somewhat shy and aloof character who, unlike most other well-known admen, has never gone in for speechifying or socialising. Many top people in advertising have got to the top by being performers, in the theatrical sense, charming clients and colleagues by their command of words in the meetings and presentations in which much of advertising life is spent. Such was never Charles's way. His younger brother Maurice is a more relaxed, more gregarious character, but he too has kept to a large extent out of the limelight.

With hindsight, it looks as though the brothers' objective may always have been to establish Saatchi & Saatchi as a brand name with a brand image distinct from any opinions people might have about Charles and Maurice themselves. If Ogilvy's career shows what can be done with the cult of personality, its perils are illustrated by the example of Peter Marsh, a one-time professional actor whose Allen Brady and Marsh ad agency seemed at one time a serious contender with the Saatchis for the most glittering prizes in British advertising. Marsh is a performer, and an accomplished one, in the sense just now defined, and in the 1970s he and his agency hit a winning streak. But it did not last. One problem may have been that ABM always looked too much like a one-man band, even though it employed many good people, and when clients got tired of Peter Marsh they fired his agency.

Perhaps hindsight is wrong, and the Saatchi publicity policy was never derived from conscious analysis of the options. Perhaps it was never a matter of anything but Charles doing what came naturally to him. But it has certainly worked well. This is not to say Charles has never made mistakes. He has, but he has been lucky enough through most of his career to find few reporters or stockbrokers' analysts willing to challenge the Saatchis' version of their own affairs.

2

In the Beginning

Charles Saatchi was aged twenty-seven and his brother Maurice twenty-five when they registered Saatchi & Saatchi and Company in August 1970. It was financed to the tune of about £100,000, including £1,000 of ordinary shares and £9,000 of preference capital (which was to be repaid within three years). Among the company's backers, as debenture holders, were Mary Quant and Michael Heseltine and Lindsay Masters, of Haymarket.

The financial link between the Saatchis and Haymarket's bosses did not last long and was never publicised. That did not prevent rumours from starting, which were to persist for years, of a clandestine connection between the new company and *Campaign*. Many of the rumour-mongers could think of no other explanation for the frequency with which the name Saatchi & Saatchi figured in the columns of what had already bcome British Adland's leading organ. The true explanation was, as we have seen, both simpler and more complicated. Charles worked hard for his publicity. Clearly, though, friendly personal relations with people in Haymarket did the brothers no harm at all.

The ordinary shares in Saatchi & Saatchi were at first divided between four working directors, apart from 15% held by Cannon Nominees. The four were Charles, with 42%, Maurice, with 38%, and John Hegarty and Tim Bell, with 2.5% each. Hegarty we have already met. Bell had been hired from the Geers Gross agency to be media director of the Saatchi & Saatchi agency, which opened its doors in London's Golden Square in September. He was to play a vital role in the agency's development.

Excluding secretarial help, there were five other employees, all creatives. They were copywriters Jeremy Sinclair, Chris Martin and Alan Tilby, and art directors Ron Collins and Bill Atherton. Of the founding employees only Sinclair, at the time of writing, is still working for the brothers. Almost all the nine, however, were to enjoy distinguished careers in advertising. Bell was to become, after a turbulent time with the Saatchis, a partner in the Lowe, Howard-Spink and Bell company, and Collins was to help start Wight Collins Rutherford Scott. Both these firms have 'done a Saatchi', that is turned themselves into marketing services conglomerates; both are highly successful, though not in the same league as Saatchi & Saatchi is today; there will be more to say about both later on.

The Saatchi & Saatchi agency of 1970 was itself in a very different league from that of the multinational conglomerate it was to become. That did not prevent it from behaving with a panache that could be envied – that *was* envied – by firms many times its size. It started with a bang by doing something that most ad agencies, despite their professed faith in the power of advertising, rarely did in those days and still do not do very often – it advertised itself. Midget though it was, compared with the JWTs and other Adland heavyweights, Saatchi & Saatchi took a full page in *The Sunday Times* to announce, in portentous prose, the arrival of a new kind of agency. It would not, it declared, seek remuneration through the normal 15% commission on the media advertising rates. This was dismissed as a 'dying system'. Instead, it would work for fees averaging 22% of billing. The long copy was signed by Jeremy Sinclair but was actually written by Robert Heller, editorial director of Haymarket.

The commission system, in fact, was not dying, but it was undoubtedly in trouble. The system worked then – and indeed works now, though with a modification which will be explained in a moment – as follows. Agencies, despite working for the advertisers who were their clients, made their money out of the commission paid by the media. The standard rate of commission paid by television and national newspapers and magazines was – and is – 15% of the price of advertising time or space. This discount, in theory at least, was available only to agencies and not to advertisers. The system dated back to the previous century, when agencies had come into being to act on behalf not of advertisers but of newspapers and had been sellers rather than buyers of space. Gradually agencies had changed their role, but it had suited everyone to keep the system going.

One of the apparently anomalous results of the system was that an agency could earn far more from a heavy TV campaign for which it had made only one commercial, frequently screened, than from a series of different press ads that might have taken far more time and work to produce. In practice an advertiser had three ways of altering an agency's remuneration. One was to make it supply additional services, for instance package design, for the same commission. The second, in cases where the commission was acknowledged not to cover the value of the services received, was to supplement it with a fee. The third, though in 1970 it was not often admitted to happen, was to demand that part of the commission be rebated to the client.

Back in 1970 rebating was prohibited under the rules applied by the media bodies that granted recognition to agencies. These bodies, such as the Newspaper Publishers Association and the Independent Television Companies Association, decided which agencies would be 'recognised' and, therefore, eligible for commission. Other purchasers of time and space were supposed to pay full price, that is without the 15% discount. In reality it did not always happen that way, but only a few bold spirits were ready to say so out loud and to argue that the anti-rebating rules were an unjustified restrictive practice. In the late 1970s the rules were changed under pressure from the Office of Fair Trading.

Nowadays, though the 15% commission is still standard, it is an open secret that many clients demand part of the discount for themselves. Such behaviour is no longer considered reprehensible or even controversial. In 1970, however, rebating was a live and hotly debated issue, and *The Sunday Times* launch ad for Saatchi & Saatchi had real shock value. It should be added that, while the new agency, in accordance with its announced policy, never did treat the 15% commission as a sacred cow, it did not stick to its promise to work for the equivalent of a higher rate of commission. That did not matter. The object had been achieved, as it was to be achieved many times in the future, of making the world sit up and pay attention to Saatchi & Saatchi.

With the two accounts it had been promised (Jaffa fruit and the Health Education Council) plus a number of smaller clients, the firm had first-year billings (the amount of advertising money spent on behalf of clients) of £1 million, a substantial amount for a brand new agency. It continued to grow apace in the next few years, picking up blue-chip clients such as Great Universal Stores, Dunlop and British Leyland. It claimed billings of £3.2 million for calendar 1972 and £5.1 million for calendar 1973, making it number twenty-six in the agencies' league table compiled annually by *Campaign*. In that same year of 1973 J. Walter Thompson, secure in the number one spot, reported billings of £41.1 million.

This comparative table of billings, incidentally, is of prime importance for the way different agencies are perceived by the advertising community. Many agency directors affect to be unconcerned about it, declaring that the quality of their firms' work or the amount of profit made are what really count. Do not be fooled. Like professional politicians deriding the opinion polls over which they pore in private, agency directors are extremely concerned about which place they occupy in the one pecking order that everyone in the business sees and remembers. Billings figures are reported to the press by the agencies themselves, and a good deal of ingenuity goes into ensuring that they are as big as possible.

For example, fees for ancillary services such as new product development are 'grossed up' (multiplied by 6.7) to make them equivalent to ordinary advertising expenditure, where what the agency keeps is only 15% or thereabouts of what is spent. And, in calculating billings, agencies tend to put them in at card rate, that is the amount that would have been paid for the time and space bought if these had been paid for at the official prices. A large part of the effort of an agency media department, however, is devoted to haggling over media rates, and clients judge agencies partly on the amount of discount they can screw out of newspapers and TV. Cheaper rates mean, of course, less commission for the agency, but the sacrifice is worth making if it increases the agency's competitive edge.

Despite all this, reported billings are usually not wildly unrealistic, and the exaggerations more or less cancel each other out. In general the published table is seen as a reasonably reliable indicator of which agencies are moving up, and which down, the business ladder. During all the years that JWT was number one its perceived position at the top of the tree was a strong element of its attraction for large clients. Being top dog is not quite enough in itself to keep you as top dog, but it's a mighty help.

Saatchi & Saatchi's early growth was fuelled not only by the quality of its work but by the skill and energy with which Charles publicised the company. For example he got a lot of newspaper and magazine mileage out of the story that his agency had insured its creative talent for hundreds of thousands of pounds and that other agencies wishing to poach its copywriters and art directors would have to pay transfer fees for them, on the model of football clubs buying players. This was just the sort of tale jounalists love. It was also pure invention. But it did nobody any harm and the Saatchi company quite a lot of good.

An even smarter *coup*, and a much more memorable one, was the 'pregnant man' ad. Produced for the Health Education Council's pro-contraception campaign, it showed a woebegone man with a pro-truding belly, over the caption 'Would you be more careful if it was you that got pregnant?' The ad was the work of Jeremy Sinclair and art director Bill Atherton. It got a great deal of press coverage. As far as Fleet Street was concerned, it was the work of the HEC, not Saatchi & Saatchi. In those days the general press was very little interested in advertising agencies. But the trade press made sure that advertising people, including those on the client side, knew which agency was involved.

Even today, when asked their opinion of the Saatchi group's creative record, many advertisers mention the 'pregnant man', a commercially insignificant item produced by a small agency many years ago. It is doubtful whether the ad did anything to reduce the rate of illegitimate births, which was the objective of the client organisation. There is no doubt whatever that it did a wonderful job of selling Saatchi & Saatchi.

This is not meant as a sneer. It should be said that all ad agencies, when creating campaigns, have the undeclared aim of promoting themselves as well as their clients. Their styles may be different. While some agencies are self-consciously 'creative' in the sense that they go in for advertising that is striking, unusual, witty or entertaining, others prefer a more sober-sided approach. But none, however loudly it may proclaim its devotion to its clients' interests, can afford to forget that it is in business for itself and that even the most loving clients can take it into their heads to change their agencies – and frequently do.

The advantage of the 'creative' style is that it is more readily noticed not only by consumers but by prospective clients. From the point of view of the agency employees who devise the ads, the show-off style has the further advantage of bringing their work to the attention of the juries which hand out the various advertising awards, such as those of the Designers and Art Directors Association. The winners of these awards may be unknown to the general public – though the efforts of a clever copywriter may have impressed many more people than have ever read anything by the winner of a Booker Prize – but they become very well known in Adland; their market value is enhanced and they end up much richer, irrespective of how well the products have fared for which their campaigns were produced. From the outset the Saatchi & Saatchi agency was good at winning awards.

Pretty early on, if not from the very outset, the brothers began to dabble in acquisitions – an activity that was to take them much farther, much faster than anyone foresaw at the time. The very first acquisition was of a small property company called Brogan Developers in 1972. The first of any real importance, however, took place the following year, when they bought the Manchester ad agency E. G. Dawes. This was then merged with the Saatchis' own new Manchester office, which had been set up at the beginning of 1973 to service a GUS subsidiary, Great Clewes Warehouse.

Already the financial mechanics of the takeover were similar to the much bigger deals that were to follow in later years. The procedure followed was an 'earn-out', with the total sum payable related to performance. The down payment was £130,000. The balance of £90,000 was payable over two years. Saatchi Dawes, as the new unit was called, reported 1973 billings of £1.6 million on top of the London agency's turnover.

The following year two more small agencies were bought, both in London. They were Notley Advertising and the George J. Smith firm. Notleys was acquired at the price of underwriting its pension fund. The Smith buy was regretted as a mistake, in which £90,000 was handed over for a business which proved to be debt-ridden and worthless. Notleys and Smiths were both absorbed into the Saatchi & Saatchi agency, which ended 1974 as number nineteen in the league table, with reported billings of £10.8 million and new, bigger premises in Lower Regent Street.

If these actual acquisitions were pretty unglamorous, a fair amount of excitement was whipped up about expansion projects which never came off. Charles, chairman of what was still only a second-division agency, was already talking to the trade press in 1973 about his plans to acquire a foothold in the American advertising business. Nothing concrete came of that. However, *Campaign* splashed all over its front page an 'exclusive' given to the magazine by Charles about the establishment of a subsidiary in Paris called Saatchi Damour. Various details of the deal remained, he said, to be settled.

Many months passed before it emerged that the whole thing had fallen through. The revelation appeared in *Adweek*, which had taken the trouble to check with French sources what was happening, or rather failing to happen. Charles had cannily kept quiet about the collapse of his negotiations, and *Campaign* never bothered to follow up the story even after it was printed elsewhere. The upshot was that thousands of *Campaign* readers had got the message that Saatchi & Saatchi was an agency of international standing. The message was somewhat premature.

Other abortive expansion attempts went unpublicised. Acquisition offers were made to two medium-sized but promising ad agencies, Boase Massimi Pollitt and Murray Parry. A feeler is said to have been put out to Masius Wynne-Williams, which in those days was runner-up to JWT and had a reputation for sound marketing strategy (it had helped to invent Babycham) rather than creative brilliance. It was run by the late Jack Wynne-Williams, an affable and immensely experienced autocrat, who reportedly came back with the rejoinder that he had looked at the petty cash and thought he had enough to buy the Saatchis' firm. (After a series of mergers, what was his agency is now called D'Arcy Masius Benton & Bowles, is American-owned and is in no position to be sarcastic about Saatchi & Saatchi.)

When the brothers' big opportunity did come, it was from a totally unexpected quarter. The 1975 merger of Saatchi & Saatchi with Compton UK Partners, which finally propelled the brothers into the big time about which they had been dreaming, was the result of a stroke of luck. Of course, luck is what you make of it, and they made of theirs a springboard. It is tempting, if profitless, to wonder what might have become of Saatchi & Saatchi without that lucky break. Would it have been a successful but not enormously big agency, comparable with, say, Boase Massimi Pollitt, or would the restless brothers have found another springboard for themselves? What actually did happen was as follows.

Compton UK Partners, an advertising agency group in which Compton Advertising of New York held a minority share, found itself in 1975 with a problem. The company had gone public three years earlier by means of a reverse takeover of a small but already quoted 'shell' company, Birmingham Crematorium. (Technically the advertising firm was sold to the crematorium for shares. The vendors ended up with control of the supposed purchaser and then changed its name to their own.) As one of the very few British advertising firms quoted at the time on the Stock Exchange, Compton UK Partners was particularly badly hurt by the 1974 downturn in advertising expenditure resulting from the economic recession triggered by the 1973 Yom Kippur war and the oil price rises which followed it.

The group contained several provincial subsidiaries, but its main operating division, Garland-Compton, was a London agency founded in 1928 by Sidney Garland, a former *Daily Mail* ad salesman, as S. T. Garland Advertising Service and passed on to his son Leonard, who in 1960 forged the American link. Garland-Compton, located amid the restaurants of Charlotte Street, had a strong client list, including Procter & Gamble and Rowntree, but a lack-lustre creative reputation. This did not help it to gain new accounts when billings stagnated in 1974 and 1975.

In the 1974 billings table Compton UK Partners occupied eleventh place with £17.44 million. Profits were down by more than £500,000 to £446,000. Plenty of other agency businesses were suffering from similar troubles, including half of the top ten, but most of the others, being private companies, did not have to worry about outside share-holders and could afford to ride out the storm. During the financial year 1974–5 anxiety among the directors turned to desperation as they saw themselves making money out of investments and property but not out of their main business of advertising. The answer to their problem, they eventually agreed, was to merge with a smaller, more dynamic agency able to get the new business that was eluding Garland-Compton. A list was made of possible partners. It did not, repeat not, include Saatchi & Saatchi.

It was not that the Saatchis were not perceived as dynamic and successful, but their image among the Establishment of Adland was by no means entirely positive. All that *Campaign* publicity was seen in some quarters as rather vulgar. The boards of ad agencies were still to a large extent peopled by gentlemen (in the social sense), and the Saatchis and their employees were not considered to be gentlemen. Theirs was a brash and bouncy outfit, forever shouting about itself. To the layman – and even to the adman – this may read paradoxically. Is not shouting about oneself the essence of advertising? Yes, of course it is, but we are speaking of a time when many admen were frightened of being classified as hucksters. They wanted, in Britain at least, to be known as members of a 'profession' comparable with lawyers rather than market traders.

The chosen merger partner was an agency called the Kirkwood Company, headed by Ronnie Kirkwood, a man nobody could describe as brash. Another former professional actor, who had deserted the stage young because of an illness, Kirkwood was, in his late forties, elegant, charming and a superb presenter. He had been head of television at CPV and deputy creative director at S.H. Benson before becoming creative director at the London office of the American-owned McCann-Erickson, where he really made his name. He started his own agency in 1970, the year that also witnessed the birth of Saatchi & Saatchi, in partnership with two well-known marketing specialists, Gordon Medcalf and Tom O'Leary. They quickly attracted packaged goods accounts and by 1974 were billing well over £5 million. While Kirkwood was himself no slouch at getting trade press headlines, he was universally considered to be a gent, not least because he had declined to try to poach any accounts away from his former employers, McCann-Erickson, when he left them.

In great secrecy Compton UK made an offer which Kirkwood discussed with his partners. Apparently they were considerably more mindful of the risks of the deal than of its opportunities. The chief perceived risk must have been that of succumbing to the sheer administrative weight of the larger company and being unable to shift it out of its inertia. Coupled with that was the risk that they might lose the support of the clients who currently had such a high opinion of the existing Kirkwood Company. Kirkwood and his board refused the offer and decided, pending receipt of a less risk-laden offer, to stay as they were. Compton UK was forced to think again.

As a postscript to this episode, about which nothing became known for several years, it is interesting to record that the Kirkwood Company did accept another offer, made not very long after the Compton deal had been turned down. Kirkwood and his partners sold ownership of their agency to the Lopex holding company for £800,000. The agreement stipulated that they would continue to run the Kirkwood Company but as employees. Having made their pile, O'Leary and Medcalf left not long afterwards to do other things. Ronnie Kirkwood stayed on, but his agency never fulfilled the promise of its early years. Eleven years later, by which time Kirkwood himself had all but lost interest in the firm he founded, it changed its name to Deighton Mullen in a management buy-out. If Ronnie Kirkwood has ever looked back with regret to the rejected Compton offer of 1975 and wondered whether he, and not the Saatchis, could have used it as the basis on which to build a worldwide empire, he has kept very quiet about it.

But how did the offer rejected by Kirkwood come to be transferred to a company that had originally not even got as far as Compton's shortlist? At about the same time that negotiations were going on between Compton and Kirkwood, Maurice Saatchi had contacted Ron Rimmer, managing director of Garland-Compton. His reason was not, as Rimmer at first thought, that he had heard about the Compton group's discreet search for a marriage partner and wanted to present his agency as a suitor. No, he was looking for a business manager for Saatchi & Saatchi and, with the cockiness characteristic of that agency, was asking Rimmer to leave his good place at a bigger firm to take the job.

Up to then the general management of Saatchis had been handled by Maurice himself and, increasingly, by Tim Bell, who after his first year with the agency had given up his specialist media duties. In the early stages of their company the brothers had tried, but failed, to attract various eminent marketing men to join them. In the absence of such a person it was Bell who had moved forward to take an ever more prominent role. He did not yet, however, have the formal title of managing director.

The approach to Rimmer caused him to take a closer look at Saatchi & Saatchi. He was, somewhat to his surprise, impressed by the professionalism of the people he met there and reported the fact back to the Compton UK board, which by now was having to think again about its merger options. Talks started with the Saatchis and led to the deal that, to the surprise and discomfiture of some Compton directors, allowed the Saatchi brothers to gain control of the larger company. It was not, on the face of it, a complete reverse takeover; by selling their agency to Compton UK, the Saatchi directors ended up with only 35% of the combined outfit. This block of shares, however, was quite enough to give them effective control, for the Compton UK directors owned an insignificant proportion of the equity of their own company.

The public relations version, as put out in September 1975, of the Saatchi-Compton romance and marriage, was that it started after Charles Saatchi said in an interview with *Adweek* that he admired Garland-Compton's work on Procter & Gamble and Rowntree. The interview was read by Kenneth Gill, the Compton UK chairman, who supposedly got in touch with him to return the compliment.

What was true was that it was the decision by the shrewd and humorous Gill to back the brothers that really clinched the deal. It was agreed he should be joint chairman with Charles of the merged company, to be called Saatchi & Saatchi Compton. Gill was to become the brothers' close confidant and to be rewarded several years later, after his retirement, with the honorary presidency of the group.

On the Compton side the original idea had been that its administrative strengths would be paired more or less equally with the advertising flair of Saatchi & Saatchi. Matters were put in a very different light by a *Campaign* report headed 'Saatchi swallows the Compton group.' Charles had again used his press contacts to tell the story his way. Even before the physical merger of Garland-Compton and Saatchi & Saatchi took place, the Garland-Compton creative director, Bob Bellamy, who had been slated to run a combined creative department with the Saatchis' Jeremy Sinclair, left. So did Keith Nicholson, media director of the Charlotte Street agency, who was to have been similarly yoked with his Saatchi opposite number, Roy Warman. Bellamy and Nicolson set up their own agency together with two other Garland-Compton men, Trevor Reeves and Stephen Robertshaw.

Another, delayed casualty of the merger was, ironically, Ron Rimmer, who had helped to bring it about. Tim Bell's last act before leaving the old Saatchi premises in Regent Street for Garland-Compton's Charlotte Street building was to put out a memo announcing that he (Bell) would be managing director of the new, merged outfit. Rimmer gave up his managing directorship to become, instead, financial director. After a fairly short time he left for McCann-Erickson.

His successor as financial director was a young man who was to play a vital role in the restructuring and reorientation of the company. His name was Martin Sorrell, and he met the Saatchis when he was acting on behalf of James Gulliver, the food business entrepreneur who was a shareholder in Compton UK Partners. Sorrell instantly impressed the brothers and vice versa.

Soon after Sorrell's arrival it was the turn of the Americans to be put in their place. Before the merger Compton Advertising of New York had been the biggest single shareholder in Compton UK Partners. Afterwards the American holding was easily outranked by the combined shares of the brothers. Nevertheless Stu Mitchell, then boss of

Compton Advertising, was confident that the Saatchis would not get the better of the New York firm in any future conflict. He said as much during merger talks in Kenneth Gill's flat, taking a patronising tone towards the brothers – perhaps understandably, for they were in 1975 still very young men. In 1977, however, a new holding company was created by share exchange under the name of Saatchi & Saatchi Company, with Gill as sole chairman. In this company the Americans had no part.

The name Saatchi & Saatchi Compton, previously that of the whole company, was now confined to the operating subsidiary which controlled its advertising activities, and the 20% American share was also confined to that subsidiary. The Americans were no longer in a position to interfere, even if they wished, with the brothers' empire-building schemes. True it was that the group's advertising activities were as yet virtually its only activities, but Charles and Maurice were already starting to talk of expanding into other marketing services, though their ambitions in this respect bore no immediate fruit.

It should be emphasised that since 1975 there has been no advertising agency called Saatchi & Saatchi. The official name of the agency in Charlotte Street became for a long time Saatchi & Saatchi Garland-Compton and subsequently, as we shall see, Saatchi & Saatchi Compton, London. This is not a merely pedantic point. The confusion in the popular mind – and not only the popular mind – between the holding company and the Charlotte Street agency, which even its staff refer to as Saatchi & Saatchi, is of real importance. It is a confusion that the brothers have done nothing to discourage and that has had two effects.

On the one hand the advertising achievements of Charlotte Street, which are considerable, have helped to make the Saatchi name famous and, therefore, to prepare the ground for the holding company's long series of acquisitions. On the other hand those acquisitions, especially the more spectacular international deals of recent times, have enhanced the Charlotte Street agency's reputation in the minds of prospective clients. After all, the headlines, whether in the advertising trade press or in national newspapers, have never made any distinction between the holding company and its most important London advertising subsidiary.

The identification of the fortunes of what was to become an international conglomerate with those of one particular office in an ad agency chain has had another consequence. Charles Saatchi, the assiduous publicist, has always been inordinately sensitive about any publicity to do with the flagship agency. Charlotte Street's employees, however grand, have always been forbidden to talk to the press without permission, though Charles is perfectly relaxed about such matters when it comes to others of the holding company's many subsidiaries.

But we are jumping ahead of the historical record. Let us return to the 1970s and the manner in which Saatchi & Saatchi became a force to be reckoned with.

At the end of 1975 the newly merged Saatchi & Saatchi Compton group of advertising agencies, including provincial offices, ranked fourth in the *Campaign* billings table, with a figure of £30.5 million, roughly £11 million behind the leader, J. Walter Thompson. In second and third place respectively stood Masius Wynne-Williams (£32.5 million) and McCann-Erickson (£30.8 million). In terms of turnover growth the latter was the most outstandingly successful big agency of the period in the UK, having put on nearly £6 million in billing in one year. McCann's record was attributable to two men in particular, both then in their early forties – Phil Geier, a bustling American go-getter who, as chairman, had led its business-getting team, and Barry Day, vice-chairman, creative director (he had succeeded Kirkwood in the post) and one of Adland's most accomplished speakers and writers. Also important were Nigel Grandfield, a personable and urbane presenter who took over from Geier when the American was recalled to an even bigger job in the US, and the equally personable Ann Burdus, another vice-chairman, in charge of market research. We shall have occasion to mention all these names again.

Barry Day's department was responsible for one of the most memorable ad campaigns of the decade, for Martini vermouth. It was not witty and irreverent in the style of Collett Dickenson Pearce or Doyle Dane Bernbach – or many Saatchi ads – but it was a classic of television image-making, cleverly designed to seduce its targeted audience of young women drinkers. The commercials showed groups of glamorous young people riding, skiing, flying in multi-coloured balloons to a romantic castle top. 'We offer the consumer a dream world she knows isn't true,' said Day, 'but she likes to dream, and the dream comes back into the product, and maybe it's just a bit true,' which was a pretty good summing up of the way in which much modern advertising works.

The fifth, sixth, seventh and tenth agencies in the 1975 UK pecking order were also, like JWT and McCann, American-owned. They were respectively Ogilvy & Mather, Young & Rubicam, Leo Burnett and Ted Bates.

In 1976 the Charlotte Street agency Saatchi & Saatchi Garland-Compton on its own stood in seventh place in the annual billings table. The following year it moved up to sixth place, and the year after that to fourth. In 1979 it hit the top spot, with declared billings of £67.5 million, ousting JWT, which had ruled the roost for more than twenty years. *Campaign* gave the story front-page prominence, referring to the agency not by its proper official name but simply as Saatchi & Saatchi. Charles Saatchi, with calculated modesty, was quoted as saying that 'as the positions of the four leading agencies are so close, it is not especially meaningful which one emerges at the top for any given period.'

It was, on the contrary, exceedingly meaningful from the public relations point of view, as Charles well knew. Just as being known to be top dog had helped JWT to keep its lead for so long, so the Charlotte Street agency was now to enjoy the benefits of market leadership. Apart from 1980, when it shared the top honours with JWT, it was to continue to be number one in the league table, and its position there is now almost as much taken for granted as JWT's used to be.

The years 1978 and 1979 were exhilarating for the Saatchi group, not only because of the vast amount of new business that flowed into Charlotte Street, including accounts from Allied Breweries, British Leyland, BP, Black & Decker, Dunlop, IBM, Procter & Gamble and United Biscuits, but because the name Saatchi & Saatchi suddenly became a household word throughout the nation as a result of the work it did for the Conservative Party. The Tory account, of which more later, was handled by Charlotte Street, that is by Saatchi & Saatchi Garland-Compton, but politicians and political commentators knew even less than did *Campaign* reporters about the distinction between the holding company and the agency with the unwieldy name, and Saatchi & Saatchi was the name that stuck.

Comedians and others enjoyed playing games with the exotic names (Snatchy and Snatchy, what are they, Japanese?) without ever trying to find out where they really came from. The Garland-Compton bit would have done nothing to help these jokes. For the Saatchis the Tory account turned out to be an almost unmixed blessing, attracting the benevolent interest of both prospective clients and City investors despite

24

the jokes. The fact that the Conservatives won the 1979 election worked greatly in their agency's favour.

Advertisers' opinions of Saatchi & Saatchi Garland-Compton could hardly have been better. A 1978 survey of 110 client companies gave the agency top place in three tables of perceived virtues, including creativity. Another similar survey in 1979 put the agency behind Collett Dickenson Pearce for creativity and behind both JWT and Allen Brady and Marsh for strong management, but in answer to the question 'Which agency would you most like to handle your business?' it gathered more support than any of its competitors.

At that time the creative reputation of Saatchi & Saatchi Garland-Compton actually rested on a fairly small proportion of its output. Campaigns for the Health Education Council, Dunlop and the Tory Party were among those most frequently mentioned by admirers. But a lot of work was fairly run-of-the-mill. It would have been surprising had it not been so. The original Saatchi & Saatchi agency, comparatively small and bright, had merged with a larger, less adventurous staff and had taken on several clients, notably Procter & Gamble, which were not ready to change their settled, conventional advertising habits. P & G, however, though a hard taskmaster to its agencies, was a highly valuable client to have. Not only did it spend large amounts of advertising money, it stuck firmly to the 15% commission arrangement even when many other clients were abandoning it, taking advantage of the abandonment of the rules against rebating. Usually when advertisers moved away from 15%, it was to pay their agencies not a higher rate of commission, whatever Saatchi & Saatchi's launch ad of 1970 might have said, but a lower one.

A most curious feature of the Saatchi & Saatchi Garland-Compton of the late 1970s was that, although it was popularly known as Saatchi & Saatchi, it had become very much not the brothers' shop but Tim Bell's. It was Bell, by now a first-class presenter combining charm with sophisticated understanding of advertising problems, to whom both staff and clients professed loyalty. The brothers were, by contrast, backroom boys, though Charles kept a close eye on the creative product, in consultation with the agency's creative director, Jeremy Sinclair.

The question was sometimes asked why Bell did not break away to start on his own. Remember that we are speaking of a time when, though the Saatchi group was becoming very prosperous, most of its turnover was accounted for by the one agency that Bell ran, first as managing director, then from 1978 to 1980 as chairman, with Ron Leagas as managing director, then from 1980, when Leagas left, as both chairman and MD. Many offers were made to Bell to back him in setting up his own agency. Given the regard in which he was held, he would probably have been able, had he wished, to take with him a large part both of the Saatchis' billings and of their staff. That might well have spelt the end of their empire-building ambitions.

Bell chose never to take such a step. Partly, no doubt, because he was very well rewarded. His salary aside, he was able, as one of the original shareholders in Saatchi & Saatchi, to make a profit on his shares variously estimated as £2 million and £3 million. Another possible reason is that the right partners never presented themselves, and he is not by nature a man to go into business on his own. The most plausible explanation, however, is that he was perfectly happy to go on working for a company that had done so much for his own fortune and reputation. By the time he was to make his break with the brothers, at the beginning of 1985, he would have been removed from his power base in Charlotte Street and have ceased to pose any threat to the Saatchi & Saatchi organisation, which in any case would have grown too big to be undermined by the departure of one employee.

3

Better with the Conservatives

Let us pause to consider in a little more detail the political tie-up that, as already said, did the Saatchis so much good. On the company's side the Conservative Party's advertising account was seen and welcomed as a commercial opportunity rather than a means of showing ideological commitment. The majority of British advertising practitioners is certainly Tory-inclined – since the ad industry is thought more likely to flourish in the kind of economic conditions favoured by the Conservatives – but neither of the Saatchi brothers was active in politics and neither even made any public mention of his political preferences. Tim Bell, who was an active Conservative, was paradoxically the one who counselled caution when the Saatchi directors discussed whether to take the account.

The precedents were not particularly encouraging. No British ad agency had done itself very much good by handling a party political account, not even Colman Prentis & Varley, which had become for a short time in the late 1950s a household word because of its work for the Tories. A party political account meant, in effect, the Conservative Party account, since only the Tories used an agency in the same way as did commercial clients. Other parties preferred to have their advertising handled on a voluntary basis by *ad hoc* groups of politically sympathetic advertising people, using agencies only to buy newspaper and poster space. This was thought to guarantee sincerity.

Indeed up until the 1959 General Election the Labour Party had totally rejected the notion of enlisting the skills and techniques of commercial advertising even when these were offered free of charge.

Not long before the 1959 election a group of admen sympathetic to the Labour Party volunteered its services, but the publicity sub-committee of the party's National Executive turned them down. It was felt inappropriate to try to sell party policies as if they were, to use the common expression, tins of baked beans. That ads for baked beans are on the whole far more truthful and sincere than the electoral promises of politicians was an argument that found little favour among those politicians.

The Conservative victory in 1959 changed Labour Party minds, however, and a voluntary publicity group was set up, consisting of professional advertising and PR people, who produced such winning campaign slogans in the 1960s as 'Let's Go with Labour' and 'You know Labour Government works.' All parties came to accept that voters could not be expected 'to follow closely reasoned arguments or to be automatically interested in the great issues of the day. Unless our propaganda can immediately echo a feeling or strike a subject close to their hearts, we have lost them.' The words were those of Brian Murphy, a former copywriter who had contributed the 'Let's Go with Labour' slogan to the party.

The Tories, heartened by their 1959 experience, went on using agencies. Their account moved at different times to Davidson Pearce, a subsidiary of Ogilvy & Mather, to Roe Humphreys, a subsidiary of Saatchi & Saatchi Compton, and back again to Davidson Pearce. Nothing of any great note was produced by either. More interesting were the Tories' party political broadcasts in the election year 1970. These, made with the help of a leading ad agency creative man, Barry Day of McCann-Erickson, and a television advertising production company, James Garrett and Partners, marked quite a break with the way things had been done before.

Traditionally party politicals had consisted of dull little speeches by politicians to the mass audience they hoped would not switch off. They were not political advertising in the sense understood in America, where parties bought TV spots in exactly the same way as commercial advertisers, and used the same film techniques. In the UK no advertising is carried by the BBC, and the rules of Independent Television bar political ads. Instead, both channels carry an agreed number of party politicals as a public service. The Day-Garrett broadcasts, however, took a step towards American practice by virtue of the techniques used if not of the manner in which airtime was obtained. Imaginative camera work and quick cutting made the broadcasts look more like commercials even though they still contained the requisite respectable talking heads.

Even the Labour Party's publicity people were impressed and, by the time of the October 1974 General Election, started following the Tories' example, using throbbing music as well as snappy camera shots to lend some much needed drama to clips of party leaders out and about. Meanwhile, it was on the Labour side that another step had been taken towards the American pattern of political advertising by introducing an element of 'knocking copy'. In the US it was common for candidates to sneer at each other in TV spots in a way quite unknown in British political advertisng. An example was the 1968 Democratic Party commercial in which the words 'Agnew for Vice-President' appeared on the screen to the sound of hysterical laughter. As the words faded they were replaced by another message, 'This would have been funny if it weren't so serious.'

The consensus among British party publicists at the time was that such personal attacks on political opponents would not work in the UK. In 1970, however, Labour did launch a knocking campaign in print in which the Conservative leaders were depicted as ridiculous puppets. This was the famous 'Yesterday's Men' campaign, believed by many to have been counter-productive and to have had some share in the responsibility for Labour's General Election defeat that year. Strangely the Tories repeated Labour's mistake four years later, this time on TV. In the February 1974 election one Conservative party political included a clip showing a puppet Harold Wilson throwing away pound notes. It did not save Edward Heath's Conservative Government from defeat and, in the opinion of some, may even have contributed to that result.

Come 1978, and the Conservative Opposition, now led by Margaret Thatcher, was fully appreciative of the need for hard-hitting yet restrained advertising that would make the most of the perceived failings of the Labour Government without being so offensive as to antagonise uncommitted voters. This task was carried out to near-perfection by the agency chosen, Saatchi & Saatchi Garland-Compton. The agency was to become quickly and universally known as Saatchi & Saatchi, though that, as already explained, was not actually its name.

The poster campaign launched by the agency in 1978 capitalised cleverly on the current mood of dissatisfaction with the Labour Government headed by Jim Callaghan. The posters were simple but striking. Possibly the most noticed and most effective was that headed 'Labour isn't working'. It showed a long queue of people outside an 'unemployment office'. Unemployment had in truth increased alarmingly, although it was still – ironic to recall – low in comparison with the heights it was to reach under the Tories. The pay-off line, that is the words in smaller type at the bottom right-hand corner of the poster, was 'Britain's better off with the Conservatives', which echoed the famous slogan of 1959, 'Life's better with the Conservatives.'

Another poster, in the same style, was headed 'Britain isn't getting any better' and showed a queue of patients trying to get into a hospital. Yet another had a child writing on a blackboard 'Educashun isnt wurking.' Like the unemployment poster, these played on legitimate public anxieties about the way things were going in the country. Ruder but less simple and probably less effective was a poster that declared '1984 – what would Britain be like after another 5 years of Labour?' By this time it was 1979, and in the spring General Election the Tory ads became themselves a major talking point. The fact, discovered by the press, that the people in the dole queue ad were not genuine unemployed men and women did nothing to diminish controversy. But reports that they included agency staffers were untrue.

As the election approached it was the party political broadcasts that became more important than the posters. These broadcasts, on the Conservative side, looked more than ever before like long commercials, with all the technical tricks of the advertising trade brought in to make graphic and compelling the party's claims about alleged Labour mismanagement of the economy. In one, for example, stereotypical foreigners – a Frenchman, a German and an Italian – were seen collecting money they had won, while an Englishman argued about how much he was entitled to. Such broadcasts were criticised by some as being, unlike the posters, confusing in their effect, but they were far more watchable than most party politicals.

As the political battle went on, the exotic-sounding name of the Conservative Party's ad agency cropped up more and more frequently in ribald comments by comedians, journalists and anti-Tory politicians. Who were these two mysterious people 'Snatchy & Snatchy' and 'Thaatchi & Thaatchi'?

The brothers themselves, shunning as usual personal publicity while delighting in the corporate variety, did nothing to enlighten them. The mystery of their name, like the ribaldry, served to heighten public interest in their company, and public interest, they rightly reasoned, could not be bad for business.

In any case Charles for one has always been exceedingly touchy about public mention of the family's origins. When the draft of a book about the UK advertising business had been shown to him three years before the 1979 elections he had made only one suggestion to its author – that a reference to the Saatchis as being Iraqi Jews be deleted. At that time he had thought such information could be of benefit only to his enemies in Adland. His company certainly had its detractors, including those envious of its rapid growth, but it may be wondered why, so successful a man did not feel more pride in what he was as well as in what he had accomplished. As the years went by, and he accomplished even more, he did not appear to become any more relaxed about this particular subject.

Perhaps, if the company had been called Smith & Smith, it would have attracted far less satirical interest during the election campaign – and benefited less greatly from it. It is arguable, therefore, that the brothers' alien origins, far from being a handicap, ended by bestowing a substantial advantage on them. What is indisputable is that, despite the low personal profiles they kept, the 1979 General Election and the advertising run-up to it made *their* name famous and not that of Tim Bell, who at the time was not only running the main agency (Saatchi & Saatchi Garland-Compton) but was the advertising man most closely involved with the Conservative Party campaign. Bell greatly prized the letter of thanks sent to him after the election by Margaret Thatcher, but it was the Saatchi name and not his that became synonymous in the public mind with the successful political advertising.

For, of course, the most important thing about the 1978–9 Tory political ad campaign was not any of the poster slogans or TV gimmicks but the fact that the party won. It is impossible to assess with any accuracy whatever the extent to which advertising contributed to the Conservative victory. After the public service strikes of the 'winter of discontent', which preceded the General Election, and the disarray into which the Labour Government seemed to have been thrown, all the smart money was on a Tory return to power anyway, with or without advertising. But the ads certainly did no harm and, by focusing skilfully on the Government's difficulties, may well have helped some of the floating voters make up their minds. If the Tories had lost, it would nevertheless have been difficult to describe the campaign as successful. Since they won, it could hardly be called anything else.

At the time there was indeed a popular impression that the Saatchi contribution, rather than being of marginal importance, as students of advertising would have been likely to say, was central to the Conservative achievement. Paradoxically the company's prestige owed as much or more to the statements of its political clients' opponents as to anything said by the Tories. Labour Party people made much of the supposed 'packaging' of the Tories by advertising and publicity professionals. Their victory was ascribed not to political factors but to the cleverness with which they had been 'sold' by Gordon Reece, their publicity chief, and the ad agency he had chosen. This line of argument, intended to belittle Mrs Thatcher, had one certain result, it elevated Saatchi & Saatchi to quasi-mythological status.

Any doubts there may have been inside the company about the wisdom of handling a party political account must have been stilled by the results of the 1978–9 campaign. Not only did the Saatchi & Saatchi name become famous, not only was it associated with success, the company won golden opinions among the Tory business Establishment, which were to stand it in good commercial stead. It is commonly thought that it was the political advertising work done by Saatchi & Saatchi Garland-Compton that tipped the balance in the agency's favour when Lord King, installed by Mrs Thatcher as chairman of British Airways, came to appoint a new firm to handle the airline's account in 1982.

The link between the agency and the Conservative Party has remained despite occasional speculation that the Tories might look elsewhere for their advertising needs. The benefits to the agency have diminished, as they were bound to do. After all, the shock value of its first arrival on the political scene could hardly be repeated. The 1983 General Election, furthermore, did not come into the same category as 1979. In 1983 nobody could labour under any illusion that it was advertising that was responsible for the Conservatives' massive majority rather than the pitiful divisions of the Opposition. Being on the winning side is, however, always good for morale.

As the likely date of the next General Election approached a truly Machiavellian company might have decided that it would be a good thing to resign the Conservative Party account on the grounds that, whatever the exact result might be, the Tories were certain to lose some ground and that, rightly or wrongly (but in all probability wrongly), responsibility for the loss of market share would be attributed to their ad agency. Having served as a ladder with which to scale the heights of Establishment respectability, it might have been argued, the account could now safely be cast aside. But that would have been to ignore some of the facts of advertising life – the web of personal contacts that grow up between advertiser and agency and the value placed upon agency loyalty by other clients and prospective clients.

And then, when an agency does resign an account, it is usually pretty difficult to convince the outside world, except when there is overwhelming confirmatory evidence, that it has not in reality been fired by a dissatisfied client. On the whole, the Saatchis must have decided, life was better for them with the Conservatives. If their political client was to be relatively less successful than formerly, they could hardly complain, given the enormous boost the company had had from its political work at a time when the boost could not have been more useful. And, indeed, rather than backing away from the Tories, the Saatchis tightened their links with the party by seconding Michael Dobbs, a deputy chairman of the Charlotte Street agency, to Conservative Central Office as chief of staff to the party chairman.

In the event, the client's success in 1987 turned out, against many expectations, to be scarcely less than in 1983 – at least in terms of votes and seats won. The advertising campaign itself came in for considerable criticism, not least because it appeared to be outshone by a Labour Party advertising effort that represented a vast improvement on the previous time around. The single most striking advertising event of the election was the Labour election broadcast made by film director (and former commercials maker) Hugh Hudson that almost eschewed politics in favour of an American-style presentation of party leader Neil Kinnock as a warm and wonderful guy.

Nothing that came out of Saatchi & Saatchi Compton was specially impressive. A broadcast that portrayed Labour as a crooked conjuror was felt to be slow and unconvincing. A rogues' gallery of allegedly extremist Labour candidates was not much more persuasive. The Tory campaign slogan, 'The next move forward', was criticised as lacking bite.

Meanwhile Labour press advertising, created by an anonymous group of volunteers, was pressing strongly on the theme of alleged Tory lack of care for the poor, the sick and the elderly. Much of the work, though anonymous, was understood to come from people at Boase Massimi Pollitt, an agency with a high creative reputation which had run an eye-catching campaign for the Greater London Council against the Government's decision to close the GLC down. One typical Labour ad juxtaposed the pictures of a small boy, Mark Burgess, and the Prime Minister and quoted them as saying respectively: 'I've been waiting 13 months to go to hospital for a heart operation,' and, 'I can go on the day I want, at the time I want, with the doctor I want.' Another, showing people in various states of deprivation, was headed: 'She's nice to Reagan, she's nice to Gorbachev, why's she so nasty to us?' No picture was necessary for the reader to know that the she in question was Margaret Thatcher. That ad was probably effective. However, a cartoon sequence in one of the Labour TV broadcasts lampooning Mrs Thatcher was admitted even by Labourites to have been counter-productive in the same way as the 'Yesterday's Men' campaign of 17 years previously.

The most effective Tory press ad in this battle of negatives was probably the one that showed a British soldier with his hands raised in surrender and headlined 'Labour's policy on arms'. Charles Saatchi is believed, though none of the news media published the story at the time, to have taken a personal hand in the production of the Tory ads. Doing the account director's job, now that the Thatcherite Tim Bell was gone, was John Sharkey, the recently appointed joint managing director of Saatchi & Saatchi Compton, London. But also closely involved was Maurice Saatchi. Nobody seems to have found it curious that the two key men in what had by this time become an international conglomerate holding company should be behaving like executives of a single advertising agency, even if that agency was the Charlotte Street bedrock of their fortunes.

According to various press accounts Margaret Thatcher lost faith in the way the campaign was being run by the Saatchis and by the Conservative Party chairman, Norman Tebbit, after a couple of opinion polls had shown a drop in the Tory lead. Research findings by the Young & Rubicam ad agency, which had been supplying the Tories with information from interviews commissioned by it using its Cross-Cultural Consumer Characterisation technique, also indicated a weakening in support for the Government among the large category of people categorised by Y & R as 'mainstreamers', the self-interested, unadventurous people not much concerned with ideology but keen on having such things as an efficient National Health Service.

At that point, it is alleged, Tim Bell, by now a director of Lowe Howard-Spink & Bell, was called in, and as a result of his advice and that of his partner Frank Lowe, the Tories hit back in the closing days of the campaign with some no-nonsense newspaper ads with no clever-clever visuals but full of large-print claims that, for example, 'Nurses' pay is up by 30% above inflation,' and, 'Britain now has the fewest strikes for 50 years.' The new campaign slogan was, 'Britain is great again. Don't let Labour wreck it.' This was eerily reminiscent of the old Colman Prentis & Varley slogan of some thirty years before. Some things do not change as much as they are believed to.

The consensus inside the advertising industry was that Labour had won the advertising war. On the day, however, it made no difference to the outcome. From the outsider's point of view the most remarkable feature of the election was the consistency of the voting pattern with opinion polls over a long period. It is difficult to believe that what really mattered was anything else but the division of the opposition and the reluctance of the electorate to let go of nurse for fear of getting something worse. And whatever the course of the election campaign, a win for the Tories could only be good news for Saatchi & Saatchi. As with every other advertising account the client's success inevitably rubs off on to the agency.

Nevertheless, the Saatchis were clearly riled by the adverse coverage of their election performance. When 'Panorama' was thought to have implied that Charlotte Street had lost control of the Tory campaign a libel suit was threatened and the BBC paid £1,000 to the NSPCC by way of apology. Subsequently a joint statement was put out by Saatchi & Saatchi and Lowe Howard-Spink & Bell in which one side congratulated the Saatchis 'on their great success with the Tory election campaign' and the other thanked Frank Lowe 'for his valuable contribution during the campaign.'

Whether the Saatchis will be working for the Conservative Party, their most influential client, in 1991 is anybody's guess.

4

The Takeover Trail

From its very early days as a small advertising agency, Saatchi & Saatchi was, as we have already seen, acquisition-minded. One of the reasons why the brothers, to begin with, enjoyed a somewhat mixed reputation among their fellow advertising professionals was precisely that they were seen as being too big for their boots and in too much of a hurry to expand by takeover rather than, in the approved manner, by attracting more clients and more business from existing clients. Even in a trade where modesty is hard to find and blowing one's own trumpet is standard practice they were distinguished for their (corporate, not personal) cheek. Or, to use the Yiddish word with its twin meaning of boldness and effrontery, chutzpah.

Between 1970 and 1975 this chutzpah struck different observers, according to their dispositions, as amusing, admirable, irritating or deplorable. Nobody, however, except possibly the brothers themselves, would have believed that within comparatively few years Saatchi chutzpah would triumph over the whole advertising world. But so it was to do.

The empire building began in a small way with the 1973 purchase, previously alluded to, of Dawes of Manchester. In the same year links were forged with small ad agencies in Holland and Belgium, proving that there was some substance in the Saatchis' international ambitions. Their French venture, however, turned out to consist mainly of wishful thinking. In theory Saatchi was supposed early in 1973 to be taking a majority stake in the Paris ad agency Opta Dragon, which was being joined by Pierre Damour, who had been running another Paris agency,

Quadrant. Damour was expected to bring with him £500,000 of British Leyland advertising business, but in the event only half of Leyland's billing followed him to Opta Dragon, renamed Saatchi Damour. Subsequently the agency lost a quantity of other business, and Saatchi & Saatchi withdrew from the deal without ever completing it.

The real great leap forward was the merger with Compton UK, which came about partly through luck. But luck is what you make of it, and there is no doubt that the Saatchi team brilliantly exploited the opportunity presented in 1975. After 1977, with the restructuring of the group and the establishment of Saatchi & Saatchi as a holding company, the way was clear to resume the search for growth through acquisition, but now from a much stronger base. With hindsight the period 1975–8 can be seen as a breathing space during which Saatchi energies were concentrated on consolidating and building up the main Charlotte Street agency, Saatchi & Saatchi Garland-Compton. From 1978 onwards the brothers hit the takeover trail with a vengeance. They were greatly aided by having at their disposal the financial acumen of the newly recruited Martin Sorrell.

In 1978 Hall Advertising of Edinburgh was bought for £1 million. Or rather for a down payment of £250,000, to be followed by further instalments of £250,000 in 1979 and £500,000 in 1980. In 1979 Saatchi & Saatchi acquired 80% of the Dublin ad agency O'Kennedy-Brindley and two years later bought the rest, the total price being £315,000.

These were, hindsight again shows, mere limbering-up moves. A more serious attempt to expand was launched in 1978 against Collett Dickenson Pearce, the London agency where Charles had made his reputation as a copywriter not so many years before. In one sense this was the most natural of all the Saatchis' numerous takeover projects; CDP, with its strong reputation for creative and imaginative advertising, must have seemed to Charles to provide, of all the larger UK agencies, the best fit with his own group. Though by now he was primarily a businessman, and an ambitious one, he had never lost, and never was to lose, his craftsman's concern for advertising's creative product.

In another sense, though, the move was uncharacteristic of the Saatchi acquisition policy. Usually that policy was, and has continued to be, to make a takeover bid only with the agreement of the people running the company to be taken over. There is nothing altruistic about such a policy. In a 'people business' such as advertising, where the assets, as is commonly said, all go home at night, a contested bid involves the risk of losing some of those assets. The Saatchi bid was not welcomed by the CDP board, which was intent on retaining its independence, and the price offered was declared by CDP's financial advisers, Warburgs, to be too small.

At the time CDP was Britain's sixth biggest ad agency, not much smaller than Saatchi & Saatchi Garland-Compton, in fourth place. Nevertheless CDP was thought vulnerable because, while it too had become a publicly quoted company, it was facing an uncertain future owing to the recently disclosed intention of the Inland Revenue to charge its chairman and managing director with tax irregularities. Saatchi was only one of six companies that, scenting blood, had been drawn to CDP as to a wounded prey. CDP managed, however, to overcome its difficulties. Both the chairman, the late John Pearce, and the managing director, Frank Lowe, resigned. (Both were eventually fined as a result of the court case that arose out of the disposal of certain of CDP's earnings abroad.) The agency itself managed to escape from its exposed position as a public company by being sold into the private ownership of its own employees. This happened in two stages. First, in 1979, a holding company was set up in which the merchant bank Hambros held 75% of the equity. Finally, in 1983, thirty-seven CDP employees raised enough money to buy Hambros out and take a majority stake in their own agency. A 40% share was taken by Young & Rubicam, the giant – and privately owned – American ad agency group.

The CDP people's fear was of being bought and sold against their will in the same way as had happened to Dorland Advertising at the beginning of the 1970s. It was precisely Dorlands that fell into the Saatchis' hands in 1981, their first major financial *coup* since the 1975 merger with Compton UK Partners. To explain how this happened, we must retrace our steps a little and see what happened to Dorlands after its bruising encounter with John Bentley.

Bentley, as already explained, bought and sold Dorland within months. The purchaser was Eric Garrott, proprietor of a small but prosperous ad agency. He formed the Garrott Dorland Crawford Holdings group, privately owned with himself as the main shareholder but with minority stakes held by some working directors. The price paid by Garrott was £850,000. Ten years later, in ill health and with no wife and children, Garrott feared that in the event of his death the company would be destroyed by death duties. Reluctantly he decided to sell out but, moved by patriotic feeling, he resisted several approaches made to him by American agencies. Instead, after several months of negotiations, a deal was struck with Saatchi & Saatchi.

The Saatchi group was to take over the whole of GDCH, including Dorland Advertising, the Crawford and Brockie Haslam agencies and Dorland Financial Services, for a total price of £5.6 million, of which an initial payment of £1.5 million was financed by an equity issue. The rest was payable in 1982 and 1983, depending on the achievement of certain financial targets. Garrott was to continue as chairman of GDCH, within the enlarged group, and it was agreed that the individual agencies would continue to be run autonomously by the same people as before. At one stroke the merged group became the largest of its kind in the UK, with total billings of about £150 million, of which GDCH accounted for more than a third.

Garrott declared: 'This is a union of strength and a great day for British advertising.' Only four months later he died during an operation.

The GDCH deal set the pattern that Saatchi & Saatchi was to follow in subsequent years as acquisition succeeded acquisition at an accelerating pace. There would be no contested bids; a company would be bought only if it had competent management willing to stay on. The price would be paid over a period, with the exact amount dependent on performance. Shares would be issued to fund the deal.

This last point was extremely important and was in the future to become even more so. Saatchi had become the first British ad agency business able to tap the London stock market in a big way to finance its growth. It was able to do this because not only was it publicly quoted but its commercial and financial record was found impressive by City of London investors. An apparently unstoppable stream of new accounts gained by the main Charlotte Street agency had been accompanied by excellent financial management. In the three years preceding the deal with Garrott new business had come in from, among many others, Allied Breweries, British Leyland, British Petroleum, British Rail, Campbell's Soups, Dunlop, IBM, Procter & Gamble, Rowntree, Schweppes and United Biscuits as well as the Conservative Party.

There had been losses too, of course. Every agency suffers them from time to time, but in the case of Saatchi & Saatchi Garland-Compton they had been vastly outweighed by the gains. And group profits had been shooting up in line with this growth in turnover. In the financial year up to the end of September 1980, that is the last full year before the Garrott deal, the Saatchi group's pre-tax profits had risen by 23% to just over £3 million on turnover of almost £85 million. This ratio of profit to turnover of about 3.5% was considerably above the industry average of nearer 2%. (It should be emphasised that, in speaking of advertising agencies, the word turnover, like billings, refers to the volume of money handled by agencies on behalf of their clients and not the amount retained by them as remuneration for their services. Assuming such remuneration to be roughly 15% of turnover, a 3.5% margin on turnover equates to one of about 23.5% on income.)

The obvious next step was to expand internationally, something the Saatchis had been trying to do since the early 1970s. Ten years previously they had spoken ambitiously about their hopes of obtaining a toe-hold in the United States, now they were in a position to do something serious about getting rather more than a toe-hold in the world's biggest advertising market. Negotiations went on over a long period with at least four American ad agencies – Doyle Dane Bernbach, Cunningham & Walsh, Wells Rich Greene and Compton. Conversations are believed also to have taken place with Kenyon & Eckhardt and Foote Cone & Belding.

In the end it was Compton Communications (as it was now called) which consented to be bought. The event was both logical and surprising. The obvious logic lay in the fact that the New York company had been associated with the Saatchis since 1975 as a part-owner of their operating subsidiary Saatchi & Saatchi Compton. The American agency also had a string of affiliated agencies in various countries with which Charlotte Street already co-operated, particularly on Procter & Gamble business. Indeed if any other American agency had succumbed to Saatchi blandishments, it might have involved some disruption of that co-operation, perhaps even the loss by Saatchi & Saatchi Garland-Compton of its cherished P & G business.

The surprise when a takeover deal between the two companies was announced in 1982 was real enough, though. Not many months beforehand Milton Gossett, boss of Compton, had explicitly denied that a deal was on the cards, though he said he was happy to help his British associates in their search for a merger partner. Less surprising, though still fairly remarkable, was the fact that it was the smaller fish that was swallowing the bigger one. The Americans explained that it was easier for a publicly quoted firm to buy a privately owned one than vice versa. Likewise a private company would find it harder than a public one to raise money for expansion.

It was their desire for expansion – the strengthening of the Compton network both at home in the United States and abroad – that the Americans advanced as their motive for the merger. In one way the deal could be compared with the original get-together between Saatchi & Saatchi and the Compton group in the UK; a larger but duller and slower-moving outfit hoping to benefit from the dynamism of a smaller but higher-profile organisation. But in other ways it was very different. Compton UK Partners had been a public company frightened that its stock market quote might do it an injury and turning to a private firm to save it from that danger. Seven years later it was precisely the fact of being a public company that made Saatchi & Saatchi an attractive merger partner. Another important difference was that this time the Compton directors stood to get rich out of the deal. About 100 employees held stock in the American company, the biggest shareholder being Milt Gossett with 10%. Understandably they laid less emphasis on this than on their hopes for a bright business future.

What they were selling was not simply one New York agency but a group, reckoned to be fourteenth largest of its kind in the world, with total billing of about $650 million and pre-tax profits of $8 million. It was divided into three parts: Compton Advertising, the New York agency, founded in 1908; Compton International, the network of affiliated agencies in other countries; and Compton Group, consisting of several companies in the US, mostly specialising in particular kinds of advertising. Among the latter were: Fairfax Advertising, specialising in direct response ads; Klemtner Advertising, specialising in health care products; Rumrill-Hoyt, an industrial advertising agency; Mayo Infurna, a design consultancy; and Irv Koons, specialising in packaging design.

To finance the deal Saatchi & Saatchi resorted to a rights issue, which raised £26 million. The Americans received an initial payment of $30.8 million. In addition $24.5 million was to be paid to them over the following eleven years if earnings grew by 8% or more. A new agency network was created with the name Saatchi & Saatchi Compton Worldwide, of which Gossett was chairman and chief executive officer. As a result of the deal the Charlotte Street agency changed its name from Saatchi & Saatchi Garland-Compton to Saatchi & Saatchi Compton

London, not that in practice this made much difference, for everyone, including its employees, went on calling it (wrongly) Saatchi & Saatchi. The slightly paradoxical situation was created, which continues to this day, that Charlotte Street theoretically reports to New York, which in turn reports back to Saatchi & Saatchi corporate headquarters in London. In fact Charles and Maurice Saatchi did not necessarily bother to consult Gossett before taking a hand in the affairs of their own flagship agency.

More surprised than anyone else by the Saatchi takeover of Compton were the men in charge of KMP, a London ad agency which had sold out to American Compton not long before and which now found itself without warning part of the Saatchi empire. KMP merits a few words all to itself, for there had been a time in the 1970s when it, rather than Saatchi & Saatchi, looked to be shaping up as a British advertising conglomerate with the possibility of rivalling the American-owned multinational agencies.

The KMP story illustrates perhaps better than most the snakes-and-ladders nature of the 'people business' called advertising. It is a business in which reputations and fortunes can be won and lost in a short time. KMP was founded as Kingsley Manton and Palmer in 1964, when it made an even bigger splash than Saatchi & Saatchi was to do when it was launched six years later. Unlike the reclusive Charles Saatchi, the three eponymous founders were all highly visible public figures within the business. Before joining forces to start their own agency all three were directors of other firms – David Kingsley of Benton & Bowles, Michael Manton of Crawfords and Brian Palmer of Young & Rubicam. Unlike the Saatchis they chucked in their jobs and set up on their own without first having signed up a single client. They won clients by soliciting them directly, a practice even more frowned upon at that time than in 1970. Like the Saatchis, they were outspoken in their opposition to the commission system and their preference for fees.

They won attention as well as clients, not only because of their outspoken opinions but also because of some eye-catching ad campaigns, including those for the Salvation Army ('For God's sake, care') and White Horse whisky. In 1969, by which time the three founders had been joined by a fourth partner, Len Heath, they decided they were tired of running a successful small agency. They wanted to be big, and the way to get big quick, they reasoned, was through acquisition. They intended to acquire other ad agencies but also marketing services companies of other kinds. How to finance this ambitious programme? Why, through going public and tapping the investment funds of the City of London, of course. In other words they set out very consciously and deliberately on the same course that was later to be followed more successfully, but apparently less deliberately, by the Saatchis.

Their new, publicly quoted holding company was called KMPH and later changed it name to Kimpher, to accommodate the initial of a fifth partner, George Riches, who joined them briefly. Within four years Kimpher owned, instead of one ad agency, eight, including five in London, two in Manchester and one in Australia. The group also had minority interests in agencies in Sweden and Ireland. Additionally it had moved, as planned, outside the conventional ad agency field and owned companies in the fields of sales promotion, market research, design and recruitment and classified advertising. There was also a very successful subsidiary, still around, called The Media Department, which specialised in the buying of advertising space and time on behalf of clients who did not want to operate through agencies.

In the 1974 league table of agency billings Kimpher took the number five spot with a group turnover figure of £23 million. That was its high spot. After that things began to fall apart. In fact they had already begun to fall apart, for although the group had been growing in turnover its profits had been stagnating. In the financial year 1973–4 group profits amounted to only £362,000, which was not much more than twice the amount made by the original KMP agency in 1969–70 on a turnover of only a sixth of Kimpher's. KMP still retained its identity as an agency within the group but was no longer doing very well now that its principals – Kingsley, Manton, Palmer and Heath – had withdrawn from the job of keeping advertising clients happy to devote themselves to corporate administration.

A process of rationalisation was embarked upon. The KMP shop kept its autonomy, but three other London ad agencies were merged into a fourth, Allardyce. This in turn was hit when its biggest-spending client, Brentford Nylons, collapsed leaving Allardyce to pick up the bills. (In law advertising agencies are principals and are responsible for debts contracted to media even though they are acting on behalf of clients.) Meanwhile group losses bgan to mount – £372,000 for the year to the end of March 1976, of which £210,000 was accounted for by Brentford Nylons. Another £72,000 went on termination payments to Palmer and Heath, who went off to do other things. Kimpher struggled on for a while under Manton as group managing director, but eventually it was bought out by Guinness Morison International, a subsidiary of the Guinness brewing concern. In 1979 the management of KMP, still going as an agency, bought its freedom from Guinness and retained it for the three years until its deal with Compton, swiftly followed by the Saatchi takeover.

The failure of Kimpher, plain though it was for all to see once things went wrong, was not easily predictable. The men who put it together were vigorous and talented. They had a clear vision of what they wanted to do, and there was no obvious reason why it could not be done. It may be said that they were unlucky in their acquisitions, but that was not so obvious at the time they made them. It may be said more convincingly that they began to spread their efforts too thinly before having built up a really solid financial base in one operating company. It may be said that going public made them vulnerable, but if only their financial performance had been more satisfactory access to the stock market would surely have proved to be the advantage they counted on it being.

The comparison with Saatchi & Saatchi is instructive. The Saatchi brothers' company went public not of its own accord but via the unplanned reverse takeover of a larger firm. If the 1975 merger with Compton UK Partners had not happened – if Kirkwood had accepted the proposal put to him by Compton instead of turning it down – would Saatchi & Saatchi have taken its shares to market? Probably, given the ambitious outlook of the brothers and their associates, it would have done so sooner or later in order to raise money for the acquisitions on which they had already before 1975 proved they were bent. But would they have been able to raise enough money to acquire really worthwhile properties? Would they have been big enough for Eric Garrott, to name but one, to take seriously as purchasers of Dorland Advertising and its associated agencies? Maybe, but it's doubtful.

It is amusing but ultimately fruitless to speculate what might have happened to Saatchis if it had followed the Kimpher path of buying a spread of small subsidiaries rather than getting into the big time with one bound. The brothers would not necessarily have made any of the same mistakes as Kingsley Manton and Palmer, but there would surely have been a real chance of coming a cropper as Kimpher did if they had rushed their fences. But once they were sitting on top of a substantial profit-earning base in the shape of the merged Saatchi & Saatchi Garland-Compton agency, their position was transformed. They could afford to think seriously about what Kimpher could only dream of doing, namely emulating Interpublic.

Interpublic is the American company which years ago blazed the trail for the advertising-based conglomerates and so-called mega-mergers that have recently become fashionable. No need to wonder whether Charles and Maurice were influenced by Interpublic's example. They could hardly have not been. Later, as we shall see, they were to be influenced by direct rivalry with the American company, which until 1986 was to retain its position as the world's biggest ad agency group. At the beginning of the 1980s, however, it must have been Interpublic's past rather than its future that most interested them.

The concept of a worldwide organisation of operationally independent advertising agency networks able to compete with each other for accounts was turned into a reality by a man called Marion Harper. In 1948 Harper, who had started out as a market researcher, became boss of the New York agency McCann-Erickson. Up till then conventional advertising wisdom had it that limits were set to the growth of any agency business by the unwillingness of clients to allow their accounts to be handled by the same agencies that worked for the clients' competitors. The ban on such account conflicts is inspired by fear of breaches of commercial confidentiality, since ad agents get to know a lot about their clients' plans. Neither the fear nor the ban apply, incidentally, to Japan, where advertisers quite happily trust agency people working on their accounts not to communicate secrets to colleagues working within the same agencies on rival accounts.

Marvel Marion Harper, as he came to be known, decided that the solution to this problem, and the secret of rapid growth, lay in acquiring other agencies and keeping them strictly separate, so that clients of one agency within a group would have no fears of breach of trust even if a rival account was handled by another agency owned by the same group. To this end Harper created a holding company called Interpublic and started to put his ideas into action. He spent money lavishly not only on buying new subsidiaries but, increasingly as the group grew, on unnecessary administrative luxuries such as company aircraft and a dude ranch in Long Island. The boss's spendthrift habits led to a financial crisis in 1967. In that year the other six members of the Interpublic board united to throw Harper out despite the facts that he was the largest individual stockholder and a dictator whose creatures they were all considered to be.

Marvel Marion sank into obscurity, but his ideas went marching on. It was Harperism without Harper. The biggest Interpublic *coup* was carried out years later by Phil Geier, who took over as head of the holding company after having run the McCann-Erickson office in London. Late in 1978 it was announced that Interpublic was taking over the entire SSC & B: Lintas world-wide ad agency network. This was constituted by two organisations, the American SSC & B (Sullivan Stauffer Colwell & Bayles) and Lintas (originally Lever International Advertising Service), owned 51% by Unilever and 49% by SSC & B. At the time the SSC & B: Lintas network was eighth biggest in the advertising world and claimed to be number one in Europe. The deal with Interpublic was the biggest in the history of advertising and would not be topped until 1986.

But back to Saatchi & Saatchi and its own progress along the Interpublic route. The 1982 Compton deal marked no let-up in the pace of expansion. Acquisitions followed one another at a fast and furious pace, the majority of them in America. In 1983 the New York ad agency McCaffrey & McCall was bought for $10 million plus deferred payments of about $7.5 million. This was an agency billing $140 million, with pre-tax profits for 1982 of nearly $3.6 million. Also in 1983 Hunter Advertising in Dublin and Gough Waterhouse in Sydney were bought.

In 1984 yet more agencies were bought, including Cochrane Chase Livingston, a well-known firm in California, for a down payment of $1.4 million and another, performance-related payment of $1 million the following year, with a final sum due in 1989. In the Netherlands an agency called RJA was bought for £130,000 plus deferred performance-related sums payable over three years. It was merged with an existing Saatchi & Saatchi Compton office in the country. In the UK the Harrison Cowley chain of regional ad agencies and public relations and recruitment consultants was bought for £7.5 million worth of convertible unsecured loan stock. It was merged with other Saatchi subsidiaries to form (though not for long) a new grouping called Crawford Hall Harrison Cowley, under Stuart Duncan, who had been boss of Crawfords since before the deal with Eric Garrott.

Also in 1984, also in the UK, Michael Bungey DFS was taken over and merged with Dorland Advertising, which simultaneously acquired an option to buy the European operations of Bungey's American associate, the Dancer Fitzgerald Sample agency of New York. This deal marked the beginning of protracted negotiations to link Dorlands with Dancer itself. These were to culminate only two years later in an agreement which effectively brought DFS into the Saatchi empire. It will be described in detail later.

At the end of 1984 a smallish but successful young British agency, Hedger Mitchell Stark, was acquired and merged with the Charlotte Street agency. The price was £1.2 million down plus a deferred performance-related sum of £1.8 million. This, though not a major deal from the financial point of view, cast an interesting light on the Saatchi acquisition strategy. HMS had a good list of accounts, including part of British Rail, but the main purpose of the deal was not to buy billing but to buy back Jeff Stark, a talented copywriter and the creative partner in the agency, who had previously worked at Charlotte Street but had left the Saatchis' employ to do his own thing. Starting one's own shop is an option any well-regarded (and some not so well-regarded) admen are likely to consider at some time. The obvious motivating desires are for independence, fame and money. By giving up the first Stark now gained the latter two at a stroke, since the Saatchi offer in effect put a value on him personally of about £1 million.

Was the HMS acquisition an extravagance, then? In a way perhaps it was. But it involved benefits no less real for being intangible. These were the strengthening of the Charlotte Street creative team, in fact but also in the minds of clients and potential clients who read about the deal in the trade press, and the generation of a sense of excitement among not only clients but employees and potential employees of the Saatchis' flagship agency. Such excitement – call it enthusiasm or morale if you prefer – is an important element in the success of any advertising agency. It is what makes an agency, in adman's slang, 'hot' and causes the cleverest people in the trade to want to work for it and the most important advertisers to want to do business with it. Even when a high pitch of morale has been attained, as was certainly the case with Saatchi & Saatchi Compton London, keeping it going year after year is not necessarily easy. Behind the well-publicised return of Stark to the fold could be seen the old flair for ballyhoo of Charles Saatchi.

However, late 1984 also witnessed a far more significant event in the development of the Saatchi & Saatchi Company. This was the start of its first real attempt to diversify out of advertising. The brothers had been talking privately for years about their interest in expanding into market services other than advertising, as Kimpher had done, but nothing much had happened apart from the launch in 1980 of a UK subsidiary, the Sales Promotion Agency. Suddenly in December 1984 two separate announcements marked the group's move into market research and, even more surprisingly, management consultancy.

Both these diversifications took place in the United States, which increasingly and logically – given the huge size of the American market – was where the Saatchi group's centre of gravity lay, even if its headquarters remained in London. The research company acquired was Yankelovich Skelly & White, of New York, together with YSW's subsidiary McBer & Co., which specialised in studies of employee attitudes and performance. YSW itself was renowned among the top twenty American research companies for its new product testing and surveys of social attitudes. Its eponymous founders, Daniel Yankelovich, Florence Skelly and Arthur White, had sold it several years earlier to Saul Steinberg's Reliance group partly to obtain the resources with which to develop their work.

At the time of the sale to Saatchi YSW's turnover performance was fairly static. Combined revenues of YSW and Boston-based McBer during 1984 amounted to just over $20 million, with after-tax profits of $972,000. The sale price was a straight $13.5 million. No earn-out arrangement was involved, since the people running the research agency had parted with all their shares when they sold to Steinberg. There was, for the same reason, no need to consult them, but they were in fact fairly pleased about the prospect of taking part in the development of a new wing of a growing international company. Charles Saatchi let it be known that his group was keen on acquiring more research agencies which would be placed under the authority of YSW. The honeymoon with Florence Skelly, the formidable woman boss of YSW (her male partners had by then become less active in the day-to-day management of the firm) was not, however, to last. We shall come to the reason in due course.

The other diversification took place through the purchase of the Hay Group. It was the most expensive Saatchi acquisition so far, a fact doubly striking because the company acquired lay outside the advertising area with which the Saatchis were familiar and even outside the larger marketing services area into which they had expressed hopes of expanding. Hay, founded in the 1940s by a man called Edward Hay, had been run for most of its existence by Dr Milton Rock as a management consultancy specialising particularly in 'human resources', meaning advising companies on how best to deploy and reward their managers. It served some 5,000 clients through ninety-four offices in twenty-seven countries.

In 1977 Hay had bought the British executive recruitment agency MSL (Management Selection Ltd) from its founder Harry Roff, who had made it the leader in its field in Britain and had also built up an extensive overseas clientèle. With the rise of executive search agencies (or head-hunters, as they are commonly known), MSL had lost its old advertising-based pre-eminence in the UK but remained a substantial business, using head-hunting as well as advertising to find the recruits it screened for its clients.

After a long period of strong growth Hay had found itself strapped for cash for further expansion. It had to choose between going public on its own account or selling out to a suitable purchaser. It was Hay's financial advisers, who knew the Saatchis to be looking around for investment opportunities, who effected the necessary contacts. Almost like the original big deal of 1975, this was an opportunity which presented itself to the brothers and their associates rather than having been specifically sought by them. It was an opportunity they were not slow to grasp.

The price paid for the Hay Group was $80 million up front, with deferred profit-related payments of another $45 million to come – $20 million if profits exceeded $16.5 million in the year to the end of August 1985, and another $25 million if profits exceeded an average of $20.5 million in the three years up to the end of August 1987. This was for a company which in the financial year to the end of August 1984 had made profits of $12.9 million on turnover of $105.17 million, of which roughly 60% came from US and 40% from its international operations. The deal was financed by the placing of 10,440,000 new Saatchi shares. By comparison the purchase of Compton Communications two years previously had involved the issue of eight million new shares.

The Saatchis justified this, for them, massive deal on several grounds. For one thing, management consultancy was in itself a good business to be in and in the US was growing faster than advertising. Secondly, they confidently expected Saatchi ownership to improve Hay's financial performance, and not only because a public company is bound to put more emphasis on meeting profit targets than is a privately owned partnership. As a US financial analyst pointed out, Hay's performance had been uneven because of the lack of a consistent strategy to market its services aggressively, and this a marketing-minded parent company could be expected to do something about.

More controversially it was also claimed that the management consultancy could and would work synergistically with the ad agencies and other specialised companies in the Saatchi group. The idea was that they would help each other by cross-referral of clients. Companies which called on Hay's services would be encouraged to go to a Saatchi agency for their advertising; advertising clients would be persuaded of the usefulness of what Hay had to offer. In some cases, notably US Steel, cross-referral seems to have worked. To what extent it makes a real difference to the fortunes of jointly owned companies that provide quite different services from each other is a moot point.

Not moot, it should be added, from the Saatchis' own viewpoint. A London stockbroker's analyst who had the audacity to express scepticism in a circular about the scope for cross-referral found himself given the cold shoulder by the company. By now Saatchi & Saatchi was paying more attention to the analysts than Charles had always done, and continued to do, to the trade press. But City analysts, like journalists, were valued according to whether they produced reports regarded as helpful to the company. Scepticism in either category of reporter was not, in the eyes of Charles and Maurice, an admirable quality.

But at this time there was very little criticism of the Saatchis either in the City or in the press. Everything they touched seemed to turn to gold. At any rate group profits went on rising – up by no less than 121% in the financial year 1984–5 to £40,446,000 on turnover of £1,307,386,000, which had risen by a more modest 53%. And the buying spree went on.

In 1985 more advertising agencies were acquired, beginning with Wong Lam, a small company in Hong Kong. Larger agencies were bought later in the year in Canada and New Zealand. The Canadian agency, Hayhurst, cost £3.75 million cash with further deferred payments to follow to bring the total purchase price to 10.5 times Hayhurst's average after-tax profits for the four years to the end of September 1988. A fairly similar arrangement was entered into for the purchase of Campaign Advertising, New Zealand's second biggest agency, the cash advance on which was £430,000.

Back home Sharps Advertising was bought in spring on the initiative of Jack Rubins, chairman of the Saatchi subsidiary Dorland Advertising, and merged into his agency. Cash up front: £1.1 million with, as usual, more to come. Sharps had stood at number thirty-seven in the 1984 league table with billings of £28 million. The equity had been held by the working directors headed by managing director Michael Kaye, who now joined the Dorland board. Dorlands had in its quiet way been growing apace, and there was now a serious question as to whether it might not finish the year at the top of the table, ahead even of its Charlotte Street sister. In fact it took third position, with billings of £140 million, up from number five the previous year. Saatchi & Saatchi Compton London stayed at the top of the tree with vastly increased billings of £207 million, thanks to the acquisition of yet another agency, Grandfield Rork Collins, which was physically absorbed into Charlotte Street.

GRC was headed by Nigel Grandfield, whom we have already met as the successor to Phil Geier as chairman of the London office of McCann-Erickson. Suave and urbane though he was, Grandfield fell out with his American bosses over the administration of his province and departed in a huff in 1979 for – guess where? – Saatchi & Saatchi. The brothers set him up as head of a new subsidiary, Saatchi & Saatchi International. Remember that this was before the takeover of Compton in New York, and the Saatchi group was still looking for a way to expand internationally. The idea was that Grandfield's unit would seek business from clients that wanted international campaigns co-ordinated from London. The project was short-lived, partly because Grandfield ran into suspicious rivalry from Tim Bell, at that time still the big cheese in Charlotte Street. Grandfield went off yet again, this time to start his own agency.

He succeeded brilliantly at first, capturing most importantly the Tesco advertising account, one of the biggest in Britain, from his old agency McCanns. Tesco's managers had thought highly of him since his McCann days when he had proved himself a first-class presenter. He had also managed to bring into his new agency as a partner Mike Franklin, another ex-McCann man who knew everything there was to know about handling the complicated Tesco account. (Big retail accounts are inevitably complicated because they rely heavily on the use of local newspapers as well as television.) Andy Rork, also an ex-

McCann man, was the well-regarded creative director of GRC.

Among other accounts Grandfield picked up was News International, and he became quite close to its boss, Rupert Murdoch. By 1984 GRC had claimed billings of £45 million and had risen to be number twenty-two in the annual league table. Not content with this, Grandfield set up a number of subsidiaries within what was already a mini-conglomerate. Notable among them were a public relations company, Granard, and a financial advertising and PR firm, GRC Financial. He also attempted to move GRC on to the international stage by forming an alliance with agencies in other countries. Ambition outran resources, and by mid-1985 there were financial problems. What probably precipitated the sell-out, however, was an argument with Tesco about alleged overspending by the agency in Ireland. With Saatchi & Saatchi Compton, which had recently lost the Sainsbury account, angling for Tesco, GRC felt very exposed.

When at this point Nigel Grandfield's old friends Maurice and Charles came up with an offer, it was one he and his board felt they could not refuse. The down payment was £4 million, with an earn-out arrangement reckoned to be worth possibly another £6 million in deferred payments to the eight shareholder-directors of whom Grandfield himself, owning 31%, and Rork (22%) were the biggest. The 175 employees were promised that all would keep their jobs, and each received a bottle of Saatchi champagne as a 'welcome aboard' gift – a nice PR touch. Grandfield went off shortly afterwards on an extended holiday to France. GRC's office premises in Lower Regent Street were reassigned for use as Saatchi & Saatchi corporate headquarters, and the brothers moved out of Charlotte Street to almost the same spot where their old agency had lived between its nursery days in Golden Square and the merger with Compton UK Partners ten years before the GRC takeover.

And still they had not finished gobbling up other ad agencies. In their last deal of 1985 they bought the London firm of Humphreys Bull & Barker – an acquisition which was, like others in the unpredictable Saatchi & Saatchi story, not without its ironies. Richard Humphreys, the majority shareholder, aged forty-one at the time of this deal, had started his advertising career in 1968 at Garland-Compton. Later he had helped to run Roe Humphreys, a Compton UK Partners offshoot headed by Graeme Roe, the man who was then seen by most people, including himself, as the heir apparent to Kenneth Gill as chairman of the Compton UK group. After the 1975 merger with Saatchi Roe Humphreys had been merged with another small subsidiary to form Roe Downton, while Humphreys went off on his own. (Later the Roe part of the name was dropped when Graeme Roe, admiration of whom was not shared by the brothers, left in his turn.)

Humphreys, a small shareholder in the public company which became Saatchi & Saatchi, kept his shares and bought more as an investment. Meanwhile his own agency, which started slowly, picked up speed in 1983, when it recruited David Barker from Geers Gross as creative head, and in eighteen months doubled in size. It attracted the attention of the Saatchis, who had clearly retained a high opinion of Humphreys, and during 1985 they sounded him out about the possibility of bringing him into their organisation. What they were correctly anticipating was the loss by their KMP subsidiary – remember KMP? – of its biggest account, British Telecom, and the need to rescue the agency by merging it with another. At first Humphreys was not interested, but finally a particularly juicy proposition was put to him, namely that he should head a new line-up of forces within the Saatchi empire.

He agreed, and the result was the birth of a new agency under the cumbersome title of KMP Humphreys Bull & Barker. The chairman and managing director of KMP, respectively Tim Thomas and David Barraclough, were given their marching orders, and that was the end of the company started with such panache and such high hopes by Kingsley, Manton and Palmer more than twenty years before. That was not all, however. The new agency was also to swallow up Crawfords, the link-up of which with a chain of provincial offices was adjudged a failure, and Downton, which specialised in leisure and film advertising accounts. KMP Humphreys Bull & Barker accordingly entered the end-of-year league table as number ten, with aggregate billings of £80 million. There were now three Saatchi-owned agencies among the UK top ten.

Humphreys sold out not for cash but for shares. He and his partners, mainly Stuart Bull, received £1.35 million in the form of 187,342 Saatchi ordinary shares, with 97,508 more due a year later dependent on performance. A final shares transfer was to be made five years later related to profits in the period up to 1990. The deal almost certainly made Dick Humphreys the third largest private shareholder in the Saatchi group after the brothers.

Several months peviously in spring 1985 Saatchi & Saatchi had greatly increased its capital with a rights issue of £99.5 million of convertible preference shares. Thus enriched, the group had pursued its new policy of acquisitions outside the field of advertising. Most of these acquisitions took place in the US. Marlboro Marketing, a leading New York sales promotion company, was bought for a down payment of $14 million, with further cash instalments dependent on profits in the following three years. Also in New York the Kleid company, specialising in direct marketing, was bought for $4 million, with deferred performance-related payments to a maximum of $11 million due by 1987. Siegel & Gale, an American corporate communications consultancy, went for $2 million plus further performance-related payments.

Another market research agency was acquired, the Connecticut-based Clancy Shulman & Associates, founded by two former employees of Yankelovich Skelly & White. The initial payment was $2 million. Deferred payments were to be made to bring the total price to ten times average earnings for the years 1986 to 1990. In the financial year to the end of July 1984 Clancy Shulman had made pre-tax profits of $274,000 on turnover of $1,456,000. The neat earn-out arrangement may have had to be slightly altered in the light of the subsequent Saatchi decision to merge Clancy Shulman with Yankelovich Skelly and White. This was not at all to the liking of Florence Skelly or her partners, who walked out taking a score of executives with them. The rump of the agency, renamed Yankelovich Clancy Shulman, gave up its New York office and is now run by Robert Shulman in Connecticut.

The Saatchi group broke into public relations with the purchase of the Rowland Company, a leading New York PR consultancy, from Herb Rowland. Down payment $10 million with the total price planned to equal ten times average earnings between 1987 and 1989. In 1984 Rowland's pre-tax profits had been $2,170,000 on turnover of about $7,300,000. One of Herb Rowland's stated motives for selling out was to put his business on the international map. Despite having blue chip clients such as Procter & Gamble, he lacked resources with which to compete with the international giants of PR, including the Young & Rubicam subsidiary Burson-Marsteller and Hill & Knowlton, owned by J. Walter Thompson. He hoped to lead a Rowland International line-up under the Saatchi umbrella.

Other PR companies joining the Saatchi group in 1985 were the two GRC subsidiaries Granard and GRC Financial, already mentioned, and Kingsway Public Relations, another London firm, run by Anne Dickinson, ranked as the ninth largest of its kind in the UK. This deal followed a failure to take over Good Relations, at the time Britain's biggest PR firm. Saatchis had won the agreement of its chairman Tony Good to a takeover, but he could not talk round the rest of his board, and his attempts to do so exacerbated the friction between him and his managing director Maureen Smith, which led to her breaking away and setting up on her own.

Also in the UK Saatchi acquired the Infocom Group, which later was renamed the ICM Group, specialising in audio-visual presentations and the organising of conferences. The down payment was £1,180,000, with further performance-related payments to come.

All this amounted to an extraordinary amount of expansion on several fronts. It might have been thought that the Saatchi group would pause for breath after 1985 and take time to digest the many different companies it now encompassed. Not at all. An even bigger deal than any of those so far recorded was already looming up on the horizon.

5

Friends Fall Out

It had taken Saatchi & Saatchi a mere decade to go from being a middling-sized advertising agency to being an international conglomerate with a famous name and an apparently insatiable appetite for acquiring new subsidiaries. Naturally this had not happened without quite a few managerial changes along the way. The most memorable change, as far as members of London's close-knit and gossipy advertising community was concerned, had been the fall from grace of Tim Bell. It was Bell who was seen within that community as having been largely responsible for the growth of the Charlotte Street agency Saatchi & Saatchi Garland-Compton, which up till 1981 and the start of that remarkable series of takeovers had provided the bulk of the group's revenues.

Up till and including 1981, moreover, Bell was very much the public face of Saatchi & Saatchi, with the brothers playing the part of backroom boys. Bell was not, however, a member of the board of the holding company (the only company, be it remembered, that officially bore the name Saatchi & Saatchi as such). In other words, though he ran the main operating subsidiary, he was not in the place where the real decisions about the future were being taken. Members of the holding company board were, apart from the brothers, Kenneth Gill, the chairman, David Perring, the company secretary, and Martin Sorrell, the financial director who in lunch-table gossip was starting to be talked of as having become 'the third Saatchi'.

It was in 1982, the year of the Saatchis' second great leap forward, the takeover of American Compton, that Bell who had done so much to build up their core business and was so identified with the Conservative political link which had helped to open the gates of the City to them, began to be eclipsed. He was moved from control of his Charlotte Street power base to be international chairman of Saatchi & Saatchi Compton Worldwide, reporting to Milt Gossett in New York. Jeremy Sinclair, the quiet creative man, succeeded to the title of chairman of the Charlotte Street agency, Saatchi & Saatchi Compton London, and Terry Bannister and Roy Warman took over as joint managing directors. During 1984 Bell spent much of his time advising Ian McGregor, the Coal Board chairman, on publicity aspects of the coal miners' strike. At the beginning of 1985 he left Saatchis to join Frank Lowe in building up another successful advertising-based conglomerate. Of that more anon.

Accounts of what went wrong between Bell and the brothers, even from sources very close to them, differ greatly. It is even disputed whether Bell asked for the international supervisory job which removed him from Charlotte Street or was pushed into it. According to one version, years of overwork then temporarily took their toll of Bell's energies. According to another he was displeased at having been supplanted as 'the third Saatchi' by Sorrell, who was working with the brothers on their new empire-building strategy. Yet other comments, from the principals themselves, would keep the libel lawyers busy if they were printed.

Bell, it may be said, is no longer a great fan of the brothers with whom he worked so closely for so long. Charles Saatchi, on the other hand, speaks of Bell with regret as of a friend who went through a bad patch. Nevertheless there is some reason to think that, whatever truth there may or may not be in that, the breach with Bell was caused at least in part by the brothers' wish to put limits on the growth of his personal empire within their own. At all events it became plain in Bell's last two years as a Saatchi man that the danger, if ever there had been one, of his leading a breakaway from Charlotte Street and taking some of the Saatchis' clients with him had disappeared.

It is noteworthy that, since Bell gave up the reins of power at Charlotte Street, that agency has been without a single charismatic leader. Let us now take a closer look at the workings of Saatchi & Saatchi Compton London, for it is on that one agency that the reputation of the whole Saatchi group to a large extent rests. And that despite the fact that it ceased years ago to be the largest unit within the group, which now does the greater part of its business in the United States.

One may infer that the group management and Charles Saatchi in particular are unwilling to let any individual regain the kind of control over Charlotte Street that Bell at one time had, for fear of the harm that could be done by an independent-minded agency boss.

Certainly the brothers have involved themselves more closely on a personal level with the affairs of Charlotte Street than with those of any other unit in the group. Indeed the group has in general adopted a hands-off management style, allowing the managers of the various operations to get on with the job as they thought fit so long as they met their financial targets. Not so with Charlotte Street. For example, Charles himself is known to have written one of the magazine ads with which in 1985 Charlotte Street tried to save its Sainsbury account. The supermarket chain rejected the agency's efforts as failing to catch the right tone of voice. It was agreed that a quiet chatty style was appropriate but in practice the Charlotte Street creatives proved unable to produce it, being emotionally committed to a more strident kind of advertising. They lost Sainsbury's account to the Abbott Mead Vickers agency, the chairman of which, David Abbott, is considered by many to be the best copywriter in London.

Again, Maurice Saatchi intervened personally in 1985 in an attempt to save the *Mail on Sunday* account, which was also lost by Saatchi & Saatchi Compton London. Having made a highly effective personal appearance at the presentation with which the account had originally been won, Maurice thought it appropriate to go over the client management's heads and appeal directly to Lord Rothermere, chairman of the publishing company. To no avail. Maurice also keeps in close touch with two other important Saatchi Compton clients, Lord King of British Airways and Stuart Cameron, chairman of the tobacco company Gallaher.

As can be seen, Charlotte Street has lost accounts as well as won them. That is something that happens to the best regulated agencies. Among clients whose accounts Saatchi & Saatchi Compton London has over the years won and lost again have also been Black & Decker, British Leyland, Dunlop and McDonalds, the hamburger chain. (That is without mentioning the crop of losses due to account conflicts created by the 1986 takeover of Ted Bates, a major event to which we have not yet come.) These were all biggies. A small but interesting account lost by the agency was Alexon womenswear, for which it did some striking magazine ads, featuring top-class photography. The ads were too glamorous for the merchandise, and the client opted for a plainer style at another agency, Leo Burnett. You can't please all the people all the time. Nevertheless the agency has managed to please a great many clients and keep them pleased for a long time, among them such major advertisers as Allied-Lyons, British Petroleum, Cadbury Schweppes, GUS, IBM and Procter & Gamble.

For its many and varied clients, many and varied campaigns have been produced. Saatchi & Saatchi Compton London is not known for a single distinctive creative style, as are some agencies, but it is known for the determination – some clients and ex-clients call it arrogance – with which it sticks up for its creative ideas. And, although its output is not of uniform quality (no big agency's can be), it has in recent years given birth to some really excellent campaigns. A handful of examples may be mentioned. On television the agency's advertising for British Airways got off to a spectacular start with its famous Manhattan commercial in which, through visual trickery, a chunk of New York was seen flying in from the Atlantic to land in Britain. More recently there have been the marvellously funny Castlemaine XXXX commercials, made by a British team in Australia, to popularise the Australian beer with British consumers. One of them is the ad in which a man in the outback, tending a sick companion, is told by a flying doctor to give him something to drink but polishes off the last remaining can of beer himself and then commiserates with the invalid. The slogan 'Australians wouldn't give a XXXX for anything else' is just sufficiently *risqué* to titillate a mass audience without giving offence.

In print there have been clever campaigns for Silk Cut cigarettes, with ads that have managed to make out of a visual pun (cut pieces of mauve silk) pictures rivalling in visual charm CDP's 'surrealist' Benson & Hedges campaign; for the National Society for the Prevention of Cruelty to Children, similar in style to the Health Education Council ads with which Charles Saatchi made his reputation years ago (one NSPCC shocker showed a young victim of violence with the heading 'Help heal this child. Place a 50p piece over each bruise'); and for Pilkington Glass ('What would the City of London be like without Pilkingon Glass?' asked one ad, supplying its own answer in the form of buildings, buses and cars, all with bricked-up windows). Posters for Castlemaine, picking up the theme of the TV commercials, have shown a beer pipeline running through the desert and a plane coming in to land at a desert airstrip picked out by beer cans.

One print campaign which showed the agency at its most vigorous and aggressive, so much so that it sparked threats of legal action, was that carried out for James Gulliver's Argyll Group during its 1985 battle with Guinness to take over the Distillers Company. One ad pictured the Guinness chief executive Ernest Saunders with two mouths, to illustrate allegedly contradictory statements made by him. Since the agency had worked for Saunders himself not long before, producing ads for the successful attempt by Guinness to take over the Arthur Bell & Sons whisky firm, this attack on him took some nerve. Ads like this aroused some controversy, and the City of London Takeover Panel intervened to curb the knocking copy, though it had no legal authority to do so.

The feat the Charlotte Street agency has managed to pull off ever since 1975 is one that has eluded several other big competitors, namely to keep up a reputation for creative originality while handling a large volume of packaged goods advertising, much of which must necessarily be down-to-earth and repetitive. The operative word is reputation. A reputation for creativity is based not only on the quality of the work an agency does but also on the skill with which that work – and the people who do it – are promoted. It was not a mere whim that made the Saatchis hire one of London's better known copywriters, Geoff Seymour, in 1983 for a record and well-publicised salary of £100,000, a sum that immediately entered Adland jargon as a unit of currency, the Seymour. The logic was that an agency that paid such big money for creative talent would be seen as very creative.

Overall, the quality of Charlotte Street's work now is probably higher, though such an assessment is bound to be somewhat subjective, than in 1978, when a survey of 110 client companies' attitudes put the agency at the top of the creativity table. In 1980 another survey of clients carried out for *Campaign* by Mark Research ranked the agency second as a producer of 'original creative ideas' behind CDP. Five years later an exactly similar survey by the same firm gave it only fourth place for creativity behind CDP, Boase Massimi Pollitt and Frank Lowe's agency Lowe & Howard-Spink.

A perhaps more important question asked in the two Mark Research surveys was 'Which agency would you most like to handle your business?' In 1980 the winner was Charlotte Street, with 46% of client companies surveyed choosing it, ahead of CDP, BMP and J. Walter Thompson. In 1985 the order was BMP in top place followed by JWT,

CDP and Lowe, with Saatchi & Saatchi Compton sharing fifth place with Ogilvy & Mather. It came third, after BMP and JWT in another table, based on aggregate scores for the attributes described by clients as being the most important for an agency. This, again, marked a decline from the previous survey, when the table had been headed by Charlotte Street.

Other tables in the 1985 survey report put the agency (referred to throughout as Saatchis) at number three for marketing skills, after BMP and JWT, number four for 'high calibre personnel', after BMP, JWT and CDP, number two for media-buying skills, after JWT, and number four for international facilities. The one measure on which the agency scored highest was 'growing and expanding'. This was quite possibly a reflection of the great amount of publicity received by the parent company, Saatchi & Saatchi, properly so called, for its running series of takeovers as much as of the growth of the Charlotte Street agency itself.

If one takes these survey findings with some seriousness, it is not because they provide an exact assessment of the strengths and weaknesses of the agencies concerned. Like political opinion polls they tell us about the state of mind of the people questioned at the time they responded. But general perceptions of an ad agency among advertisers are, if anything, more important than anything that actually happens in that agency, since in the end it is client attitudes that determine whether it wins and keeps business or loses it to more fancied competitors.

As far as the management of the Charlotte Street agency is concerned, its most striking feature in the post-Bell era has been the multiplicity of top job titles. A glance at the portrait gallery of managers of Saatchi & Saatchi Compton London, as published in the group annual report for the year to the end of September 1985, showed one chairman, Jeremy Sinclair, one vice-chairman, John Treasure, and no fewer than five deputy chairmen, namely Michael Dobbs, Richard Hedger, Jennifer Laing, Bill Muirhead and John Spratling. In addition there were two managing directors, Terry Bannister and Roy Warman, who also shared the title of chief executive, and three deputy managing directors, Len Barkey, Michael Parker and John Perriss. The management group was completed by two creative directors, Paul Arden and Jeff Stark, under Sinclair as executive creative director.

This profusion of gold braid had several causes. One was the desire of the Saatchis to give official recognition to the degree of responsibility borne by the deputy chairmen, each of whom, with the exception of Michael Dobbs, was an account group head running in effect his (or, in the case of Laing, her) own agency within an agency. Dobbs was in a different category. He was the Saatchis' link with the Tory Party. He had been a researcher at Conservative Central Office before being brought into the agency by Tim Bell. Subsequently, as already noted, he returned to Central Office, working there on secondment from the agency as chief of staff to Norman Tebbit, the party's chairman. This highly unusual arrangement guaranteed, as far as guarantee was possible, that the Tory account, immensely advantageous as it had been to the agency in terms of prestige and visibility, would stay with it.

Of the other deputy chairmen, Hedger was acquired along with his agency, Hedger Mitchell Stark; Spratling was inherited from the management of the old Garland-Compton; Laing was a graduate trainee at Garland-Compton at the time of the Saatchi merger and was rapidly promoted by Tim Bell, who was impressed with her abilities as an account handler; Muirhead, another highly capable account handler, was an early recruit to the original Saatchi & Saatchi agency, to which he went from Ogilvy and Mather.

Another consideration relevant to the handing out of titles has been the wish, not unique to Saatchi & Saatchi Compton London, to satisfy, as far as possible, its employees' vanity. This is coupled with a reluctance to see those who are any good leave to work elsewhere, which would be damaging to the mystique of the place as the biggest and best firm of its kind in the UK. The mystique is taken very seriously inside the agency if not necessarily everywhere outside. In the case of John Treasure, who joined the agency quite recently when he was already in his early sixties, the title was bait to attract him, not to keep him. The most important reason for hiring Treasure, as with so many other things done by the Saatchis, was to cause a stir, since he was and is the nearest thing British Adland has to a Grand Old Man.

Treasure, who began as a market researcher and rose to be head of the British Market Research Bureau, stepped up from that job to become chairman of BMRB's parent, the London office of J. Walter Thompson, a position he held for many years. They were years when JWT's position at the top of the UK agency tree went unchallenged and when Treasure became known as Mr Advertising. He left JWT to take up a chair at London's City University. After a spell there he was bitten by the advertising bug again and tried starting his own agency. This was not a success. However, with a wealth of contacts in the business world and an assured public manner, he brought to Charlotte Street a touch of maturity in what till then had been predominantly a youngsters' agency.

Yet another reason for the managerial structure just outlined is the Saatchis' policy, already hinted at, of divide and rule, at least when it comes to their flagship agency. Hence the two chief executives. Terry Bannister joined the old Saatchi & Saatchi before the 1975 merger with Compton UK, having worked in the marketing departments of Fisons and Spillers. Roy Warman had joined the agency even earlier, having been brought in by Tim Bell from Geers Gross to be media director in succession to Bell himself. He subsequently graduated to more general managerial duties. Opinions of Bannister and Warman differ, but after they took over from Bell some clients were inclined to classify them as lightweights in comparison with their predecessor.

They themselves acknowledge that Bell's was a hard act to follow and that, even together, they cut less impressive figures than he. They were bright enough to realise that it was important for them indeed to stick together. Joint managing directorships have been tried by many companies and have often fallen apart under the strain of conflicting views and ambitions. The Bannister-Warman duo resolved that they would not fall out and that they would back each other's decisions. Within the partnership Bannister was seen as the more cerebral and Warman as the more impulsive fellow. They answered critics who suggested that the agency was running out of steam by pointing to the continued growth of its billings, even though a good part of its 1985 surge was due to the absorption of Grandfield Rork Collins. Nevertheless turnover increased during their period of office from £114 million in 1982 to £223 million in 1986.

The billings table for 1986, as published by *Campaign*, showed the agency still in the number one place, with J. Walter Thompson not far behind, with £200.5 million. Third was Dorland, now called DFS Dorland, with £190 million, and some way behind in fourth place was Young & Rubicam, which after a very successful year claimed its billings had risen by about 50% to £142 million, enabling it to displace Ogilvy & Mather. (A big chunk of the Y & R increase came from advertising the stock market flotation of British Gas.) For the first time, incidentally, *Campaign* included in its annual table independently monitored figures for advertising expenditure by agencies. According to these figures, compiled by the Media Register, Saatchi & Saatchi Compton led JWT by less than £5 million (£161.89 million to £157.14 million), but the Register does not cover some categories of advertising such as outdoor posters.

Of the deputy MDs Barkey is a survivor from the Saatchis' first substantial acquisition, Notleys; Parker, a one-time distinguished athlete, came to the agency after working for Foote Cone & Belding and McCann-Erickson; Perriss, who worked for Garland-Compton before the merger, succeeded Warman as media director and, even though he too later took on wider duties, is still regarded as one of the most capable people in London in the field of media planning and buying.

Since 1982 the Charlotte Street agency has, of course, been part of the Saatchi & Saatchi Compton international network. Other agencies in the network are of varying sizes and reputations in their different national markets. None, including New York, which is bigger in turnover than London, carries anything like the same clout both at home and abroad. It was in an effort to beef up the performance of the rest of the network that in early 1987 the first important managerial changes took place in Charlotte Street since Tim Bell's exit a couple of years before.

Before we go into those changes, however, and summarise the performance of the non-UK parts of the Saatchi-Compton network, we must first turn our attention to the deals which in 1986 took Saatchi & Saatchi to the top of the worldwide advertising heap. Read on.

6

Top of the Heap

The events of the year 1986 made the name Saatchi almost as well known in the United States as it had long been in Britain. The group already derived more than half its income from the US thanks to the acquisitions of the previous four years. Now the pace of acquisition was to change from a canter to a gallop.

A rights issue in April raised roughly £400 million, giving proof not only of the group's determination to go on expanding but also of the City of London's continued faith in its ability to invest wisely and profitably in new subsidiaries. The departure at around the same time of Martin Sorrell, who had done so much to build that faith, was not seen until later as a serious impediment. Sorrell refused the brothers' offer to become group chief executive and left, with the brothers' backing, to take over and run another company, WPP, in partnership with Preston Rabl. (Of that more later.) He was succeeded as group finance director by David Newlands, recruited from the accountants Touche Ross, but the role of principal financial spokesman was taken over by Maurice Saatchi, who had become chairman after the retirement of Kenneth Gill in 1985, though Gill stayed on the board as president.

Another managerial change that had taken place in 1985 was the restructuring of the group into two divisions, Saatchi & Saatchi Communications and Saatchi & Saatchi Consulting. The latter division, headed by Dr Milton Rock, consisted mainly of Rock's own Hay Group but also took in the market research company Yankelovich Clancy Shulman. The Communications division, made up of advertising, public relations, sales promotion, design and marketing operations, had as chairman and chief executive Anthony Simonds-Gooding, who had been first marketing director and then managing director of Whitbread before joining the Saatchis.

The first important deal of the year, announced in February, brought another big American ad agency into the group but not, as we shall see, under the authority of Simonds-Gooding. This agency was Dancer Fitzgerald Sample, of New York, which in the previous year had billed $876 million, making it bigger than Saatchi & Saatchi Compton New York. Negotiations had been going on for a long time between DFS and Dorland in London. As part of the 1984 deal by which it acquired Michael Bungey, the UK affiliate of DFS, Dorlands had also taken over from DFS its equity shares in a number of small Continental European agencies. There then began a search for a formula that would enable DFS, which had enjoyed informal co-operative links with Dorlands for many years, to sell out to it without being seen to do so. The problem was to avoid upsetting clients, particularly Procter & Gamble, a client of DFS since 1933, and to reassure them that the connection with Saatchi & Saatchi Compton, through the Saatchi holding company, involved no loss of operational autonomy.

In the end an unusual formula was found, amounting in effect to a deferred takeover. Dorlands was granted an option to acquire all of the equity of the privately owned DFS at any time in exchange for a $75 million loan to a company formed by the five controlling directors of DFS. The loan would bear interest but would be waived at the moment the option was exercised. In 1991 a further payment would be made along similar lines, based on the performance of DFS over the five previous years. It would, subject to certain adjustments, equal the amount by which the aggregate after-tax profits of DFS exceeded $41 million.

The resultant, to coin an expression, 'quanmo' (quasi-non-merged organisation) would be called DFS Dorland Worldwide and would, with claimed billings of $1,200 million, be the sixteenth largest ad agency network in the world. It would be completely separate from Saatchi & Saatchi Compton Worldwide, the world's fifth largest, just as Dorlands in London had always, under the terms of the 1981 Saatchi takeover, enjoyed complete autonomy and had indeed competed vigorously with Charlotte Street. As evidence of its independence, DFS Dorland would not report to Simonds-Gooding. It would be run by a holding board, chaired by Stuart Upson, of the New York agency, and containing the four other key Americans – Robert E. Kennedy, Peter McSpadden, Gary Susnjara and William Vickery. There would be three British members – Jack Rubins, as deputy chairman, Michael Bungey and Michael Geraghty – but the corporate headquarters would be in London, not New York.

For Dorlands the deal represented in a way a return to its origins, for the name Dorland dated back to John Dorland, who founded Dorland Advertising in America in 1886. Ownership of the agency, based in Atlantic City, New Jersey, passed to another man, Walter Edge, who set up one of the first international advertising networks. In 1905 George Kettle opened a London office and later set up other offices in France, Germany and Belgium. After Edge became Governor of New Jersey in 1917 Kettle bought the company from him and closed down the US offices. Links with the Continental European offices were ended by World War Two and Kettle died in 1942.

It was in 1923 that Blackett-Sample-Hummert was set up in Chicago and in 1944 that it changed its name to Dancer Fitzgerald Sample. In 1948 the agency, which had made its mark in the production and writing of radio shows and of the ads for their sponsors, moved to New York to do the same for the nascent television industry. Among the subsidiaries it spawned there were three that specialised in the production and syndication of TV programmes as well as units dealing with agricultural advertising, direct marketing and real estate. It also had advertising offices in San Francisco and Southern California.

The DFS Dorland deal created less stir than it might have done if it had not been already on the cards. The most surprising thing about it was how long it had taken for the two sides to work out the details of their agreement. The next Saatchi group takeover, on the other hand, came as a considerable surprise and happened very quickly. Announced in early April, it resulted from an almost chance encounter less than three months earlier.

The company bought was another American ad agency, Backer & Spielvogel, chaired by Carl Spielvogel, whose career has been one of the most interesting in recent advertising history. Aged fifty-seven in 1986, he had come into the industry twenty years earlier after ten years as a journalist with the *New York Times*, for which he wrote a column about advertising. Marion Harper, the architect of Interpublic, recruited him, and Spielvogel rose to be general manager of McCann-Erickson, Interpublic's largest operating subsidiary, before going on to the holding company board as vice-chairman. In the contest to succeed Paul Foley at the top of Interpublic Spielvogel lost out to Phil Geier, who had made his reputation running the McCann-Erickson office in London. Instead of bowing to defeat Spielvogel quit Interpublic and, at the age of fifty, started a new agency with Bill Backer, two years older, who had been creative director at McCanns New York and responsible for much of Coca-Cola's advertising.

The two called themselves 'middle-aged tigers'. At the time of life when most ad agency executives start thinking about retiring they not only made a success of their new venture but pushed it within weeks into the top division of American ad agencies. They did this by capturing the $80 million Miller Brewing account from McCann-Erickson, one of the biggest account moves ever. Most of the people working on the account at McCanns left to join them. The close relations enjoyed by both Backer and Spielvogel with George Weissman, boss of Philip Morris, Miller Brewing's parent company, had stood them in good stead. Other blue-chip accounts followed, and by 1985 Backer & Spielvogel billed £385 million, had offices in California and Chicago as well as New York, and was on the receiving end of takeover offers from most of the biggest American agencies.

These were resisted, but soon B & S found itself up against the problem that lack of international facilities was excluding it from consideration for a number of juicy accounts. Spielvogel was reminded of how, in the 1950s, the D'Arcy agency, which then handled Coca-Cola in the States, refused to go international. That enabled Marion Harper to get the account for McCann-Erickson in Brazil. He used that as a stepping stone to capture it for the agency in the US, and McCanns has worked for Coca-Cola worldwide ever since.

Such thoughts, however, were not what took Spielvogel into Charles Saatchi's office in London at the end of January 1986 – at least not according to what he says. He happened to be on a trip to Europe and called on Charles, whom he already knew, for a reason unconnected with advertising. Among other extra-curricular activities Spielvogel is a trustee of New York's Metropolitan Museum of Art and chairman of its business committee. (His wife, Barbaralee Diamonstein, by the way, is a writer on art and architecture.) Charles (together with *his* American wife Doris) has become one of the foremost collectors of modern art. The purpose of Spielvogel's visit was to enlist Charles's support for the museum. He met with a favourable response, and Charles subsequently

The offices, at 80–84 Charlotte Street, London W1, of Saatchi & Saatchi Compton, the flagship advertising agency of the Saatchi fleet of companies.

The North London gallery founded by Charles and Doris Saatchi to house their modern art collection. Not only in business is Saatchi a big name.

The Health Education Council LTD

Would you be more careful if it was you that got pregnant?

Contraception is one of the facts of life.
Anyone married or single can get advice on contraception from the **Family Planning Association.**
Margaret Pyke House, 25-35 Mortimer Street, London W1 N 8BQ. Tel. 01-636 9135.

The pregnant man poster produced for the Health Education Council in 1970
by the new Saatchi & Saatchi agency. Still remembered nearly twenty years on.

Charles Saatchi relaxing on holiday. The elder of the brothers and by far the more reclusive, he has always been their company's real boss.

LABOUR ISN'T WORKING.

UNEMPLOYMENT OFFICE

BRITAIN'S BETTER OFF WITH THE CONSERVATIVES.

Perhaps the most effective British political poster ever. Produced by Saatchi & Saatchi Garland-Compton in 1978, it crystallised dissatisfaction with the Callaghan Government.

Charles (standing) and Maurice Saatchi. One of the few stock pictures the brothers supply of themselves. They do not like seeing photographers or reporters.

Maurice Saatchi in chairmanlike pose. The younger and more urbane brother is the one who talks to financial analysts and major clients.

Doris, wife of Charles Saatchi. A former student of art history who became a copywriter in her native America before moving to Britain.

Josephine, wife of Maurice Saatchi. A strong-willed, ambitious Irishwoman who made good on the space-selling side of advertising.

Tim Bell, who pushed the Saatchis' Charlotte Street agency to the top of the UK advertising ladder before falling out with the brothers.

Martin Sorrell, the finance director who implemented the acquisition policy that made Saatchi & Saatchi a worldwide conglomerate. Now running his own international empire.

became a member of its international business committee.

After they had finished with art Charles said his brother Maurice would like to join them. The conversation then took a more businesslike turn, and an offer was made. At first the reaction of the other five members of Spielvogel's board was cautious, but a Saatchi promise that B & S would stay autonomous as well as get the international back-up it needed finally persuaded them to go for the deal – that and the handsome sum of money they all stood to make out of it. The down payment was $56 million in cash coupled with a six-year earn-out arrangement that could bring the total price to around $100 million.

Meanwhile talks had been held about a possible Saatchi buy-out of the Chicago ad agency Tatham-Laird & Kudner, and conjectures were mounting about which really big fish the Saatchi group was going to catch. There was general agreement among observers that the brothers' aim was to make their company the number one of world advertising and that, with their coffers newly filled with the proceeds of their rights issue, they had the means to do it. The question was which of the big American agencies, if any, would be willing to sell out. It was said that $300 million had been offered for Ted Bates Worldwide and rejected as inadequate. In fact negotiations with Bates had been proceeding off and on for well over a year, and it had become clear that Bob Jacoby, the boss and controlling stockholder of Bates, was not opposed on principle to selling out.

In late April Jacoby was reported in the American trade paper *Adweek* as wondering whether he should take his own company public. He claimed that the Saatchis had offered to put him in charge of all their agencies, including the Saatchi & Saatchi Compton network, but that, at the age of fifty-eight, he had not been tempted. He also did not care for the earn-out arrangements favoured by the Saatchis which meant that you did not know for sure what you were going to get paid. Within three weeks of the publication of this interview the two sides had reached agreement on the biggest acquisition deal in advertising history. Saatchi & Saatchi was to buy Ted Bates Worldwide for $450 million, of which $400 million was to be paid upfront and in cash. Jacoby would personally get $100 million and thus become at a stroke the richest individual in advertising. He would also remain at the head of Bates.

The news was sensational, even to seasoned Saatchi-watchers. But what was this company for which the Saatchis were prepared to pay so much? Why had they agreed to Jacoby's price? Was it not too much? And who was Jacoby anyway? How had he personally come to be worth $100 million? What would be the consequences of this third great leap forward in the history of Saatchi & Saatchi (after the UK and US Compton deals)? Let's now try to answer these questions.

The name Ted Bates is ineradicably associated, unlike that of most agencies, not just with a record of work done for certain advertisers but with a theory of how all advertising should be created. This is the theory of the USP, or unique selling proposition, elaborated not by Theodore Bates, who founded the agency in 1940, but by Rosser Reeves, who worked for him, succeeded him as chairman and ran the company for years. Reeves, a Virginian, started his career as a reporter with the *Times-Dispatch* of Richmond, Virginia, then became a copywriter and was copy chief at Blackett-Sample-Hummert (the forerunner of Dancer Fitzgerald Sample) before moving to Benton & Bowles, where he made the acquaintance of Bates. He followed the older man to his new agency and helped build its billings from some $3 million in 1940 to $100 million by 1957.

Much of this success can be attributed to the persuasiveness with which Reeves presented his ideas to clients. As set out in his highly readable little book *Reality in Advertising*, published in 1961, these included the need to find a USP for every product advertised and to go on repeating it indefinitely. The USP did not have to correspond to a unique quality. The uniqueness of the proposition might well lie in the fact that rival advertisers had not thought of using it. A classic example of the theory in action was the slogan Bates produced for its client Colgate, 'cleans your breath while it cleans your teeth'. Although Reeves accepted that emotional appeals, or brand image, to use the phrase associated with his one-time brother-in-law David Ogilvy, could reinforce a USP, his was basically a rationalistic theory that gave priority to selling the steak (or what was claimed to be the steak) rather than the sizzle. For this reason it came to be regarded as creatively somewhat dull.

While Reeves's ideas have been criticised by other admen who preferred a different theory or no theory at all, they certainly did a good job for Bates. The USP became the agency's own unique selling proposition in proffering its services to clients. They did a good job, too, for Reeves personally. Following the pattern laid down by the agency's founder, who believed in the importance of personal leadership, Reeves became its largest shareholder. However, he got voted out by his board colleagues in 1965. At about the same time a very different character arrived at the agency who, in his own way, was to have just as important an influence. This was Robert Eakin Jacoby.

Bob Jacoby, born in New Jersey and a Princeton graduate, started his career as an economic analyst at Shell Oil, from where he moved to Compton Advertising in the early 1950s. After his 1965 move to Bates he rose rapidly through the hierarchy, becoming chairman and chief executive in the early 1970s. As such he devoted himself to building up the business through acquisition while holdng fast to Rosser Reeves's advertising philosophy as a way of getting clients. By 1985, according to the tables compiled annually by the American weekly *Advertising Age*, the Bates group ranked third among American ad agency businesses, with worldwide billings of $3,107 million. Included in the total were such large subsidiaries as the Mid-West agency Campbell-Mithun, which on its own billed $332 million, and the New York agency William Esty, bought in 1982, which billed $510 million. Perhaps more importantly, as Saatchi shareholders were told, Bates was one of the world's most profitable ad firms, with pre-tax profits in the financial year to the end of March 1986 of $64.5 million. Its ratio of pre-tax profit to income (not billings) was 16.8%, compared with an average of under 10% for the major US quoted ad agencies.

The same letter to Saatchi shareholders that provided these figures explained the reason for the purchase. Saatchi & Saatchi's strategic objective, declared chairman Maurice, was to ensure its position as a market leader of the advertising industry, which was coming increasingly to be dominated by a small number of very large agencies. He conceded that it was inevitable that some clients would be lost because of perceived conflicts with other advertisers served by the merged group, but he was confident that the net result would be a strengthening of relationships with the key clients of the enlarged group. Market leadership in advertising, he added, would serve as a base for the future development of Saatchi's global network of business services.

What the letter did not mention was the event that, coming just before the deal, made the Saatchis, as some would say, throw caution to the winds. Bates had not been the only object of Saatchi attention. Over several years it had been courting Doyle Dane Bernbach, the agency that had led the creative revolution in modern advertising but was generally thought to have run out of steam since the death in

1982 of Bill Bernbach. Given the kind of reputation DDB, despite various difficulties, still enjoyed, it might well have been considered to be a more attractive partner for the Saatchis, with their own carefully cultivated reputation for advertising creativity, than either Compton or Bates. DDB, again approached, again said no. Instead it opted for a *ménage à trois* with two other big American advertising agency companies, BBDO International and Needham Harper Worldwide. This mega-merger was announced at the end of April.

The new grouping, which was shortly to adopt the umbrella name Omnicom, brought together the sixth biggest US ad agency (BBDO, with worldwide billings in 1985 of $2,500 million), the twelfth (DDB, $1,670 million) and the sixteenth (Needham, $847 million). This was enough, if the get-together did not frighten many clients away, to elbow Interpublic out of its place as the world's number one advertising-based conglomerate. It would be 65% owned by BBDO's shareholders, with 24% in the hands of DDB's and 11% in those of Needham's (the only private company of the three). A jubilant but cautious Allen Rosenshine, chairman of BBDO and designated head of the new holding company said, 'We are the biggest – but maybe only for ten minutes.'

His words were prophetic. It took the Saatchis more than ten minutes, but not much more, to swallow their reservations about the terms Jacoby was demanding for a deal with Bates. The urgency with which the decision was taken was increased by the fact that Interpublic itself was now talking to Jacoby about buying Bates. It looked for a few anxious moments as if the Saatchi dream of climbing to the top of the advertising heap might have to be renounced. In early May the agreement was signed. Jacoby got his price with hardly any strings attached despite the view of some analysts that it was too high. At least one knowledgeable American warned the brothers against the deal. The risks were apparent. If Bates lost too many clients who objected to their agency's being linked with others working for their competitors, then its earnings might decline, but the holding company would have no financial protection of the kind built into most of its other acquisition arrangements. The brothers paid no heed to the warnings.

They got their expected headlines – on the front page of the *Wall Street Journal* as well as the trade papers. 'Bates bows to Unique Saatchi Proposition' was the witty line in *Adweek*. The rival *Advertising Age* published a table of what it called 'agency super groups', based on the 1985 billings figures of their constituent parts, as supplied to the magazine. Far away in the lead was Saatchi & Saatchi, including Bates, with a worldwide aggregate of $7,632.4 million. The new BBDO-DDB-Needham line-up was second with $5,016.9 million, just ahead of Interpublic with $4,827.9 million. Runners-up were JWT Group (J. Walter Thompson and affiliated companies) with $3,817.4 million, Young & Rubicam with $3,575.3 million, and Ogilvy Group (Ogilvy & Mather and affilates) with $3,398.7 million. All the top six, incidentally, were publicly quoted, with the exception of Y & R.

Not long after the expected headlines there also arrived some of the expected troubles together with others less expected. One thing the Saatchis had probably not reckoned with was the nature of their new and, thanks to them, super-rich employee Bob Jacoby. He was not just an outstandingly capable business manager, he had distinctly Napoleonic characteristics. The smallness of his stature – only 5ft 4in tall – was not matched by the strength of his will, and he had been accustomed for a long time to ruling the roost at Bates. With a five-year service contract in his pocket and no further need to worry about the financial future, he intended to go on laying down the law. Within weeks Saatchi & Saatchi was forced to abandon its usual hands-off style of management, in which targets were set for the subsidiary companies but they were left largely autonomous, and to intervene noisily in Bates's internal affairs.

The crisis was precipitated by a Jacoby *coup* regarded by some of those who knew him as typical of the man's headstrong behaviour. On 4 September 1986 the chairman of Bates Worldwide issued an internal announcement that he was replacing Donald Zuckert as president of Bates New York with John Nichols, who had only recently moved to the agency from a marketing management job with a client company. Zuckert was to become a vice-chairman and senior corporate administrative officer (whatever that might be) reporting to John Hoyne, who was appointed as the new president and chief operating officer of Bates Worldwide. (The title of president had been held by Jacoby himself for the past seventeen years and retained by him even after he had become chairman.) Other departmental heads, including Larry Light, president of international operations, would also report henceforth to Hoyne instead of Jacoby.

The boss's memo clearly indicated that Jacoby had chosen Hoyne, for whom he had a special affection, as his heir apparent. Until shortly beforehand Hoyne had himself been in charge of Bates's international operations and closely involved in the long-drawn-out negotiations with Saatchi. He had then been given the title of vice-chairman, relinquishing the international post to Light, who had previously had worldwide responsibility for all the work Bates did for its biggest client, Mars. Light's close connections with the Mars brothers, Forrest and John, were to prove crucial in the power struggle that followed. For Light, as well as Zuckert, resented being put under Hoyne's authority as the result of a decision about which they had not been consulted. In a memo fired off by Zuckert to Bates New York staff on 4 September, the same day as Jacoby's announcement, Zuckert made plain that this had been 'as much a surprise to me as it must have been to all of you'.

Some staffers reportedly believed that Jacoby's sudden action was motivated by suspicion that Zuckert and Light were plotting to undermine him, but Jacoby himself later denied having had any animosity towards the pair and declared that he had thought he was promoting Zuckert and doing nothing to hurt Light. Clearly they took a very different view. Exactly who said what to whom and when remains obscure, but the supposition is that at some point the danger of a massive loss of Mars billing was posed. In a situation where, as a result of the takeover, several other major clients had switched accounts away from the Saatchi group, this was a danger that London could not ignore. A fortnight after Jacoby's management *coup*, and six weeks after the sale of Bates to Saatchi & Saatchi had been finalised, Jacoby was removed from office. He was replaced as chairman and chief executive with Zuckert, six years his junior. Light was now the number two man. Hoyne and Nichols left.

Jacoby rejected an offer to work under Simonds-Gooding in some undefined group planning role and also left Bates, declaring that it would cost the Saatchis another $5 million in compensation for breach of contract. He professed his liking for Maurice and Simonds-Gooding (he had never met Charles) but suggested mischievously that they might have been swayed by regret at having paid so much money to buy Bates. The affair did no good to the reputations of any of those involved in it. The derision it aroused became part of what now seemed to be a backlash in the US advertising community against mega-mergers in general and the Saatchi empire's growth in particular.

7

The Backlash

Shortly after the triumphant emergence of Saatchi & Saatchi as the new superpower of the advertising world, a joke gained currency in American Adland. Saatchi, it was said, was not really anyone's name, it was an acronym for Single Ad Agency Takes Control of Half the Industry. A small American agency took advantage of the brouhaha to advertise itself as a non-Saatchi firm. Such pleasantries could on their own have been cause for satisfaction in the Saatchi boardroom. Charles Saatchi, for one, had never underestimated the beneficial power of publicity. But he also knew that, in an industry where reputation was the most precious of assets, not all publicity was good publicity. And the reaction among Americans, and American clients in particular, to the British invasion was not all good-humoured.

The reaction might perhaps have been less sharp if it had not been for the simultaneous arrival on the scene of Omnicom, grouping BBDO (originally Batten Barton Durstine & Osborn), Doyle Dane Bernbach and Needham Harper, the latter two of which were being cobbled together into a single agency network. Suddenly one of the oldest problems of the agency game, that of client conflict, was back at centre stage, and for months the trade press could find room for little else. Advertisers felt compelled to define their attitudes, and in the US the consensus appeared hostile to the agency mega-mergers, both those that had just taken place and those that were thought likely still to occur. Conjectures about a get-together between JWT and Ogilvy came and went. It was learned that there had been tentative talks between the two some years previously.

The solution to the client conflict problem – that is the unwillingness of competing advertisers to share the services of the same ad agency – had been found, or thought to have been found, by Interpublic. It was, of course, for a single holding company to operate through separate agency networks, which would compete with each other as if they had separate owners, while remitting their profits to the same centre. Phil Geier, who as chairman of Interpublic now ran the system originally devised by Marion Harper, commented that its success depended on maintaining not only the separateness of the different units of the group but the public perception of their separateness. That was not an easy thing to do. It had taken Interpublic many years to convince clients of the genuine autonomy of the agency networks it owned.

He could have added, though he did not, that Interpublic had not gone all out, as Saatchi & Saatchi had done, to persuade the world of the virtues of sheer size. In reporting annual billings to the trade papers that, in every country with a sizeable ad industry, published league tables of agencies, Interpublic subsidiaries kept themselves to themselves and did not pool their turnovers so as to appear more important. In the ordinary end-of-year tables published by *Advertising Age* for 1985, for example, the name Interpublic had not figured at all. The group's biggest constituent, McCann-Erickson Worldwide, had appeared in seventh position in the table of world billings. In the US-only table McCanns had made only number fourteen, behind Dancer Fitzgerald Sample and its own Interpublic sister Marschalk Campbell-Ewald. Both tables were headed by Young & Rubicam.

Interpublic's strategy of calculated modesty was scarcely available to Saatchi & Saatchi, however, even if it had wished to pursue it. The Interpublic name, like Omnicom, was unobtrusively that of a holding company only. No client company entrusted its advertising to an agency called Interpublic. None of the awards generously handed out to each other by advertising people at the numerous festivals held in different countries went to Interpublic copywriters or Interpublic art directors. Saatchi & Saatchi, on the other hand, was very much the brand name of a particular agency network as well as that of a holding company.

Yes, as previously remarked, the agency's official name was Saatchi & Saatchi Compton, but the Compton part had become submerged. At an earlier stage the Saatchi label, associated as it was with bright advertising ideas, had been useful both for promoting the agency and for making the holding company known to those with whom it wished to do business. Now, by reminding clients of other Saatchi-owned agencies of their links with what was supposed to be a competitor, the name was threatening to turn into a liability. American clients of Bates, Dancer Fitzgerald Sample and Backer & Spielvogel were doing what Dorland clients in Britain had never done and asking themselves whether their accounts would be safe in the hands of people indirectly linked through a sister agency with rival advertisers.

Perhaps, after all, it would have been better if the Compton label had been kept unaltered for the Charlotte Street agency and its associated network in the US and elsewhere. Even Charles Saatchi was heard regretting the decision, made so long before, to stick the family name on his company. Something neutral like Omnicom might have avoided some of the unwelcome sorts of publicity. Of course, he quipped, some people were already calling the group Omnivore.

At the seventy-seventh annual meeting of America's Association of National Advertisers in autumn 1986, some harsh words were spoken about the agency mega-mergers. J. Tylee Wilson, chairman of RJR Nabisco, the tobacco-to-food conglomerate with a worldwide advertising budget of $1,000 million, laid it down that he would not agree to any arrangement that put one of his brands into any agency group if a part of that group was handling a competitor. Another speaker, John Weiner of Kraft, expressed it succinctly: 'It is extremely difficult to accept an agency as a true partner if another part of the organisation is competing with you and hitting where it hurts.'

As for the claimed benefits of the new agency supergroups, Wilson declared himself unimpressed. 'I hear the arguments about global reach and keeping up with merging clients', he said, 'but I'm unconvinced. I simply do not believe that giant mergers pay off in economies of scale that will impact my costs.' Nor did he believe that creativity would be improved. On the contrary, he was concerned about the possible bad effects of the mergers on the morale of the merged agencies' employees.

Inside the advertising business it was widely believed that the resentment indisputably aroused among client company executives by the mega-mergers, and particularly by the Saatchi-Bates deal, had causes other than honest anxiety about their business consequences. Many American clients, it was thought, were upset at the spectacle of agencies becoming, as they felt, too big for their boots. They were angry in some cases that they had not been consulted about the mergers before they happened and given the opportunity of vetoing them. They were furious, irrationally so, that a man such as Jacoby could make so much money out of *them*, for where did an agency's financial value come from if not its clients? Added to these natural human feelings of envy and injured vanity was probably more than a touch of xenophobia. For years advertising had been an American business, learned by Europeans from America. The world's biggest agencies, with the exception of Japan's Dentsu, had all been American. The biggest agencies in many countries had been American-owned. Who were these Limey-Come-Latelys who presumed to cross the Atlantic and buy up everything in sight?

What really mattered, however, was not what the clients felt or said but what they did. The architects of both the Omnicom and the Saatchi-Bates deals had expected some accounts to be lost as a result of them. Their expectations were not disappointed. Within a month of its being taken over Bates had lost $100 million of Colgate-Palmolive business because of the perceived conflict with Procter & Gamble, the mainstay account of many of the Saatchi Compton offices. The possibility of this loss had doubtless been foreseen. Less foreseeable was P & G's decision to switch several brands out of Saatchi-owned agencies because the Cincinatti-based giant manufacturer also took a dim view of mega-mergers and of account conflicts. A company statement made clear that 'Procter & Gamble does not believe holding companies are a means of avoiding such conflicts.'

P & G's discomfort had begun before the Bates deal. It had looked askance at the Dorland get-together with Dancer Fitzgerald Sample. DFS worked for P & G on Luvs Baby Pants and Bounty Paper Towels but not on any of the company's food brands competitive with those of another DFS client, RJR Nabisco. However, Saatchi & Saatchi Compton did have P & G food brands in the US. Therefore, on the theory that separate but jointly owned agencies were to be regarded as if they were one agency, there was now an account conflict within the Saatchi group. The latter argued long and hard that its subsidiary agency networks were autonomous and leakproof. P & G was not convinced. By the end of the summer and despite a last-minute appeal by Maurice Saatchi, who went to Cincinatti, the company announced its decision, which brought the Saatchis another crop of hurtful headlines.

Two food accounts were pulled out of Saatchi & Saatchi Compton, namely Crisco cooking oil and Duncan Hines baking mix. At the same time DFS lost Luvs and Bounty on the somewhat obscure grounds tht Saatchi Compton handled Stayfree Silhouettes sanitary towels for Johnson & Johnson, and P & G's paper division, responsible for Luvs and Bounty, also marketed a brand of sanitary towels. The non-American reader may be inclined to smile at names like Luvs and Crisco. Can such silly-sounding words have anything to do with serious business? Why yes, they certainly can. The advertising budgets for the four brands (Luvs, Bounty, Crisco, Duncan Hines) amounted to $85 million a year. P & G, moreover, was known as an advertiser that, unlike many, stuck to the old 15% commission rate. The affected brands were worth nearly $13 million in annual income to the group.

The P & G move was interpreted by many as being not merely a demonstration of the company's strict no-conflict rule but as a kind of punishment for Saatchi hubris or alternatively as a salutary reminder to ad agencies in general of who was boss when they dealt with Cincinatti. A P & G advertising executive, Robert Goldstein, said in words not very different in spirit from those employed by the boss of RJR Nabisco, 'It's not clear to me why two or three agencies operating with one ownership as parallel networks will contribute anything either to the clients or the public which those same agencies operating separately would not contribute.'

Other major losses in the weeks following the Bates purchase included the $64 million of Warner-Lambert billing handled by Bates. After thirty years with the agency, Warner-Lambert dumped it on the grounds of account conflict between its chewing gum brands and those handled by DFS for the Lifesavers company. Equally as heavy a blow was the departure of RJR Nabisco from William Esty, a sizable New York agency acquired by Bates in 1982. Esty lost the $50 million Salem cigarettes account as well as a clutch of petfood brands. The client was thought to have been motivated partly, but only partly, by displeasure at the mega-merger. In fact it switched another $30 million of advertising, for biscuit products, from Esty to another Saatchi group shop, DFS.

Yet another blow was the refusal by General Mills, a big client of both DFS and of the Bates subsidiary Campbell-Mithun, to allow its advertising to be handled by the same group that worked for its rival Quaker Oats. Backer & Spielvogel had $60 million worth of Quaker business, run mainly from its Chicago office. The problem was eventually solved by letting the Chicago management buy itself out.

The reverberations of the mega-merger were felt not only in the United States but throughout the Saatchi empire. In several countries the group's new relationship with Mars, through Bates, caused Saatchi Compton agencies to resign Rowntree, one of Charlotte Street's oldest and most profitable clients. In Saatchi & Saatchi Compton London the estimated £6 million of Rowntree's billing was replaced with the same amount of Mars business, transferred from Bates's London office. Shortly after that another of Charlotte Street's big clients, United Biscuits, moved out, citing the danger of conflict with competitive clients, though the name Mars was not spoken. Bates lost the Olivetti account in several European countries because of Charlotte Street's position as an IBM agency.

But not all clients take the doctrine of agency loyalty as seriously as do Procter & Gamble or Mars. In America rival car manufacturers went on happily using different agencies within the Saatchi group, with Saatchi & Saatchi Compton New York working for American Motors, McCaffrey & McCall for Mercedes, DFS for Toyota, and Backer & Spielvogel for Hyundai. In Germany the Bates subsidiary Scholz & Friends pacified worried clients by issuing written undertakings that no confidential information would be passed to other agencies in the group. The assurance was sought in particular by Scholz's client BMW, concerned about potential leakage of information to Saatchi Compton Frankfurt, agent at that time for Jaguar, now for Austin Rover.

Within six months of the announcement that Bates was selling out, the Saatchi group was reckoned to have lost about $450 million of billing because of fears of account conflicts. But in the same period, said the Saatchi people, almost the same amount of new business had been won. Perhaps so, but end-of-year calculations showed a distinct dip in the fortunes of Ted Bates. Although US billings declined by only 1% from the previous year, according to the figures supplied to *Advertising Age*, the annual value of the accounts lost was reckoned to total 15% of the agency's domestic turnover. The discrepancy arose because of the time lag between decisions to move accounts and the actual transfer of responsibility for them. Bates overseas turnover was reckoned to have risen by about the same 15% proportion, thanks partly to acquisition of new subsidiaries.

Saatchi & Saatchi Compton fared much better. US billings rose by 11.7% to $1,377.3 million. The worldwide figure went up by 9.5% to

$3,320 million. Included in the US figure, as supplied to *Advertising Age*, were the turnovers of autonomous subsidiaries such as McCaffrey & McCall of New York. In the UK the agency again topped the table with declared billings of £223 million, which was more than £22 million ahead of runner-up J. Walter Thompson. However, for the first time *Campaign* printed alongside the agencies' own estimates of their billings those calculated by the independent Media Register and based on its monitoring of press and TV advertising (but excluding radio, posters, direct mail and other forms of expenditure). On the Media Register figures the gap between the two leaders was much smaller, with JWT less than £5 million behind Saatchi Compton's £161.89 million.

One of the main beneficiaries of the fall-out of accounts from the mega-mergers was Young & Rubicam, the American company that is able to present itself as a single worldwide ad agency rather than a group of competing agencies on the Interpublic model. Among the chunks of businss it picked up in the US in 1986 were $50 million from RJR Nabisco and $30 million from Warner-Lambert. Actually Y & R does have holdings in other important ad agencies as well as some wholly owned specialised subsidiaries such as the Burson Marsteller public relations company and the medical advertising agency Sudler & Hennessey. But its equity share in DYR (Dentsu Young & Rubicam), a joint venture with the Japanese giant Dentsu, is only 50%. And Y & R owns only 49% of HCM (Havas Conseil Marsteller), another joint venture, in which the majority share is held by the Eurocom group of France.

What may have particularly commended Y & R to American advertisers irritated at the sight of Bob Jacoby and a handful of other Bates executives making fortunes for themselves by selling out was the impossibility that Y & R would follow a similar path. Whereas the Bates tradition was for the chief executive to have a controlling share of the equity, the rule at Y & R was, and remains, that nobody should have more than 5%. Ownership is shared between 700 employee-stockholders.

In the autumn of 1986 reports began to appear that the Saatchi group was planning to effect a physical merger of the Bates and Saatchi Compton agencies, in the same way that Omnicom was busily putting together its Doyle Dane Bernbach and Needham Harper units. Certain clients are known to have been sounded out about their reaction to the idea. Presumably warnings were received of trouble if it went ahead, for it was shelved, at any rate for the time being. Though it would have made sense in some respects to create one network in place of two, it would also have looked like an admission of failure to make the Interpublic concept of jointly owned but competing agencies work.

For the first time the possibility that Saatchi & Saatchi could indeed encounter failure was beginning to occur to hitherto admiring onlookers, particularly in the financial community. Between spring and autumn 1986 the company's share price fell in London by more than a third. Questions were revived about whether the Bates purchase had really been worth the money paid. The farce of Bob Jacoby's sudden exit increased nervousness among British investors who a few months previously had never heard of the man.

By the end of the year Saatchi supporters in the City had recovered their nerve, helped by the announcement of satisfactory financial results for the year to the end of September. But the assumption of infallibility that for long had seemed to attend all the company's doings was gone. Neither journalists nor financial analysts were inclined henceforth to be as uncritical in their assessments of it as heretofore. Among some people in the City there was a suspicion, rightly or wrongly, that without Martin Sorrell beside them the brothers were more likely to go off the rails.

Summing up the position after some of the dust had settled, the chairman of Saatchi & Saatchi Communications, Anthony Simonds-Gooding, said he thought the trouble had been that events had moved too fast for the liking of American advertisers. In the space of a year they had been confronted with not one but three mega-mergers of agencies, first that btween D'Arcy MacManus & Masius and Benton & Bowles, then the formation of Omnicom, then the Saatchi-Bates deal. The mega-mergers had become a big talking point in the US, and advertisers had been provoked into taking a stand. In fact, he pointed out, some of the toughest account conflict problems had arisen from the deals with DFS and Backer & Spielvogel, but negotiations with the clients had gone on quietly and discreetly until the Omnicom merger and the Bates takeover had touched off the publicity explosion.

Simonds-Gooding, speaking as the man with responsibility for the performance of all the group's ad agencies, strongly defended the rationale behind the Bates deal, whatever might have been the temporary setbacks it entailed. Contradicting the stand taken by some of his biggest American clients, he averred that time would prove that the mega-mergers were good both for agencies and for advertisers. In the advertising industry, as in others, medium-sized firms were doomed to be squeezed out. The future belonged to very big agencies on the one hand, and small specialised outfits on the other.

The advantage to a client company of having a very big agency, he added, was that the latter had the resources to serve it more efficiently – by allocating more people to work on the account, by spending more on market research, by having the buying clout to extract the cheapest prices from the media for advertising space and time. Moreover, being number one in size made it easier for the Saatchi group to attract the best talents.

These were large assertions. They accorded fully with the line of argument that Saatchi & Saatchi had been advancing since long before Simonds-Gooding's arrival. Global marketing had been the name of the company's game since even before it could truly be described as having established a global presence. Now, however, it was a worldwide advertising power. How powerful was, and is, it in the various countries where it operates? The next chapter will supply a bird's eye view of an empire which you may or may not recognise as possessed of the advantages claimed for it by its eloquent propaganda.

8

The Global Market

The most influential writer on marketing in the world today is probably Theodore Levitt, Professor of Business Administration at the Harvard Business School and editor of the *Harvard Business Review*. A famous article published by him in the magazine in 1983 was entitled 'The Globalisation of Markets.' Its thesis was that developing technology had led to the 'emergence of global markets for globally standardised products'. Examples included Japanese electronic goods as well as Coca-Cola and Levi jeans. Despite national differences, tastes all over the world were converging, and consumers were in any case willing to sacrifice traditional preferences for the sake of buying high quality goods at the low prices that were facilitated by the economies of scale available to companies producing, transporting and communicating for a worldwide market.

Levitt does not deny the existence of market segments, that is groups of consumers marked off from each other by social, economic and demographic differences, but in his view such segments are becoming global rather than national, with similar groups of people in many different countries having similar demands for similar things, whether these be hamburgers, bicycles or classical music. Defending his thesis against the many criticisms directed against his 1983 article, he has insisted that he never meant to advocate rigidly standardised products with rigidly standardised marketing messages. For instance the Japanese company Seiko offers consumers more than 100 different styles of wristwatches but manufactures only a few basic mechanisms which, by being aimed at a global target, can be produced in large enough quantities to combine low prices with high quality.

Ted Levitt had practically nothing to say in his original article about advertising as such. But there were obvious implications for advertising, and they seemed to accord, despite his qualifications, with the gospel of world brands that Saatchi & Saatchi was already preaching. For several years the company had been using its glossy and beautifully produced annual report booklets as a medium not simply for information about its financial progress but also for lengthy analysis of the state of marketing and advertising as a whole. The 1981 report, produced of course before the company's invasion of America, spoke only of 'pan-European branding', but by 1982, after the takeover of Compton Communications, the annual report was pontificating about 'world brands', and the global approach was emphasised in every successive booklet. The arguments deployed are worthy of close attention.

The 1981 version conceded that selling a single brand in several countries would not necessarily achieve significant savings in the cost of advertising. The strategic value of pan-European branding lay rather 'in the scale economies it may afford across the company's business system – to help make the company the low-cost producer.' The economies could come, according to the category of product, in research and development or manufacturing or distribution or advertising. And the text went on to specify five stages of corporate development as follows. Stage 1, Company starts to operate in its own country; Stage 2, Starts to export; Stage 3, Opens marketing companies overseas with their own manufacturing plant; Stage 4, Co-ordinates marketing and production across different countries; Stage 5, Centralises production/distribution/marketing by continent.

A paragraph headed 'Consumer homogeneity' declared that cultural barriers between consumers in different European countries were crumbling. Language differences, it was added, would progressively decline in importance as a barrier, partly because 'satellite television will shrink the parochial marketing and advertising boundaries of recent decades.'

The 1982 report took the five stages of corporate development described the previous year and retitled them 'Organisational progress to world brands.' It added five stages of 'Economic progress to world brands', namely Stage 1, Pressure of cost inflation in static markets; Stage 2, Need to be low-cost producer to win market share battle; Stage 3, Search for more efficient business structure; Stage 4, Economies of scale; Stage 5, World brands. The booklet repeated the argument in favour of pan-European branding, with the exception that it was now termed pan-regional branding. Market research, it said, would in future be done to find not the differences between separate national markets but their similarities, so that these could be efficiently exploited.

Successes in world branding had so far been few, it was admitted, but an example of a company that had achieved such success was Procter & Gamble, and an example of a successful world brand was P & G's Pampers disposable diapers, sold on a similar strategy almost all over the world. Pampers was an important Saatchi Compton advertising account, but the cleverly written report did not abandon its tone of impartial authority in order to point that out. That tone was probably far more effective in seducing potential clients than any amount of noisy self-congratulation would have been.

The next few paragraphs did, however, blow the Saatchi Compton trumpet, though discreetly so. In framing international brand-positioning strategies, said the report, local customs, languages and marketing conditions must be taken into account. It was also necessary to monitor the progress of a brand's reputation in the different countries where it was being marketed. A brand's reputation was made up of four factors, to wit functional attributes, emotional attributes, market status (whether it was seen as a leader or an also-ran) and badge status (with which kind of people it was associated). Research carried out by Saatchi & Saatchi Compton New York, tracking a number of packaged goods brands, was enabling the agency to work out a Brand Character Index. Using this technique, a multinational company could 'measure the extent to which a brand's character differs across national boundaries' and establish a coherent plan for their international marketing and advertising.

Many manufacturers and ad agencies, though the text did not say so, go in for similar tracking studies. Never mind, Saatchi & Saatchi had managed to identify itself with the notion of world brands and, by implication, brands handled on a worldwide basis by a single ad agency network. This was quite a smart thing to do for a network that had at that time a somewhat less global presence than several of its competitors. Clearly the company was trying to position itself as one with the breadth of outlook needed to service big multinational clients. By talking in global terms it was bound to attract the interest, if no more, of firms with global activities. Pretentious this might be, but pretentious in the classic advertising way, as recommended by Rosser Reeves and others. A USP (unique selling proposition) was, remember, defined by Reeves as something other advertisers had not thought of saying about themselves or their products even if they could have done so. The Saatchis were making global-mindedness their USP.

Not that everyone was convinced. In 1985 Saatchi & Saatchi Compton lost the Black & Decker account to McCann-Erickson because the client did not believe the Saatchi agency was sufficiently well established internationally to service the account as well as necessary. The risk run by all advertising except the self-deprecating kind used by Doyle Dane Bernbach in its classic campaign for the Volkswagen Beetle (and self-deprecation can also be risky) is that the product may appear to the consumer not to live up to the enthusiastic picture of it painted in the ads. The same goes for an ad agency's self-advertising.

By the time the 1986 annual report was published, some months after the company, by its acquisition of Bates, had actually climbed to the top of the international advertising tree, the spiel appeared less pretentious. After some general reflections about the consequences of the fact that 'the world is becoming one marketplace', the report proceeded to talk about the relevance of globalisation to 'the business service company' that is Saatchi & Saatchi itself. 'Is global size important? Is size itself a competitive advantage? Is bigger automatically better in our business?' Unsurprisingly the answer given to these questions in the report was yes. It was not, of course, put quite so bluntly.

What the report did say was as folows. 'Size and scope are not automatically better. Nothing is automatic. But size and scope can and do make increased resources and opportunities available so that we can be better.' Size conferred a 'power of scale' that in advertising meant 'the ability to attract, reward and retain the very best talent, superior media-buying clout and better media-planning systems' as well as 'improved global information systems, increased technological resources and increased access to a broad range of communications and consulting expertise.'

Publication of the report was backed up by a full-page press ad hammering home the advantages of size. Over the past five years, the ad pointed out, the share of total world advertising expenditure by the largest 190 American advertisers had risen from 12% to 17%. And over the past ten years the multinational ad agencies had increased their share of the world advertising market from 12% to 20% even while the number of such agencies had declined from twelve to eight. The Saatchi group itself now worked with more than sixty of the world's biggest 100 advertisers. The ad, like the report, quoted Professor Jagdish Sheth, of the University of California, to the effect that most industries fell over time into a pattern where there were only three leading companies plus a number of 'niche players'. There was, declared the Saatchi spiel, a 'Law of Dominance', according to which the number one brand in a market was wonderful, number two was terrific, number three was threatened and number four was fatal. Saatchi & Saatchi, it was quite clearly implied, was in the wonderful category.

The 1986 annual report quoted Professor Levitt on global marketing. More importantly the accompanying ad was able to announce that Levitt had joined the boards of both the operating divisions of the company, Saatchi & Saatchi Communications and Saatchi & Saatchi Consulting. This was quite a *coup*. One does not need to agree with everything Ted Levitt says to recognise him as a first-rate intellect, and first-rate intellect was an ingredient that for most of its existence had been lacking from the Saatchi & Saatchi recipe. For his part Levitt was unstinting in his praise of the Saatchis and their 'Promethean' achievement in creating a global enterprise so speedily and effectively. Well, even first-rate intellects can choose their words carelessly. Remarkable the boys' achievement had certainly been. Promethean? Not a word Charles or Maurice would have used about themselves. But the testimonial, despite coming from a man now on their payroll, can have done them no harm at all.

At the end of 1986 Saatchi & Saatchi was able to boast that it was the leading advertising agency group in nine countries, including the US and the UK, and ranked among the top five in twelve others. At last it was truly in a position to offer global services to clients who required them, or even to mount worldwide advertising campaigns. Not that there are very many such campaigns. As Jack Rubins, of Dorlands, says, some brands are able to use the same advertising throughout the world, while others, even though they may have a global strategy, need to employ different tactics, sometimes very different tactics, in each country.

An example of a client company for which some pretty uniform global advertising can be, and is, done is British Airways, for which much of the creative work originates in Charlotte Street. However, Saatchi & Saatchi Compton, which handles BA, is as willing as any other agency to adapt its advertising to meet local conditions. Its much admired British campaign for Silk Cut cigarettes, for instance, featuring subtle and visually beautiful variations on the theme of cut silk, is not used in markets where the agency agrees with the client, Gallaher, that the brand's less well established position makes such advertising inappropriate.

Let us now try to get a bird's eye view of this advertising empire, the parts of which are in most cases somewhat less impressive than the whole. It could hardly be otherwise. It is an empire built by acquisition, and what was acquired was what was available. The company, in its determination to become number one in size, set aside the idea of acquiring only agencies that were already as creative or efficient as it would have liked and, instead, relied on its expensively won 'power of scale' to try to make its acquisitions into what it wanted them to be.

To start with, then, the Saatchi & Saatchi Compton network. Its economic centre of gravity is in the US, but the flagship agency of the network, as indeed of the whole Saatchi group, remains Charlotte Street. There, at the beginning of 1987, some important changes took place, connected precisely with the aim of overhauling the whole chain and strengthening its weaker links.

The chairman and joint chief executives of the London agency, respectively Jeremy Sinclair, Terry Bannister and Roy Warman, were replaced at the head of it by two new joint executive chairmen, Jennifer Laing and Bill Muirhead. Sinclair, Bannister and Warman, while remaining based in London, moved up to become with another man, Alban Lloyd, the governing quartet of a new operating division called Saatchi & Saatchi Compton International. Their authority was to extend over all Saatchi Compton agencies outside North America, and their mission to improve the creative standards of the network. For a long time it had been evident, not least to clients and potential clients, that the undoubted quality of the work produced by Charlotte Street was matched by scarcely any of the forty-four other wholly owned and forty-seven affiliated agencies in the chain and that none of them enjoyed anything like the same dominance in its market.

The managerial structure of the new division was, to say the least, curious. Bannister and Warman were to transfer to the international scene the double act as chief executives they had been performing in London. Jeremy Sinclair was to be joint chairman of the international set-up with Alban Lloyd, who for the previous two years had been head of European operations outside the UK. Lloyd, at about fifty, was ten years older than his three colleagues and was also the only one with real international experience, having run McCann-Erickson's agency in Italy before returning to the UK to be chairman of McCanns London. He had quit McCanns, giving as his motive the attractiveness of the Saatchi job.

While there was, no doubt, plenty of work for the four to do, given the number of countries for which they were now responsible and their geographical spread, there seemed to be no very good reason for the division of authority between them. If 'divide and rule' had been an intelligent policy for the brothers to follow with the Charlotte Street agency after the period during which it had been run by a single leader, Tim Bell, who could have walked away with much of its staff and clientèle, the same hardly applied to an international set-up, which could not constitute the same kind of power base for an individual manager. The contrast was marked with North America, where one man only, Ed Wax, president of Saatchi & Saatchi Compton New York, was now being made chief executive of all S & SC agencies.

Perhaps the reason for the unusual four-way power split was simply that, once it had been decided that the job to be done required the efforts of all four individuals, it would have been too bruising to the egos of three of them if the fourth had been designated *numero uno*. And ego-boosting is an important part of the art of managing advertising agencies, where strong egos tend to be more numerous than in almost any other kind of business. The removal of the topmost layer of management from the Charlotte Street agency certainly allowed the egos of those just below to grow and bloom in a way calculated to keep them happy and loyal.

The most eye-catching of the new appointments was that of Jennifer Laing if only because of her sex. The Saatchi group has always, of course, specialised in catching eyes. She was not the first woman chairman of a major UK ad agency – Ann Burdus had headed McCann-Erickson's London office for a while after Nigel Grandfield's departure and before she herself left to become a director of AGB Research – but there are still few enough women in the upper reaches of agency management to make Jennifer Laing's achievement something to talk about. She is known as an intensely ambitious perfectionist and an effective presenter, good-looking in a trim, businesslike way. She was the butt of a rather cruel profile in the *Tatler*, which laid great emphasis on her attachment to the red Ferrari with which the agency tempted her back to work for it after she left in the late 1970s to work for a period for another agency, Leo Burnett.

Interviewed by the magazine, she pointed out rightly that it was unusual for anyone in the Charlotte Street agency to be allowed to talk to the press. 'We are not to be seen as individuals outside the company,' she was quoted as saying, 'it's all to do with the mystique.' She could have added, but did not, that she had declined to talk about the Saatchi company to a journalist even when she was working elsewhere. Charles Saatchi, she had responded then, would not be pleased if he learned that she had been talking about the agency without his authorisation, even to praise it. Though she was not at that moment employed by him, he was a big man in the industry, she said, and she had no intention of getting on the wrong side of him. Her words threw an interesting light not only on her own canny character but also on the publicity policy of that master manipulator of publicity, Charles Saatchi.

Bill Muirhead, sharing the limelight with her, won his spurs supervising the British Airways account. A laid-back Australian, forty years old at the time of his appointment to the joint chairmanship, he was described by Laing, his junior by one year, as being more intuitive and more creatively inclined than her disciplined self. At the same time that the Laing-Muirhead duo was put in place the Charlotte Street agency acquired two new joint managing directors in the persons of John Sharkey, previously one of the numerous deputy chairmen, and Paul Bainsfair, who had been a group account director.

At the same time changes took place on the creative front. With Sinclair given the job of supervising standards of creative work throughout the non-American provinces of the Saatchi Compton network, Paul Arden, that other quiet-spoken but talented maker of ads, moved up to be executive creative director of Charlotte Street, with under him as creative directors, *tout court*, James Lowther and Andy Rork. The latter, the Rork of the Grandfield Rork Collins agency acquired in 1985, had been working as European creative director under Alban Lloyd.

Even more interestingly, it was announced that Jeff Stark, who had hitherto shared the creative directorship of Charlotte Street with Arden, was moving to Saatchi & Saatchi Compton New York, together with his former business partner and present deputy chairman of the London agency, Dick Hedger. An official announcement said this was part of a new policy of posting senior people from Charlotte Street to important roles abroad. The move gave rise to instant speculation that it was an attempt to inject a bit more creative flair into the New York agency, still widely regarded in the US as no more than competent.

Promotional literature produced for Saatchi & Saatchi Compton Worldwide declares that the network, while eschewing a single style or tone of voice, since what is right for one campaign is wrong for another, strives for the same objective in all its advertising, namely 'to make a single proposition come alive in a compelling way'. The same literature emphasises the virtues of the unexpected in ads, and quotes the following poem of Christopher Logue's as summing up the kind of creativity sought for in Saatchi Compton offices.

> Come to the edge.
> We might fall.
> Come to the edge
> It's too high!
> COME TO THE EDGE!
> And they came
> and he pushed
> and they flew.

It is difficult to recognise this as the manifesto of the New York office, a substantial concern but neither one of the very biggest nor one of the most admired ad agencies in the US. Its image, very different from that of its sister shop in Charlotte Street, was historically a dull one, dating from the days when the old Compton Advertising was known as Procter & Gamble's 'house agency'. P & G, more than any other advertiser, laid down strict rules about what was and was not acceptable in its ads. It became famous for what the more irreverent admen called its 2CK formula (two cunts in a kitchen) for advertising household products. At one time P & G used Compton as a creative testing bureau, getting it to produce ads to compete with new campaigns from other P & G agencies. The client would then see how the two sets of work compared in consumer recall tests.

Like other agencies with an 'uncreative' reputation, Saatchi & Saatchi Compton New York complains that it has not received recognition within the ad business of the effectiveness of some of its work, even though it may not have been of the type that wins creative awards. For example, it helped build Tylenol analgesic into the market leader in the US in the 1970s, then helped it regain that position after the 1982 poisoning scare, when some capsules of the product were tampered with, causing a number of fatalities. TV commercials used hidden cameras to film ordinary people talking about their headaches, then describing later the relief they got from Tylenol. However satisfactory to the client, this is not the kind of stuff that gets agencies talked about and attracts the attention of other clients.

Since the 1982 Saatchi takeover efforts have been made to put more oomph into the New York agency. The energetic and personable Ed Wax, an ex-Compton man who had left to work for other agencies, Geers Gross and Wells Rich Greene, was persuaded to rejoin in 1982 by Milt Gossett and Maurice Saatchi. After a year as European co-ordinator he returned to New York, first as head of client service, later as president and chief executive of the New York agency, and then as head of all Saatchi Compton offices and subsidiaries in North America. Wax says that after he took charge he tried to play down the Compton part of the agency name and concentrate on the Saatchi & Saatchi part, signifying greater creativity.

Several creatives were hired from Doyle Dane Bernbach, including Bob Levenson, who worked on Volkswagen and other famous campaigns in the days when Bill Bernbach's agency was revolutionising the art of advertising. He wound up as its international chairman before moving to Saatchi Compton as vice-chairman and chief creative officer in 1985. His reputation still stood very high, though not all ad industry observers were convinced he still had the same fire in his belly as when he was younger. One of the Doyle Dane people who followed Levenson to Saatchi Compton, creative manager David Herzbrun, declared optimistically that the creative challenge confronting him and his colleagues was 'the best in town'.

Even though some competitors doubt how successfully the challenge has been met, Wax is quietly confident that real progress has been made. As an example he points to the agency's campaign for the Jeep Comanche pick-up truck. A TV commercial shows a Comanche stopping at a level crossing. A train arrives but also stops and backs up, allowing passengers to dismount and take a look at the little vehicle. The spot relies on strong visual execution but closes with a few economical words: 'There's a new truck on the road. It's called Comanche. It's built by Jeep. It's worth a look.'

Some other punchy advertising has been produced of late. The creative department, of course, still has to carry the burden of Procter

& Gamble and its formula approach to advertising. But is it such a burden? Is P & G so wedded to rigid formulae? According to some senior people at the agency, P & G has become remarkably open-minded of late, and some of their best work is being done for the Cincinatti giant. For example, one commercial for Tide detergent, featuring a truckdriver's wife worried because her husband is late home, is full of human, if sentimental, interest and manages to get clean away from P & G's old didactic style. Another wittily contrasts different women – one who 'would be enthusiastic about anything', one who 'is crazy' and one who 'tried new multi-action Tide.'

Whatever progress the agency may be making on the creative front, the Saatchi regime has undoubtedly improved its financial performance. There is a much greater emphasis on profit than in the old Compton days. Under pressure to meet its financial goals, the agency decided for one thing to abandon its expensive midtown Manhattan premises in Madison Avenue and move in the near future to cheaper offices in downtown Hudson Street.

In 1986 the New York office billed $600.7 million, rather less than half the US total for all Saatchi & Saatchi Compton group agencies of $1,377.3 million, representing a very healthy 11.7% increase over 1985. Gross income of the group (that is the part of their clients' advertising expenditure which stuck to the agencies' fingers) in the US was $194.6 million, an increase of 14.6% over the previous year, almost twice the industry average in the country. However, most of that increase came not from the main New York office but from the specialised and regional subsidiaries. In general, American advertising expenditure has of late grown slowly – unlike the position in many overseas places – with clients tending to switch many of their marketing dollars into short-term sales promotion.

Despite its creditable performance, it should be noted that the Saatchi & Saatchi Compton network as a whole, including such major subsidiaries as McCaffrey & McCall and Rumrill-Hoyt, ranked only number nine in the *Advertising Age* table of the top ten agencies by US income. Outside the US Saatchi & Saatchi Compton Worldwide took first position with non-US billings of $1,942.7 million. The *Ad Age* tables of the top ten agencies in 1986 in terms of both worldwide (including the US) billings and worldwide income had the Saatchi Compton network in second place, a long way behind Young & Rubicam, which also comfortably topped the table of the top ten inside the US. Y & R's performance outside the US was slightly less impressive. Its non-US billings totalled $1,802.9 million, making it number three behind Saatchi Compton and McCann-Erickson, and ahead of Ogilvy & Mather, J. Walter Thompson and Ted Bates.

Detailed worldwide and US income figures for the year were as follows. Note that they refer to the performance of individual agency networks, irrespective of ownership, so that, for example, Ted Bates is listed separately from Saatchi & Saatchi Compton, and BBDO separately from its Omnicom sister DDB Needham.

Worldwide gross income 1986 ($m)

1. Young & Rubicam	628.4
2. Saatchi & Saatchi Compton Worldwide	490.5
3. Ted Bates Worldwide	486.0
4. J. Walter Thompson Company	471.0
5. Ogilvy & Mather Worldwide	459.6
6. BBDO Worldwide	445.1
7. McCann-Erickson Worldwide	427.7
8. DDB Needham Worldwide	375.0
9. D'Arcy Masius Benton & Bowles	336.3
10. Foote Cone & Belding Communications	323.0

Source: Advertising Age

US gross income 1986 ($m)

1. Young & Rubicam	358.1
2. BBDO Worldwide	307.0
3. Ted Bates Worldwide	282.6
4. J. Walter Thompson Company	259.7
5. DDB Needham Worldwide	250.4
6. Ogilvy & Mather Worldwide	249.7
7. Foote Cone & Belding Communciations	242.4
8. Grey Advertising	203.6
9. Saatchi & Saatchi Compton Worldwide	194.6
10. D'Arcy Masius Benton & Bowles	192.2

Source: Advertising Age

It does not take an enormous effort of understanding to see that a prime object of Saatchi group policy must be to try to push the agency network bearing the company's brand name higher up the US domestic pecking order. On the evidence both of its behaviour and of its statements, as contained in successive company annual reports, Saatchi & Saatchi is a great believer in the virtues of size, not least because of the publicity value of rising to the top. In Adland, more perhaps than in any other industry, nothing succeeds like success, and clients appear to be irresistibly drawn to agencies with a reputation for being 'hot'. It would be quite extraordinary if the Saatchi company, having succeeded in establishing its lead agency at the top of the UK advertising tree, were not to try to repeat the feat in the US, the world's biggest advertising market.

The Charlotte Street agency grew, it will be recalled, both by producing admired work and through merger. If the New York agency cannot grow fast enough by its own exertions, then what more natural, from a Saatchi corporate point of view, than that it should be expanded by merger? To Saatchi-watchers it did not, therefore, come as an entire shock to learn in spring 1987 that it was proposed to merge Saatchi & Saatchi Compton in the States with the American end of DFS Dorland, formerly Dancer Fitzgerald Sample. Such a merger would, on 1986 results, catapult the merged agency into second place in the domestic American pecking order. The two New York offices alone, shorn of regional and other subsidiaries, had combined 1986 billings of more than $1,300 million, compared with slightly less than $800 million for the New York office of Y & R.

The fact was that Anthony Simonds-Gooding had early in the year moved his base from London to New York to supervise the streamlining of his Communications division in the US. To get the mergers he wanted he had to spend months talking people round. Finally in June 1987 it was announced that the two agencies were indeed to merge under the unwieldy name of Saatchi & Saatchi DFS Compton. Saatchi was paying $25 million to exercise its option to buy DFS. The combined New York office would be run jointly by Gary Susnjara of DFS as chairman and Ed Wax as president. A new umbrella organisation, Saatchi & Saatchi Advertising Worldwide, was to be created with Stuart Upson of DFS and Milt Gossett as co-chairmen. Some 125 employees out of 1,500 were to lose their jobs. But the DFS directors, who appeared to have been given the upper hand, had cause to be happy.

At the same time that this major bit of reconstruction was being planned, it was announced that two other Saatchi-owned agencies in New York were certainly to merge. They were Rumrill-Hoyt and McCaffrey & McCall, both nominally part of the Saatchi & Saatchi Compton group in the US. One says nominally because, although David McCall's agency had its turnover added to that of the Saatchi Compton offices for the purposes of returning figures to *Advertising Age*, it operated autonomously – not long beforehand McCall had made it clear that he did not regard himself as part of the Saatchi & Saatchi Compton chain, though willing to take advantage of its overseas facilities. In 1986 Rumrill-Hoyt, an old Compton Communications subsidiary, billed $163.9 million, up from $121.6 million in 1985, while the McCaffrey & McCall figure for 1986 was, at $203.7 million, little changed from the previous year. Nevertheless David McCall was to take control of the newly merged shop.

Outside America and Britain the Saatchi & Saatchi Compton network is something of a mixed bag, with only a minority of its offices having a really strong reputation in their own markets, either for creativity or business-getting.

The problem confronting the group in its efforts to improve the position of all the Saatchi Compton agencies not at the top of their own national advertising trees – which indeed means all of them except for Charlotte Street – is exemplified by the case of Saatchi & Saatchi Compton in Frankfurt. For years this was considered a dull but reliable company, strong on marketing knowledge, weak on creativity, dominated by its account managers and very much oriented towards its Procter & Gamble client. The description, unsurprisingly, was about the same that could be applied to its old parent company, Compton Advertising of New York.

Some three years ago, in an attempt to brush up the German agency's image, a new and abrasive creative director and president was brought in by the name of Matthias Kersten. There were rumours of clashes between the new man and the agency chairman, Werner Goerke. Some of the old hands left. Nevertheless the agency did manage to push its way up the billings table from fifteenth position in 1984, when its turnover was DM146.5 million, to twelfth in 1985, with a figure of DM198.1 million. The kind of advertising that the old Compton would never have dreamed of doing but that is now coming out of the shop is its recent campaign for Austin Rover, featuring detective-movie-style magazine ads in black and white. A typical example showed a

Humphrey Bogart lookalike, cigarette drooping from finger, in earnest conversation with a 'Lauren Bacall' clutching a broken tennis racket. Behind them a tennis court fence and beyond that a car with an open door. Caption: 'He had lost not merely the match but his nerve. So they had to find him at once. Luckily they had their MG Maestro standing by.' Other agencies asked sneeringly whether this was really a way to sell cars, but the ads were certainly attention-getting.

On the whole, however, the agency has not yet succeeded in creating much excitement about itself. Others in Germany have been more successful in that respect. In the 1986 billings table Saatchi & Saatchi Compton remained stuck in twelfth position, having grown very little. The German advertising market is dominated, incidentally, by the American-owned multinational agency chains, as can be seen from the following table of the top twenty.

West German billings 1986 (DM million) and change from 1985

1.	Team/BBDO	527.0	+9.6%
2.	SSC & B: Lintas	475.0	+6.8%
3.	McCann-Erickson	442.8	+5.4%
4.	Ogilvy & Mather	416.2	+28.6%
5.	J. Walter Thompson	390.2	−10.2%
6.	Young & Rubicam	351.0	+26.8%
7.	Grey	308.2	+8.2%
8.	D'Arcy Masius B & B	254.9	+26.1%
9.	Doyle Dane Bernbach	240.4	+12.3%
10.	R.W. Eggert	212.7	−0.6%
11.	Wilkins Ayer	212.6	+4.1%
12.	Saatchi & Saatchi Compton	204.8	+3.4%
13.	Michael Conrad & Leo Burnett	191.8	+10.5%
14.	GGK	179.0	+5.3%
15.	Scholz & Friends	168.1	+33.3%
16.	Publicis Intermarco-Farner	152.1	+7.0%
17.	Ted Bates	141.4	+7.9%
18.	Heye Needham	140.9	+2.6%
19.	BMZ	135.6	+11.4%
20.	HCM	129.0	+9.9%

Source: Werben und Verkaufen

In the German market, as can be seen, the Saatchi-owned agencies, including Bates and Scholz, lag far behind the Omnicom group, with agencies in first, ninth and eighteenth positions, and Interpublic, solidly entrenched in second and third positions. The twentieth position is held by HCM (Havas Conseil Marsteller), an international chain jointly owned by the American Young & Rubicam and the French group Eurocom. In France the American networks are far less solidly implanted than in other European countries, and the biggest players in the ad agency game are French. The biggest is Eurocom, an offshoot of the State-owned Havas group, with HCM, Bélier and Ecom Univas among its many operating subsidiaries.

In France, however, the Saatchi Compton affiliate, Dupuy Saatchi & Saatchi Compton, has a more distinguished record than several of its sister agencies. Its problem, rather than being how to put some sparkle into a dull image, is how to prevent itself from losing some of the shine it formerly had. Dupuy, which is only 52% owned by the British holding company and 48% by its managers, suffered a first blow in 1984, when its creative director Gérard Jean and deputy managing director Hubert de Montmarin broke away to start their own agency. Under Jean the creative department had produced some striking campaigns, particularly for Wrangler jeans. Posters showing the garments being worn by a foetus and by a skeleton became national talking points.

Somewhat to Gérard Jean's surprise, there was no reaction from London to his and Montmarin's departure, and no offer to set them up as a separate agency within the group, which is probably what Eurocom would have tried to do in similar circumstances. Instead, local management was left to cope as it thought best. The chairman of Dupuy, Didier Colmet Daage, tried to tempt Jean to split with his partner and return to the agency but failed. Jean's successor as creative director was Michel Rogale, but in spring of 1987 he too left to become head of the Paris office of D'Arcy Masius Benton & Bowles. The general impression – despite the great respect shown by the French trade press for the Saatchis' worldwide achievements – is that Dupuy Saatchi has got to work hard to keep its eleventh position in the agency pecking order. It has been overtaken in size and reputation by Boulet Dru Dupuy Petit, a breakaway from Young & Rubicam and the latest great success story of French advertising. The Dupuy in its name is Marie-Catherine Dupuy, founding partner and creative director and grand-daughter of Jean-Pierre Dupuy, who in 1927 started the agency now controlled by

Saatchi. Marie-Catherine worked there for thirteen years before leaving in 1983 to help set up BDDP.

It seems most unlikely that any foreign-owned agency will ever come within shouting distance of the top in French Adland. The pecking order of the top twenty is as follows. Note that both billings and gross income figures for 1986 are given. Percentage changes relative to 1985 are calculated on the basis of the incomes reported for the two years. Income is not a precise and constant proportion of billings because, despite the 15% benchmark agencies are fond of, it depends on the financial arrangements made with each client.

Performance of French agencies 1986 (Frs million)

		Billings	Income	Change
1.	Publicis	2,140	290	+9.5%
2.	HCM	1,800	270	+14.5%
3.	RSCG	1,670	251	+24.2%
4.	Young & Rubicam	1,190	179	+12.6%
5.	Bélier	1,100	165	+18.7%
6.	BDDP	988	148	+46.5%
7.	Doyle Dane Bernbach	880	132	+9.4%
8.	Lintas	825	120	+21.7%
9.	FCA	675.2	101.2	+18.4%
10.	McCann-Erickson	604	96	+10.3%
11.	Dupuy Saatchi	603.6	90.5	+13.7%
12.	Ogilvy & Mather	534	87.5	+16.7%
13.	Ecom Univas	570	85	N/A
14.	J. Walter Thompson	560	85	+6.2%
15.	CFRP	550	82	+7.9%
16.	Futurs	479	72	+2.8%
17.	TBWA	475	68	+22.5%
18.	Foote Cone & Belding	N/A	64	+82.8%
19.	Ted Bates	443	60	+11.1%
20.	Synergie Kenyon & Eckhardt	500	59	+8.8%

Source: Communications & Business

As well as the Dupuy agency the Saatchi Compton group in France includes two other small ad agencies, Compar and Références, a sales promotion company, Doping, a direct marketing firm, RSVP Direct, and other marketing service units.

In Italy Saatchi & Saatchi Compton has a mediocre track record. It was previously distinguished mainly for excellent computer facilities and for having an office in Rome, near Procter & Gamble's Italian headquarters, as well as Milan, the capital of Italian advertising. However, late in 1986 it bought a majority share in another agency, MVL, and this helped it to shoot up the turnover table, finishing the year in fifth place. At the same time it acquired a hefty slice of the big-spending Renault account, formerly with Foote Cone & Belding but now divided between the Saatchi agency and Publinter Ayer, an affiliate of the American N.W. Ayer. More recently a bright new creative director has been hired, Maurizio Dadda from Ata Univas.

From the following table it will be seen that the Italian advertising market is one of the fastest growing in Europe.

Italian billings 1986 (L1000m) and change from 1985

1.	McCann-Erickson	247	+20.5%
2.	Armando Testa	203	+39%
3.	Young & Rubicam	192	+37.1%
4.	J. Walter Thompson	185	+17%
5.	Foote Cone & Belding	155	+4%
6.	MAC	150.5	+77.5%
7.	Saatchi & Saatchi MVL	144	+38.5%
8.	BBDO	140	+27.3%
9.	Ata Univas	130	+21.5%
10.	TBWA	125	+34.4%
11.	D'Arcy Masius B & B	120	+14%
12.	SSC & B: Lintas	110	+30.9%
13.	ODG	99	+41.4%
14.	Livraghi Ogilvy & Mather	97	+19.7%
15.	Milano & Grey	93	+14.8%
16.	Canard	82.5	+26.9%
17.	RSCG	75	+50%
18.	Pirella Gottsche	65	+18.2%
19.	Ted Bates	63	+3.3%
20.	Publinter Ayer	63	+44.2%

Source: Pubblico

In the Netherlands Saatchi & Saatchi Compton is a success story. A smallish shop to begin with, it bought its way into the top twenty in 1984 by taking over a much larger agency called RJA. According to the annual 'Bugamor' survey of advertising industry opinion (the respondents are senior people on both the client and agency sides), the Saatchi partner in the marriage was seen as above average in creativity and 'top talent' but only average in marketing knowhow and 'dynamism'. RJA was seen as average or below average on all these scales except marketing knowhow.

However, a couple of years on, and after some judicious staff recruitment and self-promotion, the January 1987 survey found the merged agency to be considered above average in all important respects. In accordance with this improved reputation the agency has been growing fast. It ended 1986 as Holland's seventh biggest ad agency, with billings equal to 44.2 million US dollars, nearly 52% up on the previous year. The market leaders, though growing less fast, are the Dutch affiliates of the American networks Young & Rubicam and Ogilvy & Mather, with 1986 billings of, respectively, 77.6 million and 75.6 million US dollars. At the beginning of 1987 Saatchi & Saatchi Compton Amsterdam was appointed to handle an $11 million international campaign for TV sets made by Blaupunkt of West Germany.

In Spain, like Italy a fast growing advertising market, the Saatchi Compton network has added to its Madrid subsidiary, seventeenth biggest ad agency in the country, a smaller but much higher profile agency in Barcelona. This is RCP Saatchi & Saatchi Compton, only number twenty-three in the turnover table but a winner of many awards for its creative work.

Ireland, a small but lively advertising market, has two agencies belonging to the Saatchi Compton network which have maintained quite separate identities. O'Kennedy Brindley, the third largest Dublin agency, put on a burst of new business three or four years ago after the Saatchi takeover and after management of the agency had been entrusted to Martin Larkin. Creatively and financially it had another resurgence in 1986–7, winning the Bank of Ireland's account and earning praise for its hard-hitting General Election campaign for the victorious Fianna Fail party. Also owned by Saatchi is the slightly smaller Hunter Advertising which has a good creative record.

Outside Europe and North America the Saatchi Compton network's most important investment is in Australia, where its Melbourne and

Sydney offices jointly weighed in at fifteenth place in 1986 with aggregate billings of 53 million Australian dollars, up from eighteenth place and 45.5 million dollars the previous year. The Melbourne office, part of the old Compton set-up, suffered from a dull image, which it attempted to brush up for a time by bringing in a well-known creative man, Ron Mather, as manager. Unfortunately this caused it to lose some previously loyal clients. The Sydney office, formerly Gough Waterhouse, was founded some years ago by a couple of British creative men and enjoyed a much brighter reputation, at least with other creatives. The latest word is that Melbourne has been stabilised, and David Stewart-Hunter, formerly account planning director of the Charlotte Street agency, sent out in 1986 as joint managing director of Sydney, is trying to help the agency win the kind of new business growth that has so far eluded it.

In a number of countries, notably in Latin America, the network has collaborative agreements with local agencies but no equity stake. In Japan, after the failure of attempts to move in by acquisition, on the European and American pattern, it had to settle for a 5% stake in Asahi Advertising of Tokyo, the country's eighth biggest agency. It is typical of the global power posture adopted by the Saatchi group that successive annual reports listed names and addresses of Saatchi Compton network agencies throughout the world, together with pictures of their managers, without distinguishing between those that were wholly owned by the company and those that were not owned at all.

The 1986 report dropped this habit, but by then Saatchi & Saatchi had acquired Ted Bates and no longer had to puff itself up frog-like to appear bigger than it was. From some of the figures already given, it may be seen that Bates is in some places as weak as, or weaker than, Saatchi Compton, for example Germany. However, the Bates network has some areas of strength that complement those of its sister chain of agencies.

In Australia the biggest advertising agency is George Patterson, which is 80% owned by Bates. In 1986 Patterson billed 351.6 million Australian dollars, nearly seven times as much as Saatchi & Saatchi Compton Australia. Patterson has the reputation of being an uncreative but very canny outfit, which knows its market well. It also owns half of another agency, Campaign Palace, widely regarded as Australia's most creative. In 1986 Campaign Palace was sixteenth biggest with turnover only fractionally behind that of Saatchi & Saatchi Compton.

Bates, through various acquisitions, ranks as the biggest agency grouping in Spain, with aggregate billings of 2,300 million pesetas, even though its constituent units – Delvico, the recently acquired Alas chain of regional offices and the Ted Bates office in Madrid – occupy only the twelfth, fifteenth and twenty-fifth positions respectively. Bates is also, and more obviously, top dog in Scandinavia, with its agencies occupying the number one spot in Denmark, Norway and Sweden. Unlike Saatchi Compton, Bates owns a share of a Latin American agency – 40% of Arellano Ted Bates, one of the top ten in Mexico.

In the US Bates has a number of subsidiaries. In March 1987 Simonds-Gooding approved the merger of three – AC & R Advertising, of New York, Sawdon & Bess, of New York and Los Angeles, and the Diener/Hauser/Bates chain of agencies in New York, California and Florida. Together they had 1986 billings of $311 million. The chief executive of the new formation, Stephen Rose, who had been head of AC & R, declared that the merger was his idea and that it would result in annual savings of more than $1 million. There were said to be no conflicts between the 150-odd clients involved.

Another merger plan – to put the New York office of Ted Bates together with Backer & Spielvogel – hung fire for months. The question of which man should run the combined show is always the hardest to answer in such circumstances, and neither Carl Spielvogel nor Bates's Donald Zuckert has shown himself an easy pushover in the past. Finally in July 1987 it was learned that the merger was going through with Spielvogel as chairman and Zuckert as president of the new Backer Spielvogel Bates Worldwide.

Another problem connected with Bates was what to do about the William Esty agency, the once highly profitable New York outfit bought by Bates and hit by a series of account losses, some of them stemming from reactions to the Saatchi takeover. At one point the new parent company was rumoured to be thinking of combining Esty with McCaffrey & McCall. Another conjecture was that Esty might be sold. Finally what did happen was that the agency received a new boss in the person of Joe O'Donnell. He is an ambitious high-flier who was forced out of the chairmanship of J. Walter Thompson, the ad agency arm of the JWT Group, after he tried unsuccessfully in early 1987 to stage a putsch, supplant chairman Don Johnston and lead a management buy-out of the publicly quoted company, the financial performance of which had been flagging.

It did not take the Saatchi group long to hire the 44-year-old hustler, who had made his name as manager of JWT's highly successful Chicago office. He got to Esty just in time to see yet another account, Nissan, pulling out. His mission, it was made clear, would be to put the faltering Esty show back on the road. This is an American task, and O'Donnell is seen as an America-firster. One of his grievances against his former boss was that he believed JWT was spending too much money on investing in ad agencies in out-of-the-way countries. Not every adman is obsessed with global conquest.

Globally the question remained whether, despite the dangers of client conflicts, it made sense to keep the Bates and Saatchi Compton networks strictly apart. Many observers will be surprised if in the long run there is no merging of the two, at least in the countries where both are represented by weak offices. Already there are the beginnings of a degree of co-ordination between the supposedly autonomous parts of the Saatchi empire. One example of this is the agreement by British Airways to shift its American advertising account to the merged Backer Spielvogel Bates agency and out of Saatchi & Saatchi DFS Compton, allowing the latter to hang on to Northwest Airlines, ADFS account. Another more dramatic example is described in the next chapter.

9

Coping with Conflict

In the spring of 1987 the most extraordinary example of the importance attached by some advertisers to the account conflict problem occurred in Britain. Dixons, the electrical retailing firm, took legal action against its agency, DFS Dorland, in an effort to prevent it from handling the Woolworths account, which was viewed by Dixons as competitive – not least because of a bitterly contested and unsuccessful takeover bid for Woolworths by Dixons some time before. One of the bizarre aspects of a bizarre episode was that Dorlands had been happily working for a Woolworths subsidiary, B & Q, for years with no objection from Dixons.

However, when Woolworths decided to dump its agency, McCann-Erickson, and turn to Dorlands instead, Dixons cut up rough. It made clear that its account would not be left to cohabit with the main Woolworths account. It would hire a new agency, but until it had had time to make arrangements to move out of Dorlands it did not want to see Woolworths moving in. In early April, therefore, Dixons applied for an injunction temporarily to bar Dorlands from accepting the Woolworths business. The injunction application, heard by a judge in chambers, failed. Meanwhile, however, Saatchi group management had been making strenuous behind-the-scenes efforts to salvage the situation.

The grounds for concern were obvious. The two advertisers both spent enormous amounts. The 1987 advertising budget for Dixons and its subsidiary Currys was £26 million, expected to rise by 25% or more in 1988. Woolworths was budgeting for £20 million in 1987. According to MEAL (Media Expenditure Analysis Ltd), a company which monitors the amount of advertising appearing on television and radio and in the main national and regional newspapers and magazines, Dixons had actually spent in the year to 31 March 1987 slightly less than £16 million and Woolworths a little over £9 million. Precisely how much the accounts were worth to their agencies was even more uncertain – according to one report the breach between Woolworths and McCanns was partly due to a dispute over the agency's terms of remuneration – but that they were both worth hanging on to was not in doubt.

And the Saatchi group did manage to hang on to both. The solution found was that Dixons should transfer its account from one Saatchi-owned agency, Dorlands, to another, Ted Bates. What that meant in fact was that exactly the same group of people would go on handling the account but that they would physically move from the Dorlands building in Westbourne Terrace, Paddington, to Bates's Soho Square premises. The group was still headed by Michael Kaye, a personal friend of Mark Souhami, managing director of Dixons. Kaye had managed the account since his days as boss of Sharps Advertising, bought by Dorlands in 1985. In moving to Bates at the beginning of May, Kaye acquired the title of executive vice-chairman. At Dorlands he had been simply a board director.

Jack Rubins, chairman of Dorlands, was left feeling somewhat bruised and muttering darkly about the malice that had gone into the making of a crisis that he felt had been unnecessary. He did not believe the two accounts were truly competitive nor that a promise he had made some months earlier not to take on more Woolworths business still stood after Dixons had given up its interest in acquiring the other store chain, and after Rubins had prevailed on Woolworths to drop a defamation lawsuit against Dixons chairman Stanley Kalms, arising out of remarks he made during the takeover battle. A message from Woolworths chairman Geoff Mulcahy confirming this appeared to have reached Kalms too late to save the Dixons account for Dorlands.

It also appeared that Mark Souhami, who was personally acquainted with Maurice Saatchi, had appealed to him to intervene. In Maurice's absence from London his brother Charles had written a letter to Souhami apologising for the behaviour of Rubins and, in effect, taking the client's side against him. For his part Rubins was outraged by Charles's action, which was seen at Dorlands as a breach of the autonomy guarantee given to the agency when it was acquired by the Saatchi group in 1981.

The affair coincided with the attempt being made by the group to merge DFS Dorland New York, formerly Dancer Fitzgerald Sample, with Saatchi & Saatchi Compton, thus depriving Dorlands in London of the platform, painstakingly put together over a long time, on which to build an autonomous international network with its headquarters in Paddington. The plan had been to buy majority holdings in strong agencies in European countries, Australia and the Far East in place of a collection of mostly minority stakes in small agencies, but these plans were now superseded. Dorlands in London was left with control only of a wholly owned agency in Holland. Now that the transatlantic link was broken, the new name DFS Dorland lost its meaning.

This development was also seen as a breach of the autonomy agreement, since the DFS Dorland get-together, although financed by Saatchi & Saatchi, had been very much a Dorlands initiative. Furthermore, it had been a point of honour for Rubins that, after the appointment of Anthony Simonds-Gooding as chairman of the Communications division of the group, theoretically responsible for overseeing all its ad agencies, Dorlands had carried on exactly as before, reporting not to Simonds-Gooding but only to Maurice Saatchi, as chairman of the holding company. Attempts by Simonds-Gooding to assert his authority over Dorlands via written instructions on various matters had been studiously ignored. Now, through his actions in New York, Simonds-Gooding was asserting his authority with a vengeance.

The relationship between Dorlands and the holding company had up till now been an arm's-length one. Rubins, whose personal contacts with Saatchi & Saatchi had been largely confined to occasional lunches with Maurice, had always given the impression that he would be happier if the rival ad agency, Saatchi & Saatchi Compton, did not bear the same name as the holding company. As for Dorlands, though there had never been any secret about who owned it, it had also never been firmly bracketed in any UK client's mind with Saatchi & Saatchi. Evidence of that was the action of the Guinness company in appointing Dorlands to handle its Harp lager brand in Ireland in 1986 at the very time that Guinness was in legal dispute with Saatchi & Saatchi Compton over the latter's aggressive anti-Guinness knocking ads, done for Argyll as part of the takeover battle for the Distillers Company.

Rubins and his colleagues at Dorlands, including Michael Bungey to whom he had recently given the title of chief executive along with a share of his responsibilities, were angry and alarmed at the unexpected turn events had suddenly taken in early 1987. They were reliably reported to be demanding from Saatchi headquarters a new *modus vivendi* that would allow Dorlands to continue to grow independently as the centre of its own network. Demanding rather than requesting. Despite the fact that it was a wholly owned subsidiary of the Saatchi & Saatchi Company, Dorlands needed to be treated with extreme care by its parent if a débâcle was to be avoided. This was because Rubins and his team had established a formidably successful operation of their own and were capable, if the worst came to the hypothetical worst, of repeating their success outside the group. The danger of a breakaway, in which the team might decamp, taking with it a large number of Dorlands clients, seemed in early 1987 remote but not impossible.

The success story is all the more remarkable for having come about without any of the publicity hype from which the Charlotte Street agency has benefited. Dorlands, declares Rubins, is 'not a flamboyant agency.' As someone else said, it has risen and risen without trace. Rubins himself is not a flamboyant man. Aged fifty-five in 1987, he had spent all his working life at the agency, of which he had become media director twenty years previously. For 1981, year of the Saatchi takeover, Dorlands reported billings of £46 million and just scraped into the top ten in the league table of British ad agencies. By 1986 the figure had risen to £190 million, and Dorlands was number three, treading on the heels of the leaders, Saatchi & Saatchi Compton and J. Walter Thompson.

Expansion had been aided by the absorption of two other agencies, Michael Bungey DFS in 1984 and Sharps the following year. But lots of new business had been added, including in 1985 £18 million of billing from Austin Rover, £9.5 million from Imperial Tobacco and £8 million from Presto supermarkets. Another gain that year was Blue Nun wine, won from sister agency Saatchi & Saatchi Compton. Gains in 1986 included £7 million of advertising for the Department of Health and Social Security and £6 million for the Halifax Building Society.

In the first quarter of 1987 Dorlands topped the table of agency billings compiled by MEAL on the basis of advertising space and time monitored by it during the period. The figures for that one quarter were as follows: 1. DFS Dorland £29,988,000 (a gain of 11% on the corresponding period of the previous year); 2. Saatchi & Saatchi Compton London £29,259,000 (down 30%); 3. JWT £27,641,000 (down 13.8%). For the twelve months to 31 March 1987 the pecking order, as compiled by MEAL, was somewhat different: 1. JWT £152,123,000 (up 12.6%); 2. DFS Dorland £151,098,000 (up 32.2%); 3. Saatchi & Saatchi Compton London £142,958,000 (down 7.7%), reflecting the loss of such accounts as the McDonalds hamburger chain.

As published, however, the MEAL list put Saatchi & Saatchi Compton in first place, with billings of £186,522,000. This figure was arrived at by including, at Saatchi insistence, work handled not only by Charlotte Street but by some of the group's smaller subsidiaries. This provoked vociferous protests from JWT, on the grounds that the list ought to show the performance of individual offices only, and *sotto voce* grumbles from the Saatchi subsidiary in Paddington. Defending what had happened, Roy Warman, joint chief executive of Saatchi & Saatchi Compton International, said the figures for KHBB (previously KMP Humphreys Bull & Barker) had been included because 'when we did the KHBB merger we artificially hurt ourselves because a lot of their business was ours . . . It doesn't do any harm one way or the other.'

The frequent assertion by ad agency bigwigs that billings tables do not matter are about as convincing as the protestations by politicians that they pay no attention to political opinion polls, by which everyone knows their actions are totally governed. Logically or illogically, the tables are regarded by both agencies and clients as a major publicity weapon. Many clients pay more attention to the MEAL figures than to those published annually by *Campaign*. While MEAL cannot take account of everything ad agencies do – it does not monitor outdoor advertising, reckons the value of all space and time at the official price rather than the discounted prices secured by skilled agency media buyers, and has no knowledge of fees for non-advertising services such as new product development – it is independent and impartial. The *Campaign* figures and those similarly compiled by other trade papers in other countries are supplied by the agencies themselves and are inflated by means of various quanmos (quasi-non-misleading operations).

Dorlands, with some justification, regards the MEAL figures as proof that it is beginning to overhaul its more famous sister agency in Charlotte Street. If that achievement owes little to public relations, it does not owe much either to the kind of advertising that agency people qualify as 'creative'. It goes in for sensible stuff rather than pyrotechnics *à la* Charlotte Street. For example it won the Austin Rover account with a presentation of witty ads which it subsequently refused to run, on the grounds that, though fine for wooing clients, they were unsuited to selling cars.

The advertising of which it is proudest is probably the 'liquid engineering' campaign for Castrol motor oil, a brand leader which was in danger of being ousted from its position when Dorlands took it on in the mid-1970s. The agency's solution was, in Rubins's words, to 'put the product on a pedestal,' and it is now well ahead of its competitors. Castrol TV commercials are beautifully filmed, strongly branded and somewhat pompous – not what always passes for 'creative' in the contemporary adman's jargon. Another campaign of which Rubins is proud is that for Duracell batteries. The advertising features graphic demonstrations of how Duracell goes on working for a long time, and Rubins sees Dorlands as producing sensible ads that go on working year after year for its clients.

The Dixons episode throws light, it must be said, not only on the position of Dorlands as a powerful barony within the Saatchi empire but also, and once again, on the question of account conflicts and how the group has managed them. Whatever else the row with Dixons proved or failed to prove, it did give considerable encouragement to the school of thought, founded by Marion Harper of Interpublic, that maintains that it ought to be possible to retain within a group of ad agencies clients who would refuse to share a single agency. Despite some spectacular walk-outs by clients after the Bates takeover, it is remarkable how many competitive advertisers have consented to remain within the Saatchi group.

Just take, for example, the number of car accounts serviced by different Saatchi subsidiaries. There is a whole raft of rival manufacturers, including Austin Rover (handled by Dorlands London and Saatchi & Saatchi Compton Frankfurt), Renault (Saatchi Compton Milan), Nissan (Saatchi Compton London), Saab (KHBB London), Hyundai (Backer & Spielvogel New York), American Motors (Saatchi Compton New York), Mercedes-Benz (McCaffrey & McCall New York), Toyota (DFS Dorland New York) and Chevrolet (Cochrane Chase Livingston California). Even though William Esty in New York has lost Nissan, and Jaguar has moved out of Saatchi Compton in Frankfurt, it is quite an impressive achievement to have hung on to all these competing clients.

The case of the Ted Bates office in London also merits attention, because it has worked, since the 1986 takeover of Bates by Saatchi, in close co-operation with the Charlotte Street agency. Even the present chairman of Bates London, Tony Dalton, is a Charlotte Street man. Formerly a deputy chairman of Saatchi & Saatchi Compton, Dalton was put in to run the agency when the previous boss, Chris Woollams, in place at the time of the takeover, was fired after criticising Saatchi managerial methods. ('Management by Sellotape' was the phrase he reportedly used.)

Soon after the arrival of Dalton, some £5 million of Bates's Mars business was transferred from Soho to Charlotte Street, a move that Woollams was understood to have opposed. From New York, Larry Light, international president of Ted Bates, was reported as having said that clients should use whichever of the two agencies – Bates or Saatchi Compton – suited them the best. In Britain it seemed that Bates, a second-division agency with reported billings for 1986 of £60.2 million, making it number nineteen in the *Campaign* pecking order, was being used as a second string to the Charlotte Street bow rather than as a strong performer in its own right. This was, of course, not at all the direction in which Rubins and his team at Dorlands wished to see themselves going.

In the immediate aftermath of the Dixons affair there were two ways of looking at what had happened. On the one hand the Saatchi group could be said to have coped successfully with the account conflict problem and to have proved the viability of the old Interpublic thesis on how to accommodate rival clients. This was the thesis which had been so sorely injured by the mass defections of American clients from the new mega-merger groups.

On the other hand it was arguable that, in taking action to resolve the Dixons-Woolworths conflict and save both accounts for the group, the Saatchis had provoked a, for them, much graver conflict – between the group management and that of one of the group's most successful constituents, Dorlands. If it came to the crunch could Jack Rubins and his colleagues actually do anything to make their weight felt, or would the power of Saatchi money stifle their discontent? The answer soon came. In the face of Saatchi refusal to contemplate a management buy-out, Dorlands resistance collapsed. Jack Rubins, disgusted at the destruction of his plans for an international network of his own, left the agency after the DFS-Compton merger in New York, handing over the chairmanship to Michael Bungey in exchange for the meaningless title of consultant. And that was that. However, the affair helped to underline doubts about the strategy being pursued by Simonds-Gooding in the US, where Saatchi-owned agencies were being forced, against their will, into mergers that might appear to make economic sense but that left the human factor out of account.

One of the most important ingredients in any agency's success is the intangible one of morale. A demoralised ad agency risks losing its clients. Some mergers gell perfectly – the 1975 amalgam of Garland-Compton and the old Saatchi & Saatchi agency turned out, to the surprise of many, to be a brilliant success – but others have been far less successful. At least one agency chief felt that Simonds-Gooding, for all his intelligence, was behaving in New York like 'a buffoon', counting the cost savings that could be achieved by putting DFS together with Saatchi Compton in the latter's new Hudson Street building and forgetting about the added costs that would be incurred in the form of employee discontent. These might be metaphorical costs to begin with, but in the agency business they could pretty soon turn into financial ones, as alienated staff resulted in alienated clients.

As for Rubins, he found himself in the gratifying position as he went off on a long summer holiday of being inundated with job offers from both inside and outside the advertising business.

10

New Horizons

Saatchi & Saatchi began as an advertising agency and is still identified, in the minds of people who have heard of it at all, with advertising. The advertising agencies it owns do indeed account for the greater part of the company's revenues as well as almost all its public notoriety, not to mention its most knotty problems. However, advertising is by no means the only field in which it operates, and it is likely that in the future the non-advertising subsidiaries will assume increasing import- ance. Let us now look at the business service fields into which the group has diversified.

They are divided, as previously mentioned, between the two divisions of Saatchi & Saatchi Communications and Saatchi & Saatchi Consult- ing. Communications includes, as well as the ad agencies, companies concerned with sales promotion, direct marketing, design and public relations. Consulting has been up till now a far smaller division, con- sisting principally of the Hay Group. Its most important other con- stituent has been the market research agency Yankelovich Clancy Shulman. The decision to bracket market research with management consultancy was presumably a matter of administrative convenience. It would have been at least as logical to put it in Communications on the grounds that research firms, like ad agencies and sales promotion outfits, are usually hired by the marketing departments of client com- panies, but this would have made the imbalance between the two divisions too great.

There is no doubt that, of all the non-advertising fields in which the Saatchi group is now involved, management consultancy must be the one that appears most promising for the future. Worldwide the business consulting market is estimated to have been worth around $100,000 million in 1986 and to have grown by 20% – almost six times the increase in world GNP. These were the figures quoted by Victor Millar shortly after he had been hired in late 1986 to be chairman and chief executive of Saatchi & Saatchi Consulting in succession to Milton Rock, now retired. He was adopting the broadest possible definition of 'consulting', taking in information services.

More narrowly defined, traditional management consultancy had aggregate turnover of perhaps $10,000 million, half of it in the United States, where the Saatchi subsidiary Hay ranked twelfth in the list of the top twenty firms. The table (figures available refer only to 1985) was as follows.

Worldwide revenues of US-based management consultancies ($m)

1.	Arthur Andersen	477
2.	McKinsey	350
3.	Towers Perrin Forster & Crosby	305
4.	Price Waterhouse	280
5.	Booz Allen	260
6.	Mercer-Meidinger	254
7.	Peat Marwick	240
8.	Coopers & Lybrand	201
9.	Wyatt	201
10.	Ernst & Whinney	188
11.	Arthur Young	175
12.	Hay Group	142
13.	Touche Ross	140
14.	Alexander Proudfoot	120
15.	Johnson & Higgins	118
16.	Human Resource Management	105
17.	Bain & Co.	100
18.	Hewitt Associates	97
19.	Arthur D. Little	90
20.	Deloitte Haskins & Sells	78

Source: Consultants News

Far and away at the top of this particular tree, it will be noticed, is the management consultancy side of the accountancy firm Arthur Andersen. It reached that position under the leadership of the same Victor Millar whom the Saatchis tempted away, reportedly to the great dismay of his former company. The bait: a remuneration package, including share options, said to be worth $1.25 million a year, plus the challenge of trying to repeat for his new employers what he had already achieved once for Andersen. Millar is generally regarded as an impressive character, and if anyone can reach the Saatchi goal of upping the share of profits contributed by Consulting from a fifth to a half it is he. (In the 1985–6 financial year the division accounted for only £14 million out of group pre-tax profits of £70.1 million, compared with £11.7 million out of £40.4 million the previous year.)

From his base in Washington DC Victor Millar is proposing to create a global consulting organisation that will match the increasingly global character of client companies. Opportunities are expanding for experienced consultants, he says, but adds that 'if consulting firms are to be effective in dealing with the concerns of global businesses ... ultimately domination by a few firms will be necessary. The current fragmented state of the profession will not allow it to serve global clients properly – the key value that such clients will look for in their consultants will be reliability on a global scale.' This view fits in very well, of course, with the gospel of globalisation that the Saatchi group has been preaching for years regarding marketing and advertising.

The Hay Group's operations are already global in scope. Unlike the majority of the big US-based management consultancy firms listed just now, it derives more than half its revenues from its operations outside the US, including those of its British-based recruitment subsidiary MSL and its French-based subsidiary Gamma International, which specialises in management information systems. As well as advising on employee rewards, Hay offers clients a variety of services, including the analysis of recruitment needs, the auditing of internal company communications and access to its OASIS database, which correlates company strategy and human resource management with financial performance. Another subsidiary, Huggins Financial Services, specialises in management consultancy for financial institutions, including the formulation and marketing of new products.

Operating in very much the same corner of the field as Hay is the McBer company, bought by Saatchi in 1984 from the Reliance group. McBer, which specialises in researching employee attitudes, now works closely with Hay.

The first acquisition made by the Consulting division after Millar's arrival was that of Cleveland Consulting Associates, an American firm specialising in information systems. It was bought in March 1987 for an initial cash sum of $2 million plus deferred payments, on the usual earn-out pattern, to bring the total price to 9.5 times average after-tax profits.

Market research, according to Millar, is high on his list of priorities for future expansion. He takes the view, based on his own experience as a buyer of research, that the strategic planning of companies is often insufficiently research-based. Within the consulting field research has not, he thinks, been as highly regarded as it deserves, partly because it is seen as tied to the advertising and promotional side of client activities. And this despite the fact that market researchers tend to be far more like management consultants in their motivation and outlook than like the more flamboyant race of advertising folk. He has been talking to a number of research agencies, but by spring 1987 nothing concrete had come of these contacts.

It is in a way curious that the Saatchi group is not better represented in the research business. Long before Millar came on the Saatchi scene, the group was putting out feelers to a number of market research agencies in Britain but found no willing seller. An approach was certainly made, for example, to the MIL Research Group, the fifth biggest of its kind in the UK, now a public company in its own right. There have been persistent rumours, too, of Saatchi interest in Britain and Europe's biggest market research company, the publicly quoted AGB Research. These have been equally persistently denied on both sides, though less emphatically by the Saatchi side than by Sir Bernard Audley, AGB's strong-willed chairman.

Audley pointed out more than once that, given the strong involvement of AGB in television audience measurement in several countries, including the US, where its service had received financial backing from several ad agencies, a takeover by Saatchi would make little commercial sense. Other ad agencies would be bound to look askance at a service of that kind controlled by one of their rivals. Charles Saatchi, while denying any intention to bid for AGB, did let slip that it would be a nice business to own. Whether the supposed potential conflict of interest with subscribers to AGB services actually would stand in the way of a takeover is arguable. Rather more to the point is that AGB under Audley does not want to be taken over, and in the whole history of

Saatchi acquisitions there has never yet been a contested bid.

Market research firms, like advertising ones, are, in the much used phrase 'people businesses', where the assets are free, if they are upset, to leave. This is true even of a company like AGB, which has a good deal of fixed capital in the form of the electronic gadgetry which records the viewing behaviour of the panels of people on which TV audience statistics are based. The big money in market research is made in the continuous, syndicated (i.e. paid for by many clients) services that measure consumption of different kinds of goods as well as of media. Such services have been turning increasingly to high technology, for example electronic scanners in supermarkets as well as TV viewing meters. High tech means high costs and these in turn speed up the process of concentration that has been going on in the research industry, as it has in advertising.

Another similarity between the two is increasing globalisation, with research firms establishing, or attempting to establish, worldwide networks, though not so dramatically as has happened in advertising. Several British research agencies have, for example, bought subsidiaries in the US, most importantly AGB, which owns a company there called NFO Research apart from its TV research activities. AGB is, in fact, the only British firm among the top fifteen of worldwide research. Most of the others are American-owned, hardly surprisingly since the US market accounts on its own for $1,800 million of market research expenditure, or 47% of the world total.

Among the fifteen the non-American names, apart from AGB (ranked fourth in 1986) are GFK and Infratest, both German (seventh and tenth respectively) and Video Research (twelfth), a subsidiary of Japan's Dentsu advertising agency. Two others among the top fifteen are also owned by advertising-based companies – MRB Group, which belongs to JWT Group (parent of the J. Walter Thompson agency) and Research International, which has its headquarters in London but was recently sold by Unilever to the Ogilvy Group (parent of Ogilvy & Mather). Also worth noting is that IMS International, the world's biggest independent research agency since A. C. Nielsen was acquired by Dun & Bradstreet, is a publicly quoted company in New York but has its operational headquarters in London. IMS operates in 30 countries, Research International in 29, Nielsen (pre-eminent in the monitoring of grocery sales) in 27 and AGB in 23.

Worldwide revenues of the top fifteen American research firms in

1986, as estimated for *Advertising Age* by the American expert Jack Honomichl, of Marketing Aid Center, Chicago, are shown in the following table.

Worldwide market research revenues 1986 ($m)

1.	Nielsen	615
2.	IMS International	245.4
3.	SAMI/Burke	174.5
4.	Arbitron	137.2
5.	Information Resources	93.6
6.	MRB Group	52
7.	M/A/R/C	47.5
8.	NFO Research	36.7
9.	Market Facts	36
10.	NPD Group	35.5
11.	Westat	35.2
12.	Maritz	32.9
13.	Elrick & Lavidge	26.7
14.	Yankelovich Clancy Shulman	22
15.	Walker Research	21.3

Source: Advertising Age

The Saatchi subsidiary Yankelovich Clancy Shulman – one of two British-owned outfits in this list, the other being AGB's NFO – did respectably well during the year, increasing its turnover from $19.5 million the previous year, a growth rate of nearly 13%, and climbing from fifteenth to fourteenth place. Since the departure of the New York-based Yankelovich, Skelly & White, the merged firm has operated from Clancy Shulman's home town of Westport, Connecticut, offering a variety of services. These include Monitor, an annual survey of social attitudes, started nearly two decades ago by the old Yankelovich Skelly & White company, and Litmus, developed by Kevin Clancy, which uses computer modelling in conjunction with questioning of samples of consumers to predict the performance of products in the marketplace and how it can be affected by different marketing strategies.

The problems to which the company has applied such techniques have included whether a coffee brand would gain more by door-to-door sampling or by in-store tasting and whether an analgesic could be more successfully promoted by advertising or distribution of money-off coupons. Market research agencies use a variety of methods to tackle such problems, including several competing computer-based marketing models. The study of why people buy what (including the influence of advertising, pricing, packaging and other variables) is a fascinating one, though the habit of most market researchers of talking and writing about it in an all but impenetrable jargon makes it a subject of less popular interest than it deserves. The point to be made here, however, is that this kind of work falls into the area of what the Americans call custom research (in British English *ad hoc* research), where a different job is done for each client. Although custom research can be made to pay, it is not where the really big money is. For that, as already said, you want the continuous market measurement services, where the clients are locked in with annual subscriptions.

Where Yankelovich Clancy Shulman has distinguished itself recently is not so much in the growth of its business as in the vigour with which it has been advertising itself. Research firms, like management consultancies, do not normally go in for advertising. Paradoxically, not many ad agencies either spend much on advertising themselves. Ads for YCS have been appearing not only in specialised publications but in the general business press and in daily papers such as the *New York Times*. A typical ad was headed 'Hire Intelligence' and declared that YCS could offer clients a new kind of 'marketing intelligence' capable of discovering how to help a new product take off or set an old faltering one on the road to recovery. The firm is run by the young (mid-thirties), and single-minded Robert Shulman. He worked for the old Yankelovich Skelly & White for six years before teaming up with Clancy in 1982.

In 1985 Charles Saatchi, evincing considerable personal interest in the research business, said research firms acquired in the future would operate under the Yankelovich banner. The following year he and the rest of the group's central management were clearly much preoccupied with the Bates takeover and its aftermath. Market research took a back seat. Victor Millar is uncertain whether any such acquisitions will be merged with Yankelovich Clancy Shulman or allowed to remain autonomous. At any rate the Saatchi group has a long way to go before it achieves, as far as research is conerned, its ambition of being in the top ten in any field and in any country in which it operates.

In certain other non-advertising business sectors that ambition has been achieved. In the US the group claims to be number two in direct marketing, number three in sales promotion, number four in 'corporate identity' design work, number six in public relations. In the UK it lays claim to third place in PR and fifth in sales promotion.

While US expenditure on conventional media advertising has grown only slowly of late, more money has been going into what in the jargon of Adland is called 'below the line' activities, meaning various kinds of sales promotion, including money-off coupons and competitions, and of direct marketing. The latter term covers direct mail, telephone selling and direct respone advertising, where the consumer is invited to send in purchase orders or inquiries. Direct marketing has really come into its own with the development of computer technology, since it depends on easy storage of, and quick reference to, databases – or, in plain language, lists – of customers and potential customers. Many big ad agencies have been starting up, or acquiring, direct marketing subsidiaries.

In the spring of 1987 Anthony Simonds-Gooding declared direct marketing to be a priority growth area for Saatchi & Saatchi. The chairman of the company's Communications division told a meeting of the Association of Canadian Advertisers that direct marketing, with its capacity for precise targeting of consumers and measurement of response, was 'absolutely created in heaven for clients'.

Saatchi's direct marketing activities in the US are conducted through several subsidiaries, including Kobs & Brady, a direct marketing agency acquired by Bates shortly before it was itself taken over. Other Saatchi-owned firms specialising in direct marketing are Fairfax and DFS Direct. A large part of McCaffrey & McCall's work for clients has been in the form of direct mail. The Kleid Company is a list broker, that is to say it compiles and rents out lists of people in particular occupations who are of interest to direct mail advertisers.

In Britain the group entered the direct marketing field with something of a fanfare at the end of 1986 with the establishment of a new company called Saatchi & Saatchi Direct. (Start-ups of this kind have been the exception rather than the rule in the history of the group, which has grown so much by acquisition.) To run the new venture two heavyweights were recruited. Appointed chairman was Peter Rosenwald, at the age of fifty-one one of the best known people in the direct marketing trade. He had helped to build up the direct marketing agency Wundermans, now a Young & Rubicam subsidiary, which claims to be the world's largest, before setting up his own consultancy in 1982. Rosenwald has taken a prominent part in the annual Direct Marketing Symposium which attracts many hundreds of professionals each spring to Montreux, Switzerland.

Installed as managing director was John Maile, marketing director of the catalogue division of Great Universal Stores, a Saatchi client since the early 1970s. Within four months the new agency had won a string of accounts, including those of four clients already using Saatchi & Saatchi Compton for above-the-line (ordinary media) advertising, namely Racal, the Royal Automobile Club, the National Society for the Prevention of Cruelty to Children and the telecommunications group Mercury. A few months later a direct marketing subsidiary of DFS Dorland was set up under the name of Dorland Direct.

Some of the gilt was taken off the gingerbread, however, by the exit from the Saatchi group in early 1987 of the three men who had been running a sister subsidiary, the Sales Promotion Agency. The three – managing director John Honsinger, Mike Halstead group account director and creative director Rick Smith – left, after reported friction with group management over the agency's performance, to set up their own company, HH & S. Until the setting up of Saatchi & Saatchi Direct it had been the Sales Promotion Agency that looked after direct marketing for the group in the UK. It also handled some media advertising business, including the launch of the *Independent* newspaper.

Although the Saatchi group has some strong marketing service subsidiaries, mostly in the US and UK, it has as yet, and with one exception, no international network in any discipline but advertising. The exception is, of course, the Hay Group. However, for all the Saatchi talk of global marketing, it has no international direct marketing network like that of Young & Rubicam's Wunderman subsidiary, no worldwide group of market research companies like Research International, the one-time Unilever subsidiary acquired in 1986 by Ogilvy (Unilever did not consider a sale to Saatchi because of the latter's close links with rival Procter & Gamble), nor even an international network of public relations agencies.

This last lack is the most surprising, since the 1985 sale to Saatchi of the American PR firm The Rowland Company after twenty years of independence was justified by its founder-boss, Herb Rowland, on the grounds that membership of a bigger group would enable him to compete internationally with bigger competitors such as the Young & Rubicam subsidiary Burson-Marsteller and the JWT Group subsidiary

Hill & Knowlton. These two are the world's biggest PR companies, each with total fee income in 1986 of around $100 million. Rowland's figure was less than a tenth of that, making it fifteenth in the league table of American PR firms, as follows:

Fee income of American PR consultancies 1986 ($m)

1.	Hill & Knowlton	100.2
2.	Burson-Marsteller	100
3.	Ogilvy & Mather PR	31
4.	Manning Selvage & Lee	21
5.	Daniel J. Edelman	20
6.	Doremus Porter Novelli	20
7.	Fleishman-Hillard	18
8.	Ketchum PR	17
9.	Golin Harris	17
10.	Ruder Finn & Rotman	15
11.	Regis McKenna	12
12.	Rogers & Cowan	10.5
13.	Howard Rubenstein Associates	9
14.	Creamer Dickson Basford	8
15.	Rowland	8

Source: PR World

As a believer in global marketing, Rowland saw establishment of an international network as a necessity for real success in PR as in advertising. Shortly after selling control of his company he started approaching other PR consultancies in the US, Europe and the Far East with a view to setting up a Rowland International under the Saatchi umbrella. Presumably because of the group's preoccupation with bigger fish, such as the Ted Bates acquisition, nothing much happened on the PR front, however, during 1986.

It appeared in early 1987 that the Saatchi group might be about to make as great a leap forward in PR as it already had in advertising. Reports in the business press suggested that JWT was willing to sell Hill & Knowlton, the world's biggest PR firm, and that Saatchi & Saatchi was willing to buy it. The reports were denied, but financial analysts regarded the denials with some scepticism. As a public company with a poor reputation on Wall Street, JWT was under pressure to do something to breathe life into its share price, and it was thought that divesting itself of Hill & Knowlton, which itself appeared to be running out of steam, was a likely option if a takeover of the whole JWT Group was to be avoided. In fact, as will be seen in the next chapter, it was not avoided, and H & K stayed part of the group. In mid-1987 Rowland started talking again of setting up an international network.

In the UK Saatchi's share of the PR market is made up of contributions from several companies, namely Kingsway PR, Granard Communications, Harrison Cowley PR and Grandfield Rork Collins Financial. In the 1986 table of British PR consultancy revenues these companies stood respectively in twelfth position (with operating revenue of £2,444,398), fourteenth (£2,258,283), eighteenth (£1,827,000) and twenty-ninth (£889,577). The top fifteen positions in terms of 1986 operating revenue were as follows.

Revenues of British PR consultancies 1986

1.	Shandwick Group	£13,187,000
2.	Charles Barker Group	£7,159,359
3.	Burson-Marsteller	£7,054,783
4.	Valin Pollin	£5,393,000
5.	Dewe Rogerson	£4,669,000
6.	Hill & Knowlton	£4,601,000
7.	Grayling Group	£4,145,000
8.	Streets Financial Strategy	£3,273,814
9.	Daniel J. Edelman	£3,222,244
10.	Countrywide Communications	£2,520,000
11.	City & Commercial	£2,500,000
12.	Kingsway PR	£2,444,398
13.	Biss Lancaster	£2,403,700
14.	Granard Communications	£2,258,283
15.	Paragon Communications	£2,236,175

Source: PR Week

The same source, *PR Week*, calculated that the Saatchi group was the second biggest UK-based force in PR, outdone only by the Shandwick group. Adding together the figures for its four UK subsidiaries with those of The Rowland Company and of a French subsidiary, the Saatchi total came to £13,594,258 in 1986. Shandwick, a publicly quoted group operating only in the PR field, acquired the American West Coast PR consultancy of Rogers & Cowan in April, 1987. Two months later another publicly quoted British firm, Valin Pollen, which specialises in financial PR and advertising, took over the American Carter Organization, a similar company with 1986 turnover of over $35 million. Valin Pollen and Shandwick now rank as respectively the number three and number four PR groups in the world after Hill & Knowlton and Burson-Marsteller. PR, like advertising, has become a fast growth area in Britain in recent years. The industry was reported by *PR Week* to have grown by 37% in 1986.

Advertising and other marketing services on the one hand, management consultancy and market research on the other – these are the activities pursued by the two operating divisions of Saatchi & Saatchi. However, there is no reason to think that the company's ambitions are necessarily limited to this list. It came as a surprise to many when, in the contest for the contract to operate Britain's first DBS (direct broadcasting by satellite) contract, one of the partners in the consortium headed by Carlton Communications turned out to be Saatchi & Saatchi. As far as ordinary media are concerned, ownership by advertising agencies is either frowned upon or prohibited by the various bodies which regulate them. The thinking is that for an agency to have control over an advertising medium in which both it and its rivals wanted to take space or time would set up an intolerable conflict of interest. The alliance with Carlton marked a departure from the convention that ad agencies steered clear of any involvement in media ownership. It would have been a more important development if the Carlton consortium had not lost its bid for the DBS contract.

If further opportunities arise in the future in any part of the world for participation in control of the media that carry advertising as well as merely placing ads in them, it may be assumed that the group will be interested. In this the Saatchi position is not very different from, though perhaps more enterprising than, that of other ad agencies. In general agencies think they know more about what makes people buy or tune into different media than do those who run them – and they may well be right. They also tend to take a freewheeling attitude to media, and none more so than Saatchi, which has been among the more vociferous advocates of putting advertising on BBC television.

In a completely different field Maurice Saatchi has been reported as dreaming of buying a leading accountancy firm. If such dreams were to inspire action, there could hardly be a more suitable man than the former Arthur Andersen duumvir Victor Millar to do something about it. This is not to say that it will happen. But then, before the purchase of the Hay Group nobody expected the Saatchis to move into management consultancy. What they do will depend on the mix of opportunities and finance available to them at any given time. Given that they have shown themselves in the past to be brilliant opportunists, it would be surprising if in the future they did not spring quite a few more surprises.

11

Rivals and Imitators

The rise and rise of Saatchi & Saatchi has served as a spur and an example to a number of other British companies, most but not all of them advertising agencies. Three Saatchi group achievements in particular invited imitation. First and foremost was its success in raising money on the Stock Exchange with which to expand by acquisition. Saatchi was, of course, far from being the first British ad agency to go public, but an earlier crop of agency flotations had met with mixed results, none of them inspiring. Several indeed had stood as warnings against the perils of going public – Dorland, which fell victim to the corporate raider John Bentley in 1971, S. H. Benson, an old-established agency which, fearing the same fate as Dorland, agreed to be taken over by Ogilvy & Mather in the same year, and, ironically, Compton UK Partners, which had been induced by the joint pressure of poor performance and a quoted share price to throw itself in 1975 into the arms of Saatchi & Saatchi.

These bad memories were, however, wiped out by the track record of Saatchi as a public company and the admiration that this excited in the City of London, at least until the 1986 purchase of Bates cast some doubt on the group's judgement. Almost entirely because of the Saatchi record the City revised its opinion of the marketing services sector. Stockbrokers' analysts ceased to regard them as Mickey Mouse companies not worth bothering about and started to take them seriously as sound investment opportunities. So the Saatchis not only provided the example of what could be done in the matter of raising money, they paved the way to the City's coffers for their contemporaries.

The second lesson learned by these contemporaries from the Saatchis was the desirability of putting together advertising agencies and other kinds of company in groups offering a large range of marketing services to clients. This again was hardly a Saatchi invention. For many years ad agencies had been spinning off or acquiring subsidiaries in various marketing service fields. For instance, even before World War Two the British Market Research Bureau was founded as a subsidiary of the J. Walter Thompson ad agency. BMRB is today part of the MRB Group, which is still owned by JWT. Marplan was a spin-off of McCann-Erickson, though the latter sold it to Research International, now owned by the Ogilvy Group. Various sales promotion and public relations firms had similar ad agency origins.

However, the idea of the marketing conglomerate had tended to fall out of fashion. At any rate it was not something in which a new crop of successful young British ad agencies, mostly founded in the 1970s and 1980s, took much interest until the Saatchi group showed it could be made to pay. Other factors, too, were involved, including the sheer growth both financially and in terms of client awareness of some activities, such as direct marketing and public relations, which had previously enjoyed a less glamorous image than had the very visible advertising industry itself.

The third lesson was that America, for so long the imperial heartland of marketing, from which ad agencies such as JWT, McCanns and Young & Rubicam, research firms such as A. C. Nielsen, PR companies such as Hill & Knowlton, had sallied forth to colonise the western world, could itself be colonised. Was well worth colonising because the US by itself accounted for roughly half the market for all marketing services. Was easy to colonise to the extent that the London stock market, impressed by the Saatchi strategy, was willing to put up the money with which to do it. Before the Saatchi acquisition of Compton in 1982 several British ad agencies had tried to establish themselves in the States but with only indifferent success. The natural order of events was still seen to be for British firms to sell out to Americans. In the past five years Britain has re-established itself as a colonial power, at least in the marketing field.

Among the firms that have followed in the Saatchis' footsteps several are of particular interest. Since, despite all the noise it makes, Adland is relatively small – the entire population of all London ad agencies amounts to less than 15,000 – it is not surprising to discover that almost every one of these firms has some kind of connection with the Saatchi group. In the case of Lowe Howard-Spink & Bell, the link is Tim Bell, whose contribution to the Saatchi story has already been recounted. In the case of Wight Collins Rutherford Scott, both Collins and Rutherford are former Saatchi employees. Abbott Mead Vickers has no ex-Saatchi men among its founders, but it took over another agency, Leagas Delaney, which had been started by Ron Leagas, one-time managing director of Saatchi's Charlotte Street agency. Let us begin, however, by looking at another advertising-based mini-conglomerate, Boase Massimi Pollitt, the history of whose dealings with Saatchi & Saatchi is both fascinating and almost completely unknown.

BMP, as the survey of client opinion quoted in an earlier chapter shows, is one of the most admired of London ad agencies. It can be classified as a Saatchi imitator in respect of its most recent financial behaviour – going public and buying into America – but in other ways it is a much more original outfit than any Saatchi agency has ever been. It was started in the late 1960s as a breakaway from Pritchard Wood, an Interpublic agency now defunct, by three men – Martin Boase, Gabe Massimi and Stanley Pollitt. Of these three only Boase, the urbane bearded chairman, remains twenty years later. Massimi, an American, fell out with his partners fairly early on and quit the agency to go back to the States. Stanley Pollitt, who sadly died young, was a brilliantly clever man who laid down for the agency a system for testing advertising concepts which, though imitated by some others, remains pretty unusual.

At BMP every account has attached to it an 'account planner' whose job is to research the market and to suggest to the creatives (copywriters and art directors) points to which they should address themselves. The account planners are also personally responsible for conducting discussion groups among selected samples of consumers on whom all BMP ads are tested before they are finalised for broadcasting or publication. Such pre-testing, as it is called, is common among agencies, but most hire specialised research companies to do the donkey work. The BMP approach is that such research should be an integral part of the advertising process. Critics of advertising research point out that what consumers say in the artificial context of a discussion in which they are invited to assume the unaccustomed role of judges of ads is not necessarily a reliable guide to how those ads will perform in the marketplace. It is also sometimes said that the person conducting such a discussion can, by prompting participants, even without intending to do so, lead them in any direction he or she favours. There is sense in these criticisms; on the other hand, the most important thing about any ad is how it is seen and understood by the public at large, and without asking the public ad-creators can never be certain that what they think they have communicated is actually the message that viewers and readers have received.

BMP has distinguished itself not only by its system of testing ads but by the quality of the ads it produces. Its creative department, under the leadership of John Webster, a key man in the agency's history, has scored many hits and won many awards. Among its best known campaigns have been those for Smash instant potato (featuring spoof Martians in TV commercials), John Smith Yorkshire Bitter (very funny films featuring a sly boozer called Arkwright) and the Greater London Council (hard-hitting posters attacking Conservative Government plans to abolish the GLC). With the aid of such campaigns and the reputation gained through them, BMP climbed the advertising tree to ninth place in 1986, with reported billings of £93.6 million.

Back in 1969, when BMP was a very much smaller business, its office was in a building in Goodge Street where its neighbours, on different floors, were the Michael Peters design consultancy, today a publicly quoted company called the Michael Peters Group, and a well-thought-of creative consultancy called Cramer Saatchi. Naturally the neighbours knew each other and kept in touch after they moved out of the building. In 1976 BMP sold a 50% interest in itself to Univas, the international arm of the big French ad agency Havas, for about £750,000. However, nothing much came of the association in advertising business terms, and four years later it was agreed to dissolve it. The French sold their half of the equity back to BMP's employee-stockholders. The next corporate development idea came in 1982 from Martin Boase's old friend and ex-neighbour Charles Saatchi. It was quite an extraordinary one.

In essence what Charles suggested to Boase was a merger between BMP and the Charlotte Street agency, still called Saatchi & Saatchi Garland-Compton. The fifteen BMP shareholders – all of them employees, including chairman Boase whose 18% stake at that time was the largest – would be paid £4–5 million for their stock. Moreover most of the top jobs in the new set-up would go to the BMP people. Martin Boase would be chairman of Saatchi & Saatchi BMP, as it would probably be called, in place of Tim Bell, who would concentrate on being managing director (at that time he held both titles). John Webster, BMP's creative chief, and its joint managing directors, Chris Powell and David Batterbee, would play important parts in the new, merged agency. The thinking behind the proposal was that, after a very successful period of organic growth (that is to say business acquired from new or existing clients rather than bought in along with other agencies taken over), Charlotte Street's management resources were stretched very thin and the agency needed new blood.

The proposal looked almost like a re-run of the 1975 scenario in which the original Charlotte Street agency, Garland-Compton, merged with Saatchi & Saatchi in a reverse takeover. Only now it was the Saatchi men who would be yielding the commanding positions. Of course, there would be important differences from 1975. Notably there was no question of financial control passing from the hands of the Saatchi & Saatchi holding company. Charles and Maurice would still be the bosses, but they would be able to devote themselves to their empire-building schemes – this was at the time they were negotiating to take over Compton in New York – while leaving Charlotte Street in safe hands. The merged agency there would, on the face of it, be bigger and stronger in every respect, and its number one position in the pecking order would be assured for a long time to come.

What actually happened was more like a re-run of the Compton UK proposal to merge with The Kirkwood Company. Boase and his partners, after discussion, turned the idea down despite the lure of the money on offer. They could, they decided, keep their independence and still do well for themselves. And so it proved. The following year BMP went public on its own account, achieving a market value of more than £16 million. Nothing at the time or since was published about the details of the Saatchi offer, which constituted a great tribute to BMP's managerial and creative talents but not a striking vote of confidence by the Saatchi holding company in its own Charlotte Street flagship.

BMP subsequently expanded into marketing consultancy, with the purchase of the Marketing Solutions company for £10 million. The latter has, in turn, a sales promotion subsidiary, Creative Solutions, a direct marketing subsidiary, Granby Marketing Services, bought in 1986 for £6.6 million, and a New York office. In 1986 Marketing Solutions contributed something like 40% of the BMP group's £5 million pre-tax profit. On the advertising agency side the group took shares in small new firms in London (Davis Wilkins) and New York (Angotti Thomas Hedge) before making a big American acquisition in early 1987 with the purchase for $31.8 million of Ammirati & Puris. The deal, financed by a share issue, involved the possibility of five further deferred payments, dependent on profits. The American agency, ranked fifty-one by *Advertising Age*, had 1986 billings of $150 million, nearly half of which came from its BMW account.

When Charles Saatchi made his 1982 call to Martin Boase he began by talking of the possibility of a three-way get-together between his company, BMP and a third agency, Lowe & Howard-Spink. Boase was not interested in such a *ménage à trois*, and the talks subsequently took the course just described. Charles had already offered the previous year, the year of the foundation of Lowe & Howard-Spink, to buy a one-third share in the agency for £1 million but had been turned down by Frank Lowe, a man of about the same age with whom he had worked back in the 1960s at Benton & Bowles. Lowe is one of British Adland's most colourful characters whose climb to international success since he set up shop on his own in 1981 has been among the fastest recorded in an industry where fast climbing is not unknown.

An account handler by trade who has always, with his informal attire, given the impression of being a creative, and has indeed always worked closely with the copywriters and art people under his command, Lowe first made his mark as managing director of Collett Dickenson Pearce in the 1970s. He was forced to give up the job because of the unfortunate case brought against the agency by the Inland Revenue and which resulted in fines on him and CDP's late chairman John Pearce. This did nothing to reduce the esteem in which he was held by many clients, with whom he had the knack of forging strong relationships. Among those clients was the marketing director, subsequently managing director, of Whitbread, Anthony Simonds-Gooding, for whom he masterminded while at CDP the creation of a famous campaign for Heineken lager (distributed by Whitbread in the UK).

The humorous Heineken campaign, with its slogan 'Heineken refreshes the parts other beers cannot reach,' was not always accepted as the first-class advertising everyone now judges it to be. At the outset consumer tests produced somewhat negative results, and several leading admen gave it as their opinion that the campaign would not work. Lowe, however, persevered. Agencies, he declared, should not be afraid to give public taste a lead instead of tamely following it – a remark typical of the man and his self-confident manner. By the time £500,000 of advertising money had been put behind the brand, views of the Heineken campaign had changed drastically, and the British public had taken it to its heart.

When Lowe set up on his own with another ex-CDP man, the less flamboyant but more cerebral Geoff Howard-Spink, Heineken was one of the accounts that followed him out of CDP to give the new agency a flying start. Also taken from CDP was creative director Alfredo Marcantonio (a Britisher of Italian extraction). The ads for Heineken have kept up a high standard year by year both on TV and in print, with little masterpieces being produced now and then such as the wordless ad showing Van Gogh holding a glass of the beer and with two ears having grown in the place of the one he cut off.

At the end of 1981 *Campaign* put Lowe & Howard-Spink in 105th place, with reported billings of £5.42 million. A year later it had shot up to 41st place and £18.4 million. In 1983 Lowe pulled off an unprecedented merger deal with an old-established but declining agency called Wasey Campbell-Ewald, owned by Interpublic. Charles Saatchi had not, as it happened, been the only outsider to show interest in Lowe's new shop. Les Delano, president of Interpublic's Campbell-Ewald network, was keen to get hold of it. He succeeded but in an unexpected way. Lowe's price for merging with the Interpublic agency was that he and his partners should have a majority share in it. For the first time the mighty Interpublic agreed to give up control of an agency. It would own only 45% of the merged Lowe Howard-Spink Campbell-Ewald. The new and indigestible combination of names ended 1983 as number sixteen in the *Campaign* billings table, with a figure of £53.4 million.

The following year the agency went public, though at first its shares did not sell well. Later they recovered, and in 1985 the firm made its breakthrough on to the international stage by buying from Interpublic eight Campbell-Ewald agencies plus 30% of the four Marschalk agencies in the US (New York, San Francisco, Houston and Cleveland). The result was a new international network called Lowe Marschalk, 38.3% owned by Interpublic. The London agency was renamed Lowe Howard-Spink Marschalk. With the arrival of Tim Bell as a refugee from the Charlotte Street that had been the scene of his period of glory, a new holding company was formed under the name of Lowe Howard-Spink & Bell (LHSB). In 1986 reported billings in London were £102.2 million, putting Lowe Howard-Spink Marschalk just ahead of Boase Massimi Pollitt in eighth place in the agencies pecking order.

The agency made a strong impact with its corporate advertising campaigns, in particular those for Guinness during its battle to take over the Distillers Company, for the Hanson Trust and for the National Coal Board during the miners' strike, at which time Bell, the committed Tory, acted as personal publicity adviser to the Coal Board chairman Ian McGregor. Another account the agency was proud to pick up, or rather regain, was Parker Pens. Its work for Parker, one of the clients that had followed Lowe from CDP, had been widely admired, but a new boss at Parker headquarters in Wisconsin had decided on a policy of global marketing and given global advertising responsibility to Ogilvy & Mather. The strategy failed, Parker sold its pens business to a group of its international managers, backed by British venture capital, and they happily re-entrusted their European advertising to Lowe and his new subsidiaries on the Continent.

In 1986 two major acquisitions were made by LHSB in the UK. One was the publicly quoted PR company Good Relations, the chairman of which, Tony Good, had wanted to sell to Saatchis but had been outvoted. From having been Britain's biggest PR consultancy it had slipped to fourth or fifth place in a year partly because of management defections, including that of its group managing director Maureen Smith. A period of uncertainty about its corporate destiny was resolved in September, 1986, when it was bought for a mixture of shares and cash by Lowe Howard-Spink & Bell. The agreed offer was valued at £13.9 million. Tony Good remained chairman, but his company was placed under the authority of a new operating division of LHSB called Lowe Bell Communications, set up to run the group's 'below the line' activities. The chairman of the division was to be Tim Bell, with a board consisting of Frank Lowe, Tony Good and Alan Cornish, chief executive of Good Relations. Cornish spoke optimistically of regaining GR's former top-of-the-tree position, but no report of fee income for 1986 was given to *PR Week*. Subsequently the G R subsidiary Good Relations City changed its name to Lowe Bell Financial, indicating a serious intent to spread the new brand name around.

This takeover was quite a *coup* for the Lowe group, but it had been preceded by another acquisition which, though smaller in money terms, made even more of a splash – at least in the small pool of those who follow the fortunes of advertising agencies. It was that of the ad agency Allen Brady & Marsh. ABM had been one of the 'hot shops' of the late 1970s and early 1980s. It was run by an exuberant one-time actor from Hull, Peter Marsh. Certainly Marsh was a showman through and through and a master of the flashy but carefully designed presentation. After a lean period in the early 1970s, when his agency was saddled with a large debt for advertising space and time incurred by its bankrupt carpet-making client Cyril Lord (in law ad agencies are principals responsible for the payment of the advertising bills they run up on behalf of their clients) and paid it all off, he broke into the big time.

A series of big account wins followed, including Woolworths, British Rail, the Midland Bank and Guinness, transferred to ABM from JWT by the new Guinness boss Ernest Saunders without warning and after JWT had had the account for a dozen years. The agency gained a reputation for thoroughly researching the marketing problems of any prospective new client, for producing bright and breezy advertising with the common touch and for wringing every drop of publicity for itself out of its growth. Photographs of Marsh and his partner Rod Allen (Brady had left long before), dressed as railway porters or as milkmen were placed in trade press ads and sent to a sizable direct mailing list of clients, prospective clients and other interested parties. Marsh was interviewed on TV, took part in radio discussion programmes and started boasting grandiosely of his ambition to overtake the Saatchis as head of Britain's biggest advertising business.

In 1982 ABM reached sixth place in the league table, with reported billings of £65 million. Its 1983 billings were nearly £77 million, which put it in fifth place, but by then things were already going wrong. David Croisedale-Appleby, its capable chief executive, had left to join Lintas, and Woolworths had switched its account to McCann-Erickson. Other big clients also began leaving – Guinness to Ogilvy & Mather, British Rail to three other agencies, J. Walter Thompson, Boase Massimi Pollitt and Hedger Mitchell Stark, soon to be absorbed into Saatchi & Saatchi Compton. Peter Marsh's vainglorious style – amusing when his firm was on the up – somehow did little to help a business on the slide. It was an awful warning of how the cult of the personality as pursued not only by Marsh but by other well-known admen could go wrong. This was, of course, a type of publicity the Saatchi brothers had always carefully avoided.

When Lowe took over in May 1986 it emerged that ABM's profit figures had been falling much faster than its turnover – largely because, while clients were leaving, staff and salaries had not been cut as much as necessary. Marsh himself had been taking a salary of £300,000. Billings for 1985 were £50.7 million, and the agency had slipped to twenty-second place in the pecking order. Marsh sold out for a down payment of £5.89 million with further performance-related sums to come. In 1986 reported billings were £56.7 million and the agency ranked number twenty-one. Marsh stayed in charge after the takeover, but the new holding company moved in a couple of recruits from Collett Dickenson Pearce, Paul Smith and Mike Everett, to act as creative directors and put some renewed pep into the agency.

Other constituents of the LHSB group include The Wight Company, run by Ian Wight, which specialises in sports sponsorship and the management of events such as the Stella Artois tennis tournament, Face Ronchetti, a design company and LHSBrompton, which offers advertising and design services.

The misgivings entertained by some when Bell joined Lowe – how could two such strong personalities work successfully together, it was asked – have been dispelled. The pair appear to have worked out a relationship in which they do not tread on each other's toes. Lowe, as always, maintains a close interest in the creative product while Bell brings to the partnership his valuable range of business and political contacts. With Lowe and Howard-Spink he has achieved the position that always eluded him at Saatchi & Saatchi – that of being a triumvir, one of the governing group, and not merely an executive, no matter how important.

In terms of market value of its shares the biggest British-owned advertising-based company is, needless to say, Saatchi & Saatchi. In early July 1987 its market capitalisation figure was more than £1,050 million. Lowe Howard-Spink & Bell, with a figure of more than £110 million, ranked third. Number two, with a figure of almost £124 million was a company called WCRS, standing for Wight Collins Rutherford Scott. Two of its eponymous founders, Ron Collins and Andrew Rutherford, formerly worked for the Saatchis, respectively as an art director and a copywriter. It was Rutherford who dreamed up the famous Saatchi poster for the Conservative Party in 1978 showing a dole queue and captioned 'Labour isn't working'. In the minds of City investors WCRS is a mini-Saatchi, which has followed in the brothers' footsteps by acquiring other ad agencies and marketing service companies and expanding into America. The differences, however, and not only in the matter of scale, are almost as interesting as the similarities.

The original driving force behind WCRS, founded in 1979 was Robin Wight, a lanky, bow-tied, fast-talking copywriter who had worked for CDP before becoming creative director of a small agency called Euro Advertising. He had made a considerable name for himself less as that than as a forceful platform speaker and as the author of a book called *The Day the Pigs Refused to be Driven to Market* in which he espoused a number of consumerist criticisms of advertising. He characterised his own industry, as 'the irritator, the deliverer of half-truths, the uninformer, and disrespecter of persons, the social blackmailer.' He attacked the hyperbolic style of much advertising, condemning even the kind of puff that nobody was likely to take seriously.

Not that Wight was an enemy of the ad business. On the contrary, he had been convinced, even as a student, that there was no other he would rather be in. Politically, too, he was a Conservative. His aim, he declared, was to promote a new community of interest between business and the consumer by getting ads to talk straight. He was an admirer of the Bill Bernbach school of advertising which preferred understatement or even humorous self-deprecation to exaggeration. Wight's book was attacked on one side by an adman reviewer who dismissed as naive his assessment of advertising puffery. Research quoted by the reviewer indicated that people expected ads to exaggerate and that they treated them with practised scepticism. On the other side, a leading consumerist accused Wight of trying to have his cake and eat it, in other words of presenting himself as an advocate of truth and honesty while doing his damnedest to talk people into buying his own clients' goods.

Like Charles Saatchi, Robin Wight had a well developed sense of publicity, and even before his new agency was launched he had managed to get it hyped in the trade press as the Superstars agency, on the basis that it would be staffed by outstanding creative people, as yet unnamed. Like Charles Saatchi's agency when it started, WCRS promised to tear down the barriers between the creatives who produced the ads and the clients who paid for them and to do without layers of administrative personnel. Nobody at that stage expected that the firm starting off as a small bunch of dedicated ad-makers would within very few years turn into a financial machine dedicated to making money out of design, PR and anything else that might come to hand.

Beginning with a staff of eleven people, the agency reported first year billings of just over £6 million. By the end of 1982 the figure had grown to more than £23 million, and WCRS had climbed to twenty-sixth place in the pecking order of agencies. The following year it took a tentative first step into the world of financial wheeling and dealing by getting its shares quoted on the Unlisted Securities Market. Billings rose to £32.5 million. In 1984 the company went fully public, while account gains took its billings figure to nearly £44 million and its position in the league table to twenty-third. The first fruit of its increased financial strength was the acquisition of the sizable public relations firm Biss Lancaster in 1985, but it was the following year that WCRS really hit the takeover trail, buying FCO, a £17 million London agency, two design firms, Saunders and Siebert/Head, and the sponsorship and marketing consultancy Alan Pascoe & Associates. It also moved into America with the purchase in quick succession of two US ad agencies, HBM/Creamer and Della Femina, Travisano & Partners.

Meanwhile the original Wight Collins agency itself had been doing well, winning golden opinions with creative campaigns such as those for Qualcast mowing machines ('It's more bovver with a hover'), BMW cars and Carling Black Label beer (a very funny series of TV commercials with the catchline 'I bet he drinks Carling Black Label' included such gems as the skull kicked by Hamlet into a theatregoer's lap where it spoke those very words).

These American acquisitions, though smaller than Saatchi's, created quite a stir in the US advertising community, not least because the Saatchi takeover of Bates just beforehand had created great sensitivity there as far as any more British incursions were concerned. HBM/Creamer, headquartered in Boston, was an ad agency chain, itself constructed through acquisitions, with offices in New York, Chicago and Pittsburg as well as Hartford, Connecticut, and Providence, Rhode Island, and billings of $200 million in 1985 – rather more than those of the Wight Collins agency in London which in the same year had reached £63 million. The privately owned American company also had a strong PR subsidiary, Creamer Dickson Basford. The WCRS Group paid around $50 million for this package, $42 million of it up front.

For Della Femina Travisano the price was $20 million plus further payments over a five-year earn-out period. The New York office of HBM/Creamer was to be merged with the agency under the chairmanship of Jerry Della Femina, one of the best known characters in American Adland and author of the book *From Those Wonderful Folks Who Gave You Pearl Harbor*, containing some wonderfully funny anecdotes about skulduggery in ad agencies. The curious title was the headline he suggested, when employed years ago at Ted Bates New York, for a campaign for Panasonic. The suggestion was made in jest but it threw some stuffy Bates colleagues into a tizzy. Della Femina's own agency billed $137 million in 1985.

WCRS continued its international expansion by buying at the beginning of 1987 the Ball Partnership, previously an Ogilvy & Mather subsidiary run by Michael Ball and operating in Australia and South-East Asia. Later it raised money through a rights issue to buy another Australian ad agency, Garland Stewart & Roache, an Australian design company, Lunn Dyer, and a US medical advertising agency, Becker. In between it also bought into a London-based management consultancy, Goodall Alexander O'Hare, and a British film production company, Crossbow Films.

By now the greater part of the group's turnover was coming from overseas, and despite the excellence of much of its London advertising it now looked, like Saatchi & Saatchi, very much a finance-oriented business rather than the bunch of creative superstars it had originally presented itself as being. The most important roles were being played by Peter Scott, now group chief executive, and Tim Breene, the former McKinsey management consultant brought in to be deputy chief executive with specific responsibility for supervising the group's US operations. The group has made clear it has no intention, unlike the Saatchis, of sticking a single brand name on its various properties. In June 1987 the original agency changed its name to WCRS Matthews Marcantonio following the arrival of Roger Matthews from CDP as managing director and Alfredo Marcantonio from Lowe as deputy chairman and creative director.

WCRS achieved group profits for the year to April 1987 of more than £10 million, compared with £2.6 million the previous year. The whole has become much more important than the part from which it grew. One would hesitate to say the same of the Saatchi group despite its very much greater size.

Boase Massimi Pollitt, Lowe Howard-Spink & Bell and WCRS are the most financially successful advertising-based companies that have followed the Saatchis to the stock market, but they are not the only ones. Among the others, mention may be made of two, Abbott Mead Vickers and Gold Greenlees Trott.

Both of these are comparatively young agencies, both capitalised on distinguished creative records to go public, both are headed by members of the same generation of admen who were beginning to make a name for themselves at the end of the 1960s, along with Charles Saatchi and Martin Boase. Indeed David Abbott of AMV and Michael Gold of GGT were once partners in another agency called French Gold Abbott. The third partner was Richard French, boss of FCO, now part of the WCRS group. French Gold Abbott sold out in the 1970s to an American agency, Kenyon & Eckhardt, before the founding partners went their separate ways. That was the normal pattern of events in those days. Successful British agencies were courted by American ones looking to expand internationally. We have come a long way since then, but it is worth remembering that only a few years ago the idea that London rather than New York could provide the headquarters for international advertising networks was taken seriously by hardly anyone. The Saatchis changed all that.

David Abbott has often been called the best copywriter in London. He is certainly a very good one. A newspaper ad he wrote long ago as part of a recruitment drive by the white collar trade union ASTMS and headed: 'The board and I have decided we don't like the colour of your eyes' is still remembered as one of the most impressive British examples of the copywriter's art. The ad went on to say 'It's not usually as brutal as that. Usually, there's a polite phrase about a clash of personalities. But the end result is the same. A man gets the push because his face doesn't fit. It could only happen at one level in British industry – the top.' And so on for several hundred compelling words. They appeared in 1970, when Abbott was working for Doyle Dane Bernbach's London office, of which he was creative director, then managing director before leaving to team up with French and Gold, who had won their stripes as respectively an account director and a media buyer with the old KMP.

The ASTMS ad was representative of what was in 1970 a new school of copywriting, which owed much to the example of Bill Bernbach and his talented disciples at Doyle Dane Bernbach in New York and which was characterised by directness and candour, or at least apparent candour. Compare it with another ad, also produced in 1970, for the Health Education Council, describing 'what happens when a fly lands on your food. Flies can't eat solid food, so to soften it up they vomit on it. Then they stamp the vomit in until it's a liquid, usually stamping in a few germs for good measure. Then when it's good and runny they suck it all back again, probably dropping some excrement at the same time. And then, when they've finished eating, it's your turn.' That ad was produced by what was then a smallish agency called Saatchi & Saatchi. The copywriter was Charles Saatchi.

Abbott Mead Vickers attracted business through the creative excellence of campaigns it did for such clients as the Sainsbury supermarket chain, won from Saatchi & Saatchi Compton by David Abbott's copywriting skill despite Charles Saatchi's personal efforts to provide a more satisfactory alternative. It has also turned out clever advertising for Volvo and the Leeds Building Society, for which its TV commercials starring actor George Cole as a slightly shady character who keeps his money in the Leeds are beautifully executed. They manage, in a few seconds, to be funnier than the full-blown television series 'Minder', to which they bear more than a passing resemblance. Another campaign which caused a stir was for British Caledonian with a TV film spoofing the Saatchi Compton commercials for British Airways. The latter feature air stewards and stewardesses who fly through the air like Superman. The BCal film showed a pair of such characters dropping a passenger from high up.

The agency went public at the end of 1985 with a share issue greatly oversubscribed. Its reported billings that year were £62.5 million, giving it nineteenth place in the *Campaign* table. In 1986 the figure was hardly changed because, presumably, though AMV had put on quite a lot of business, it was now, as a public company, adopting a more stringent method of reporting growth. (It cannot be too frequently emphasised that the *Campaign* figures, supplied by the agencies themselves, give only an approximate notion of where they stand as regards turnover.) In the same year AMV bought Leagas Delaney, another of the new wave of independent British ad agencies and one which, like its contemporaries such as WCRS and Lowe Howard-Spink, seemed at first headed for success. But it ran into trouble and had to sell out. Ron Leagas, who had been managing director of Saatchi & Saatchi Garland-Compton under Tim Bell's chairmanship before leaving to start up on his own, was replaced at the head of Leagas Delaney with Bruce Haines, an Abbott Mead director.

David Abbott, still strikingly handsome in his late forties, though with a mop of grey hair, is known for his strong views on religion (he is a practising Roman Catholic), politics (a member of the Social Democratic Party, he was put in charge of Alliance publicity for the 1987 election, though that was not his most glorious hour) and advertising ethics (he has always refused to take a tobacco advertising account, and all Adland knows that his father died of lung cancer). He is a good speaker in an unflamboyant manner and remains his company's most visible asset. In 1986 Michael Baulk was tempted away from Ogilvy & Mather to run the agency, freeing Abbott's partner Peter Mead to devote more time to corporate expansion, but so far AMV has not ventured very far down that trail.

Neither has Gold Greenlees Trott, the success of which has been also built largely on the work of its creative department, headed by Dave Trott, formerly of Boase Massimi Pollitt. It has produced admired campaigns for, among others, Toshiba, London's Docklands development project and Holsten lager – the latter intercutting clips from old movies with a spiel from comedian Griff Rhys-Jones in a very skilful manner. In 1985 a panel in New York picked GGT as the most creative agency in the world. With a reputation like that it managed to grow in seven years from nothing to 1986 billings of more than £50 million and twenty-second place in the agencies pecking order. It went public in that year, fifty-nine times oversubscribed, and was expected to use the money in the by now standard fashion to acquire other firms and establish itself in the US. Those developments have not yet occurred.

Not all the ad agencies that have gone to the stock market in the past few years have been as well received as those just mentioned. None won such an enthusiastic vote of confidence from the City, however, as a non-advertising firm that started stirring up the marketing services sector in 1986. The firm is WPP (originally Wire & Plastics Products), and the chief reason for the interest it aroused was the arrival at its helm of Martin Sorrell, the financial whizz kid, who had done so much to help steer Saatchi & Saatchi through its first decade of corporate development.

Sorrell, now in his early forties, studied economics at Cambridge, then went to Harvard Business School before working for Mark McCormack, the sports sponsorship promoter, and James Gulliver, the food retailer, before moving to Saatchi as finance director. Looking for an investment opportunity of his own, he teamed up in 1985 with stockbroker Preston Rabl to buy into Wire & Plastics Products, a small, publicly quoted company that manufactured supermarket trolleys. Between them Rabl and Sorrell, still employed by the Saatchis, bought 27% of the equity for £500,000. Their plan was to use WPP as the vehicle for moving into sales promotion, design and other marketing service fields, identified by Sorrell, on the basis of his Saatchi experience, as a growth sector.

And that is what they did, buoyed up by a share price that in less than two years rose by over 2000%! City appetites for the stock were stimulated not only by Sorrell's own high reputation for financial astuteness but by the news that Saatchi & Saatchi was putting more than £1 million into WPP. If the brothers could not keep him aboard their own ship, then at least they would get a cut of the profits they expected him to produce as captain of another. In building up the WPP group Sorrell, at first together with Rabl, then without him after the latter withdrew to attend to other interests, used the same techniques that he had perfected during his time with the Saatchis, picking sound companies and buying them on an earn-out formula designed to keep their managers keen.

A string of companies was acquired, including design houses (VAP, Oakley Young & Associates, Sampson Tyrrell, Business Design Group), and firms specialising in sales promotion, incentive travel arrangements and audio-visual facilities. The group did not take long to enter the US, buying more design companies (Sidjakov Berman Gomez & Partners of San Francisco, and Walker Group/CNI of New York and Los Angeles), as well as others, including Harvard Capital Group, a financial communications outfit. By the spring of 1987 some fifteen subsidiaries had been acquired, and the group was still going strong with annual profits in the region of £7 million. Sorrell at first showed no sign, however, of wanting to get involved in the more visible and glamorous world of advertising that he left behind when he gave up working for Saatchi & Saatchi.

That appearance underwent a dramatic change in June 1987, when Sorrell launched a bid for JWT Group, that is the J. Walter Thompson advertising agency network and its subsidiaries, including the public relations giant Hill & Knowlton and the MRB Group market research outfit. There had been speculation for months and even years about the possibility of a takeover attempt on JWT in view of its overall lacklustre financial performance, and the Saatchis were said to have maintained a close watch on developments, even though any attempt by them to swallow up another leading international ad agency would have appeared rash and greedy even by their standards. The bid, when it did materialise, came from a totally unexpected quarter. It also flew in the face of the received Adland wisdom that any takeover of an ad agency had to be agreed if it were not to risk killing the goose that laid the golden eggs.

Sorrell's bid for JWT was very much not agreed with the target company's management under Don Johnston, who vowed to repel it. But the bid was well supported both financially – with Citibank and Samuel Montagu promising loan facilities – and managerially, since Sorrell had recruited to his cause Jack Peters, former president of J. Walter Thompson, who had been fired for taking part in Joe O'Donnell's unsuccessful putsch against Johnston. Also in Sorrell's favour was his reputation on Wall Street as well as in the City of London as a brilliant financial controller who could increase profits while leaving the admen to make the ads. Against him were American suspicions of Saatchi-type Limey invaders and the conservative streak in American advertising clients whom the recent mega-mergers of agencies had upset so much. Finally, after the bid had been increased to $566 million in cash, valuing JWT shares at $55.50 each, twice what they had cost only months before, Johnston and his board threw in the towel and gave up their attempts to finance a management buy-out or alternatively find another buyer. For his part Sorrell agreed to leave the existing management in place, at least for the time being. And so one of the oldest American ad agency firms, founded in 1864, fell into the hands of one of the newest British advertising colonisers. Almost the first thing that happened was that Ford, in a move reminiscent of the backlash caused by Saatchi's takeover of Bates, switched $100 million of advertising out of JWT, leaving it with about $250 million worldwide. Sorrell went for a rights issue of £213 million to help finance his deal. Saatchi & Saatchi sold its 7% share in WPP.

In the UK other non-advertising marketing service firms have in the past few years launched themselves on the Stock Exchange, some with fair success if not with quite such panache as Sorrell. They include PR consultancies such as Valin Pollen, market research companies such as MIL, and Addison Consultancy, a group which, starting from a design and PR base, has bought into advertising as well as market research. Ten years ago, before Saatchi & Saatchi began its rise to the top, it is unlikely that any of these would have thought of going public and still less likely that the City of London would have taken them seriously as worthwhile investment opportunities.

If all this activity on the part of the new wave of publicly quoted ad agencies and other 'communications' companies (to use a word beloved of the sector) is interesting in itself and indicative of the extent to which the Saatchi example has inspired imitators, none of the concerns just described constitutes a real rival to the Saatchi group except ironically for Sorrell's WPP. The principal competition it faces is still from the heavyweight class of worldwide advertising networks, American-owned except for JWT. The most notable others are Interpublic, Omnicom, Ogilvy and, probably most formidable of the lot, Young & Rubicam, which significantly is the only one that is not publicly owned. All Y & R's shareholders are its employees. If and when they leave its employ, they have to sell back their shares. This makes it considerably less vulnerable to short-term pressures than the others.

Worldwide Y & R had a good year in 1986, benefiting more than any other advertising group from the fall-out from the mega-mergers that so upset American client companies. It picked up Colgate and Warner-Lambert business from Bates. In Germany it took the massive Ford account from JWT and came out with a beautifully executed series of diverse press ads for it ranging from a Douanier Rousseau-style setting for a courting couple in one car to a childlike illustration of the space available for all the family in another. In the UK, where Y & R, though always one of the top ten agencies, had sometimes seemed to be a bit of an also-ran, it had an unprecedentedly good year, winning £75 million worth of new business and rising from seventh place to fourth with reported billings of £142 million.

The wins included Kodak, Access credit cards and, above all, British Gas, for which it handled the £27 million campaign to persuade the public to buy shares in the newly privatised corporation. Its campaign theme, 'Tell Sid' (Sid being the ordinary chap, never seen, who was supposed to be interested in becoming a shareholder if only he could learn of the opportunity) was ridiculed by many but, partly because of the ridicule, got through to almost everyone – which is, after all, one of the main aims of advertising. Under a new and energetic chairman, John Banks, the agency even got on close terms with the Conservative Party through the 4Cs (Cross-Cultural Consumer Characterisation) method of researching consumer attitudes. There was probably never any chance that the Tories were going to switch their advertising account to the American-owned agency before the 1987 General Election, but widespread press speculation that they might do so did Y & R no harm at all. Relations were maintained with the Tories up to and during the election, but it is difficult to know how much reliance to place on reports of the influence exerted on party election strategy by Y & R's research-based assessments of the voters' changing mood.

In New York Y & R currently possesses the same kind of self-confidence – the kind that comes from clear market leadership – as does Saatchi & Saatchi Compton in London. The same is not true of JWT, with its recent boardroom shake-ups and takeover drama. However, JWT's London office in Berkeley Square is a very different kettle of fish, famous in British Adland for its stability, its gentlemanliness and its intellectual distinction – qualities that do not readily come to mind when thinking of JWT's New York headquarters. For JWT London 1986 was also a good new business year, with £44 million of accounts won, including the British Airports Authority flotation. Much of the agency's best work is done for accounts of many years' standing, such as Persil, Oxo, Kelloggs cereals. It consistently gains many of the Advertising Effectiveness awards given biennially by the Institute of Practitioners in Advertising. The reason is not only (or even not so much) the demonstrable effectiveness of its ads but the elegance with which JWT people expound in prose and mathematical calculations the case for believing them effective.

The intellectual element in JWT London owes much to two men, both now in their mid-fifties. One is its chairman and former creative director, Jeremy Bullmore, probably the wittiest speaker in British Adland; the other his fellow old Harrovian Stephen King, its head of account planning (a function now almost universal among the larger London ad agencies but invented in slightly different forms by King and by the late Stanley Pollitt of BMP). Both Bullmore, due to retire at the end of 1987, and King have hammered away at certain shared ideas about their trade, such as that it is not what admen think they have put into an ad that counts but what consumers get out of it. As Bullmore says, a joke that nobody laughs at is not a joke.

JWT, still a challenger for the top spot among British agencies, is fiercely suspicious of Saatchi & Saatchi Compton's turnover claims. The rivalry between the two offices, expressed in recent knocking ads in the trade press, is likely to go on enlivening the British advertising scene for a good while to come.

The other American-owned international agency near the top of both the UK and world advertising trees is Ogilvy & Mather, about which it is worth recalling that its founder, still alive and well and living mostly in France, is not an American but a Brit or, as he would say, an Anglo-Scot. David Ogilvy is probably the most famous advertising man still in circulation (the richest is probably Bob Jacoby, who made his money out of selling Bates to Saatchi), and his career is proof that the cult of the personality can be as good a way of striking it rich as the non-personal corporate publicity favoured by Charles Saatchi. In his early days in New York, where he founded his agency in 1949 with the backing of his late brother Francis, at that time head of the old-established London ad agency Mather & Crowther, David drew attention to himself by a combination of copywriting brilliance and sheer exhibitionism. He became Madison Avenue's favourite Limey gent.

Francis Ogilvy had predicted that the British would one day invade the American advertising market, and his younger brother made the prediction come true but only in a personal sense. The agency he built up, and which took over Mather & Crowther after Francis's premature death, was an American agency which just happened to have a British boss. It was not until nearly forty years after David Ogilvy set up shop that the real Limey invasion began.

12

The Collector

Charles Saatchi has become in a short time the master not only of the world's biggest advertising company but of a major collection of modern art. This book is concerned essentially with the business record of that company, but a few words about the private and semi-private lives of the brothers who started, and still control, it may help to throw some light on what kind of men they are and on the corporate culture they have created.

Perhaps the most striking fact about both Charles and Maurice is that, despite the thousands of times their names have been mentioned in print, so little is generally known about them as individuals. They are often described as reclusive, but that is really an inaccurate perception. They lead perfectly normal social lives. Even Charles, far less outgoing than his brother, has friends with whom he plays tennis and one of whom declares that what impresses him about the man is how little he has changed in twenty years. The success, the power and the money may well have had some effect, but it doesn't show in his demeanour. He is unassuming, as he always was. He is wary of people, but he always was.

That wariness has been translated into a publicity policy that keeps nosy reporters away from the brothers and the brothers off public platforms. This is noticeable because it is unusual in Adland, which is a land of hustlers and boasters, of people to whom publicity commonly means personal publicity because they accept that advertising is a a branch of show business. Most of the famous people in advertising have been highly visible people. David Ogilvy is the most outstanding example, a man who built an international company largely by drawing attention to himself. His book of many years ago, *Confessions of an Advertising Man*, still compulsory reading for anyone interested in the ad agency business, mixes precepts for how to make good ads with reminiscences of his own experiences as a hotel cook and a farmer, not just as a go-getting adman.

One cannot imagine Charles Saatchi writing anything in the slightest degree autobiographical. He makes it a rule – broken only once or twice in the past – never to give interviews, though he has been asked countless times to do so. That does not, incidentally, prevent him from talking at length on the telephone but off the record to journalists who he thinks can be useful. He talks, when he talks, about the business; he is unwilling to share with strangers the details of his private life – whether they concern his Iraqi Jewish background; his schooldays at Christ's College, Finchley; his textile trader father, a pillar of a London Sephardi synagogue; Charles's elder brother David, a commodities broker in New York; his youngest brother Phil, a pop musician; or his American wife, the attractive Doris, to whom Charles has been married since the early 1970s.

Charles and the then Doris Dibley met in the 1960s when both were copywriters at the London office of Benton & Bowles (an American-owned agency merged in the 1980s with D'Arcy MacManus & Masius). The couple are alike in some ways, unlike in others. He is dark, she is very blonde. He is Jewish, she is not. He was a bachelor till he married her, she was previously married to a racing driver. He has made a career – and what a career! – out of advertising, while she, after stints at Ogilvy & Mather and B & B, has abandoned the trade and does some writing for magazines in Britain and the US. But she is said to be as reticent socially as Charles and, like him, she is an art-lover. Or perhaps it would be truer to say that she has induced him to take an active interest in the subject, which formed part of her American university degree course (she read French and art history at Smith College). They have no children.

Between them Charles and Doris Saatchi have invested heavily – at the rate, according to one estimate, of £2 million a year – in buying the work of avant-garde painters such as Julian Schnabel and Andy Warhol, much of it housed in a private museum in St. John's Wood. It would be interesting to know precisely how their tastes have affected the contemporary art market.

More germane, however, to this book is the perception of more than one observer that, setting aside the quality of his artistic judgement and his standing as a modern Maecenas, Charles can best be understood, in his business career, as a collector. He has for the greater part of two decades been busily collecting both companies and people. On this view the expansion of the Saatchi group is to be considered as something else than the expression of a straightforward, if overweening, ambition to build the biggest company of its kind, although it is, of course, that as well. Other advertising-agency-based businesses have nourishd the same ambition and have indeed achieved it – Interpublic for a long period of pre-eminence, Omnicom very briefly. But neither had at its head a man with a voracious appetite to hang as many scalps as possible from his belt.

The metaphor is perhaps too violent. Most of the individuals whose 'scalps' have been collected as Saatchi trophies have done very well out of it, at least in the UK. (In the US some hundreds of people who lost their jobs in Esty and other agencies because of the account losses incurred after joining the group might greet that statement with a Bronx cheer.) One thinks of people such as Geoff Seymour and Jeff Stark, the recruitment of both of whom to the creative department of Saatchi & Saatchi Compton, the one for a fat salary, the other at the price of buying his agency, resulted in the intended headlines in the trade press.

There were good advertising business reasons, as well as scalp-collecting reasons, for getting hold of those two. But the hiring of John Treasure, the former chairman of J. Walter Thompson, as vice-chairman of the Charlotte Street agency, was surely inspired more by the collector syndrome than by any business necessity. This is not to deny that Dr Treasure (to give him the title he acquired for his post-graduate thesis in economics) is a wise old bird with an enviable range of high-level contacts. However, it is difficult to suppose that there was any particular job that needed to be done by the eminent oldster rather than by some up-and-coming young executive. On the other hand, the trophy value of having on the wall at Charlotte Street, to vary the metaphor slightly, the head of the man who had been known in his day as Britain's Mr Advertising was considerable.

The same motive was behind the approach made to yet another leading figure in British Adland, a man equally as eminent as Treasure and a member of roughly the same age group. What would Saatchi &

Saatchi require him to do? That, he was given to understand, was a question of no importance. The main thing was that Charles wanted to collect him. The man, whose identity is confidential, declined. No matter, there were other scalps to be hunted. Another unsuccessful approach, and this one did become public, was made to David Puttnam, the film producer, who had once worked at Collett Dickenson Pearce and was a chum of Charles's. The proposal reportedly put to Puttnam at the end of 1984 was, however, more precise. It appeared that he had been invited to be chairman of the Charlotte Street agency.

Puttnam also declined, saying publicly that 'the idea of being involved in advertising again is attractive, but I have incredible emotional ties to the film industry'. His decision to stick with the industry was rewarded in less than two years when he became chief executive of Columbia Pictures. There were those, it must be said, who regarded the invitation to Puttnam as not just a scalp-hunting publicity stunt but as a highly imaginative and intelligent move which implied recognition of the similarity between the jobs done by a good film producer and an effective ad agency chairman, who is ideally a kind of impresario. (That role had certainly been played by Tim Bell during his chairmanship of Charlotte Street, though not by his successor, Jeremy Sinclair.) There were, indeed, grounds for believing that Puttnam, the ex-adman producer of *Chariots of Fire*, might make an excellent agency chairman.

At a lower executive level Charles did succeed in collecting for his gallery of employees Margaret Patrick, the bright New Zealand-born journalist who, after working on *Campaign* in its early years, became the long-time advertising columnist of the London *Evening Standard*. She was one of the reporters with whom he kept in personal touch and whom he eventually hired to take charge of public relations for Saatchi & Saatchi Compton, London. He could have got a professional PR executive to do the job but, quite apart from the consideration that poachers often make the best gamekeepers, he probably took a collector's satisfaction in putting yet another well-known Adland name on his payroll.

Another source of satisfaction for Charles in the Patrick appointment may have derived from his rather peculiar attitude to the press. Businessmen generally tend to be fearful of the press, sometimes with good reason, for reporters who get things wrong can do a fair amount of damage, and anyone who has had experience of a damagingly wrong report is likely to be very chary of giving another interview to any journalist. (Mind you, the damage done by inaccurate reporting, which can after all be corrected, is often exceeded by that done by accurate reporting when the facts reported are not those the company wishes to be known.) Many firms, therefore, leave press relations to PR people in either a PR agency or an in-house PR department. Others, including notoriously Procter & Gamble, prefer to have no dealings with the press at all.

The latter attitude is unusual in advertising, even though many ad agencies are less publicity-conscious than, given the nature of their trade, one might expect. It was, however, the attitude of Charles Saatchi's mentor, the one-time creative director of Collett Dickenson Pearce, Colin Millward. He once said that the press could do him no good, for his agency's work spoke for itself, but could do him harm by misreporting what was happening there. Charles certainly did not share this view, as he proved by the assiduity with which in the early days of his company he worked to get press publicity.

But neither is he one of that minority of businessmen, a minority well represented in Adland, who lap up all publicity and welcome journalists with open arms. And this is not just a matter of his personal shyness and unwillingness to make an exhibition of himself in the manner of a David Ogilvy or a Peter Marsh. For Charles publicity is a powerful and dangerous tool, which has to be used but must be handled with great care. It would be trite to say that he likes good publicity and dislikes criticism. That is true of everyone and of all companies. What is remarkable about him is how thin-skinned he is about publicity despite the many years he has spent working personally to get it. One might have expected that, as his company grew and prospered and his own wealth and influence reached the point of near-invulnerability, he would become more relaxed *vis-à-vis* journalists and their doings. It did not happen that way. He stated emphatically to the author of this book, for example, that he did not want any book to be written by anyone about the Saatchi story.

One suspects that Charles will really feel comfortable only when all the journalists he knows are working for him, as Margaret Patrick now is. It is part and parcel of a personality which, to one who has known him for many years, though not intimately, appears unnecessarily defensive. Unnecessarily defensive, for example, about his Jewish identity and unwilling for it to be known.

Maurice Saatchi, taller, fairer, more gregarious, is also married, as it happens, to a non-Jewish wife, having been divorced from his first, Jewish one, the illustrator Gillian Osband. The present Mrs Maurice Saatchi, who prefers to use her maiden name of Josephine Hart, is an ambitious and sharp-witted Irishwoman, who made quite a career for herself at Haymarket Publishing, where she rose through ability and force of character from being deputy manager of classified advertising for the magazine *Campaign* when it started in 1968, to a seat on the board. It was at Haymarket that she met Maurice, who it may be recalled worked there as business development manager between leaving university and teaming up with Charles in 1970.

They did not marry until several years later, by when Josephine had been married to, and divorced from, another Haymarket director, Paul Buckley, who had started as Michael Heseltine's personal assistant when he was still running the firm. Today Buckley runs Graduate Appointments, an employment agency in which Josephine is a partner and in which she still works part-time. She also, as a former would-be actress, takes a strong interest in the theatre and has drawn her (present) husband into acting as a theatrical angel. Josephine herself has moved from organising poetry readings, with well-known actors doing the reading, to producing plays and founding her own theatrical production company, Josephine Hart Productions. She has two small sons, one by each husband.

The balance of power between the brothers is a matter of speculation, though not the kind of speculation they care to encourage. There is no doubt that, when they started, Charles was the undisputed boss. Apart from the couple of years between them, the elder brother was the one with the reputation and the advertising experience on which the new agency was based. Stories are told of how he would in those early days sometimes lose his temper with Maurice and pull rank on him. Over the years Maurice has grown into a very urbane, very self-possessed, very confident character. Charles remains his introverted self. At the outset Charles was chairman of their small company. Now Maurice is chairman of their big company and is its front man as far as the financial community and a few favoured clients are concernd.

Has the balance changed? Those who have worked with them and can be persuaded to speak of the subject believe not. Charles is still the boss, but to the outside world the brothers present a united front. They declare their shareholding in the company jointly. They work closely together, even if they and their wives see little of each other after office hours. Charles is fiercely protective of his younger brother's reputation, rebutting any suggestion that the departed Martin Sorrell was the financial brain behind the group's success. However clever Sorrell may be, that distinction belongs, claims Charles, to Maurice.

The brothers are also partners in a private investment project (nothing to do with Saatchi & Saatchi) which has turned out well for them. In 1986 they put money into a shell company called NMC, which has rapidly moved, under the management of Norman Gordon, into the packaging field, buying up four specialist firms: Bux (corrugated case packaging), Interpoly (security packaging for banks), Barker and A.J. Bingley (both specialising in flexible packaging). In the year to March 1987 NMC made a profit of £4.2 million. The shares, worth only pennies before the brothers bought a 30% stake, are now traded at around £2.38 each.

Exactly how much each brother contributes to the strategic decisions that govern the lives of their thousands of employees it is impossible for any outsider, and very difficult even for any insider, to know. For years they have been in the habit of using male personal assistants rather than female ones. (From the point of view of security of information, they consider women to be less reliable in that they may form attachments to other male executives and tell them more than they should.) And, of course, others beside the brothers are involved in taking those decisions, notably Anthony Simonds-Gooding and Victor Millar. But if the company takes its character from any person it is less the smooth-spoken Maurice than Charles Saatchi, the brooding collector.

13

Money Matters

The financial record of the Saatchi & Saatchi Company is extremely impressive. Though global marketing and advertising creativity may be the favourite themes of the group's self-promotion, it is as a money machine that it has really distinguished itself. City of London analysts may have been too inclined, up to the time of the Bates purchase in 1986 and the difficulties consequent upon it, to swallow the Saatchi version of events and believe in the strength of advertising agency subsidiaries in countries they had never visited, but about the profit figures and the efficiency of the group's system of financial controls they were not deceived.

The holding company has a strong finance department, staffed by managers whose responsibilities include monitoring the performance of each of the operating units. These are obliged to report fortnightly and in minute detail on every financial aspect of their work. This information is then checked against the financial plans laid down by headquarters for each unit. Any problems are quickly identified. The system has been praised by a number of experts, including Emma Hill, of New York's Wertheim & Company, one of the best known American financial analysts of the advertising sector. It was, she opined in 1986 (after the Bates deal, incidentally) a 'superior' system that provided the key to the group's record of successful acquisitions and ever increasing revenue.

Martin Sorrell must be given much of the credit for this financial management structure. But the impressiveness of the financial record stretches back, well before his arrival, to the very earliest days of the small ad agency that Saatchi & Saatchi began by being. In 1971 at the end of that agency's first year of trading it declared a pre-tax profit of £25,000 on billings (i.e. the total of clients' advertising expenditure handled by it) of £1 million and paid out dividends amounting to £1,000, equal to 100% of its equity at that time. Billings doubled the following year, but the profit more than trebled. In the financial year 1973–4 billings reached £4.8 million and pre-tax profit £187,000, a ratio of 3.9%, getting on for double the industry average. By that time the company had repaid its start-up debenture loan and £9,000 of preference capital.

The following year, its last as an independent, privately owned agency, Saatchi & Saatchi made a pre-tax profit of £348,000 on turnover of just over £11 million. This, remember, was a period of economic recession, with the advertising industry as a whole in the doldrums. Results for the 1975–6 year reflected the merger of the Saatchi & Saatchi agency with the publicly quoted Compton UK Partners, with the combined turnover up to more than £35 million. Profit was very healthy at £976,000, though the ratio to turnover was, at 2.8%, somewhat less than that of the old, smaller Saatchi agency.

In 1977 the new Saatchi & Saatchi holding company was created, but for the rest of the decade and indeed up until the acquisition of Dorland Advertising in 1981 the emphasis was all on the organic growth of the main operating unit, Saatchi & Saatchi Garland-Compton, the Charlotte Street ad agency commonly known as Saatchis. Turnover increased by leaps and bounds each year. So, too, did profits. Profit margins improved as well, getting back during the financial years ending in 1979, 1980 and 1981 almost to the record levels the Saatchi & Saatchi agency had touched in the early 1970s.

How useful it is to express agency profitability as a proportion of 'sales' has always been a matter of dispute, given that the term sales, like billings and turnover, applies to money that passes between advertisers and media, using the agency as a conduit. Some people, especially in America, have long insisted that what matters is not billings but income, that is the money that actually sticks to the agency's hands, whether it is paid in the form of fees or of commission. The American magazine *Advertising Age* regularly records agency incomes as well as billings figures. In the UK, *Campaign* has yet to follow suit.

Most agencies prefer to report billings figures. For one thing they are much larger and, therefore, make agencies seem more important than they really are. For another thing, it is easier to play tricks with them. For example, if an agency is paid a fee of, say, £75,000 for a piece of new product development work, it will commonly multiply that figure by 6.7 and add the resultant half a million pounds to its overall billings figure. Why 6.7? Easy. Because that (or to be precise 6.6 recurring) is the number of times 15 divides into 100, and 15% is still the benchmark rate of commission paid by clients to agencies, even if many pay less. In other words, agencies like to treat any income as if it were a commission on media expenditure and 'gross it up' to achieve a more impressive billings figure.

The Saatchi group, too, is fond of quoting billings figures to press home its advantage as the world's largest aggregate handler of advertising expenditure. But, especially since it diversified into other fields than advertising, income has become a more useful measure of the group's performance than billing. The ratio of profit to income, more than 23% in 1980, drifted down as the group pursued its breakneck expansion in the following years but recovered to a healthy 15.8% in the year ending 30 September 1986. The following table shows some of the most important annual indicators of the group's financial progress over the years since Saatchi & Saatchi became a holding company in 1977.

Turnover, Income & Pre-Tax Profit of Saatchi & Saatchi, 1978–86

Year	Turnover	Income	Profit	Profit/ Turnover	Profit/ Income
1978	£59.1m	£8.9m	£1.874m	3.17%	21.05%
1979	£71.5m	£10.7m	£2.445m	3.42%	22.85%
1980	£84.7m	£12.7m	£3.005m	3.55%	23.66%
1981	£102.1m	£17.1m	£3.624m	3.55%	21.19%
1982	£258.3m	£39.6m	£5.521m	2.14%	13.94%
1983	£603.2m	£101.8m	£11.205m	1.86%	11.01%
1984	£855.4m	£147.0m	£18.306m	2.14%	12.45%
1985	£1,307.4m	£301.6m	£40.446m	3.09%	13.41%
1986	£2,087.0m	£443.9m	£70.1m	3.36%	15.79%

The 1986 turnover figure, be it noted, includes the contributions from Bates and other new acquisitions such as Backer & Spielvogel but only for that part of the financial year during which they belonged to the group.

Profitability has depended not only on constant growth, both organic and through acquisition, but strict control of costs. In the financial year 1977–8 the company employed, all told, about 650 people. Their average pay was less than £5,000. In that year the chairman, Kenneth Gill, was paid £25,000, and the highest paid director received £32,725. In the year to 30 September 1986 the number of employees averaged out at 9,774 and the wage bill was £208.4 million, giving average pay per employee of just over £21,300, not excessive by the standards of the ad industry, especially when one bears in mind that many of those employees are being paid American salaries. The emoluments of chairman Maurice amounted to £298,000. The highest paid director (presumably Charles?) received £298,310.

Of the £70.1 million pre-tax profit recorded for 1986, £56.1 million was reported to come from the Communication division, almost precisely double the profit it had achieved the previous year. Consulting (principally the Hay Group) rose from £11.7 million to £14 million. The Communication division's profit margin (expressed as a proportion of income or 'revenue', as the annual report calls it, not billing) was 16.75%, compared with 12.85% for Consulting. The ad agencies, which probably accounted for around 80% of Communication division profits, were still laying the majority of the group's golden eggs. One outside analyst, however, estimated that as much as £8.7 million of profit ascribed to the division really came from interest on money raised by the rights issue in early 1986.

Another interesting breakdown of the figures is by geographical area. In 1986 the United States accounted for comfortably more than half of both revenue and profit, respectively £253.2 million and £38.9 million. The corresponding figures for the United Kingdom were £98 million and £18.1 million and for the rest of the world £92.7 million and £13.1 million. On the basis of these figures the US profit margin was 15.36% and the UK margin 18.47%, while the rest of the world registered a profit margin of 14.13%. (The rest of the world, incidentally, means thirty-one countries where the group has wholly owned or majority owned subsidiaries.) So not only are the ad agencies still the most lucrative parts of the business, it is the London agencies that remain its most efficient money-makers.

Hand in hand with the growth in profits has gone a continuous and often spectacular increase in earnings per share, despite the issue of many more shares in recent years. In some of the past ten years the increase has been of 30%, 40% or even 50%. In 1986 earnings per ordinary share were 50.9 pence, a rise of 21% on the previous year. Dividends per share in 1986 were 15.7 pence, up from 13.1 pence the previous year and a mere 1.2 pence in 1978.

The number of ordinary (10p) shares, allotted, called up and fully paid, at the end of 1986 was nearly 110 million, more than twice as many as a year before. In addition nearly 100 million 6.3% (£1) convertible preference shares were held. Financial institutions (pension funds, unit trusts, insurance and investment companies) held 69% of the ordinary shares and 76% of the preference shares (convertible into ordinary shares from 1989 on at the rate of £1.4305 in nominal amount of ordinary shares for every £100 of preference shares). Individual shareholders owned 18% of the ordinary shares and 15% of the preference shares.

In the spring of 1987 a one-for-three scrip issue plus the sale of 9,740,000 new shares on the Paris Bourse brought the number of issued ordinary shares to 155,812,836. The sale of these shares raised some £61 million and left the company with cash balances of around £240 million, which could be used either to fund fresh acquisitions or to earn interest or both.

The proportion of the ordinary shares jointly held by Charles and Maurice Saatchi was reckoned to be 2.34%. Even taking into account their holdings of convertible preference shares, they still appeared to own less than 3% of the company. At current prices that small percentage of shares is nevertheless worth something in the region of £30 million.

Saatchi & Saatchi is no longer a glamour stock of the kind it was only a few years ago when its shares hit a price/earnings ratio of forty. By June 1987 they were trading on a P/E of seventeen, slightly less than Saatchi's much smaller rivals WCRS, Lowe Howard-Spink & Bell, Boase Massimi Pollitt and Abbott Mead Vickers. However, the share price had largely recovered from the beating it took after the takeover of Ted Bates and the account losses to which that gave rise. The shares were at one point, before the rights issue and Bates takeover of early 1986, trading at 936p. Later they collapsed to 570p before rising again to more than 700p, then drifting down in 1987, after the number of shares had been increased.

The share price dropped again with something of a bump in May of 1987 – paradoxically after chairman Maurice had announced excellent half-year results. For the six months to 31 March he said pre-tax profit had more than doubled to £56.2 million, largely as a result of acquisitions. Full-year profit of £117 million or more appeared in prospect. Earnings per share for the half-year increased by 21% to 21.2p. However, the shares were marked down by 30p to 624p. Why? The main reason was that the chairman's presentation gave stockbrokers' analysts the impression that the company was about to launch another rights issue, selling yet more shares in order to finance acquisitions in the consulting field. As a result of the 1986 ad agency buys in the US the half-year contribution to group profits made by the Consulting division had fallen from 26% to 13%.

The impression that the group might be going for another massive share-selling and company-buying spree was strengthened by the Saatchi prediction that the world market for business consulting services would by 1990 be worth $200,000 million and that fewer than ten firms would account for at least a third of it. This appeared to imply that the group had its sights set on expanding its presence in that field by several billion dollars within three years. The expectations of another share issue did not materialise, at least not in the short term, but the share price continued to fall towards, and briefly under, 600p, making them in the view of some observers very good value for money. Others were plainly worried about the group's prospects in the light of the slowness with which Anthony Simonds-Gooding was going about the process of streamlining its American ad agencies. After the 1987 General Election the share price rose again towards 700p.

The price may fluctuate, as share prices do, but the stock market value of the company remains near £1,000 million and is very much greater than that of any comparable competitor. The truly comparable ones are all in America, where Saatchi shares are not listed but where they are traded through the medium of American Depository Shares, each of which represents three ordinary shares. American investors have been big buyers of Saatchi stock in recent years and were in early 1987 estimated to hold about 20% of the company's equity.

In the space of little more than a year – from early 1986 to 1987 – the general view taken of Saatchi & Saatchi by financial analysts and commentators has greatly shifted. Before the Bates deal there was near-unanimity in admiring the company's unbroken record of growth in turnover and profits and its intelligent and capable financial management. Post-Bates the Saatchis still have their fans in the City and on Wall Street, but none of the fans is quite so sanguine about the future as used to be the case. It is not only that suspicions persist that the long-term financial impact of the damage done to relations with American advertising clients by the mega-merger may turn out to be greater than the figures even for the first half of the 1986–7 year revealed. More importantly, the spell has been broken. The City of London in particular no longer takes it for granted that the Saatchis can do no wrong. And, however well they do in fact do, the 30% growth rate of earlier years is seen as unattainable by the giant Saatchi & Saatchi now is.

The departure of Martin Sorrell is widely regretted among the financial community, which has given the same kind of enthusiastic backing to Sorrell's own company, WPP, that was formerly reserved for Saatchi & Saatchi. It is commonly thought that the Saatchis paid much too much for Ted Bates and that, if Sorrell had still been finance director, the deal would not have been done on the same terms (though some people think Sorrell himself paid too much for JWT). This may be quite wrong, and history has yet to pronounce on the ultimate wisdom of taking over Bates. What counts is perceptions. The stock market tends to take the short view and react, sometimes over-react, to the latest events. It is also, like advertising agency clients, swayed by fashion and reputation, which have a snowball effect. When a firm has a reputation for getting things right it will get a crowd of supporters behind it. When the same firm is thought, for whatever reason, to be faltering, they are quite likely to turn around and kick it. The Saatchis, whose reputation helped them so much for so long, have little to grumble about.

One thing which has not helped the company's image in the City is that, in the wake of Sorrell's departure, it lost a whole tier of entrepreneurially minded young financial executives – Neil McClure to FKB, Matthew Allen to Gold Greenlees Trott, Richard Ridley to Lowe Howard-Spink & Bell. But in the future it is possible that what the City thinks will become less important than what Wall Street, Tokyo and Zurich think as the shares become more widely traded.

14

Which Way Now?

Saatchi & Saatchi is a moving target. The group has changed so much even during the few months that elapsed while this book was being put together that one can be certain of only one thing. By the time you, the reader, have it in your hands, the story will have taken another unexpected twist or two. That is because the Saatchi company has been distinguished since it started by two qualities – dynamism and opportunism. The same is perhaps true of every successful business but rarely to such a great and visible extent.

The dynamism is evidenced by the company's financial record but not only by that. To go from zero to being the world's largest ad agency group in a mere sixteen years is astonishing enough, but to have an impact in a very much shorter space of time than that on a whole series of other business service industries makes the achievement even more remarkable. Saatchi & Saatchi is not content to have out-Interpubliced Interpublic, it is set on becoming an altogether more important concern than its American ad-agency-based competitors. The latter have stuck, by and large, to the advertising and related fields – public relations, sales promotion, direct marketing, market research. They have not stuck their noses into management consultancy. Saatchi, on the other hand, is quite clearly determined to become as major a player in the consultancy as in the ad game.

It makes sense, whether or not one believes there is much business to be gained from the cross-referral process (one unit in the group recommending to clients the services of sister units) in which Saatchi spokesmen have expressed such fervent belief. The advertising and consultancy businesses, while they are different, are not all that different. Both depend on the application of brainpower to a client company's strategic problems – and the problems of marketing and advertising strategy are frequently connected to those of managerial strategy. Both, therefore, involve the efficient deployment of people, those walking, talking, egotistical, mobile assets, rather than of fixed assets such as machinery. If you can run an international advertising network successfully, there's no reason why you shouldn't be able to do the same for a network of consultancies.

As for opportunism (the word is not used pejoratively), the Saatchi entry into management consultancy happened only because an opportunity presented itself and was seized upon. But this kind of opportunism goes right back to the early days of the original Saatchi & Saatchi agency. It was opportunism that decided the Saatchis to perform their merger with the Compton UK Partners company, a deal which transformed their position and provided them with the resources with which to start seriously pursuing ambitions that up till then must have seemed even to the brothers themselves pipe dreams similar to those of many another rising ad agency. It was lack of opportunism that accounted for the decision of The Kirkwood Company to reject the same deal when Compton, before contact had been made with the Saatchis, offered it to Ronnie Kirkwood and his partners.

One can speculate amusingly but fruitlessly on what would have happened to all three companies if Kirkwood had accepted the offer. Would Saatchi & Saatchi, without that stroke of luck, have gone on to become anything like the force it is today? Possibly not, but then, luck is what you make of it, and one suspects that some other opportunity would have come along that would have been seized and that would have led to other, perhaps equally interesting consequences.

Another kind of luck or opportunism – the two words refer, after all, to opposite sides of the same coin – enabled the Saatchi brothers to recruit the two men who did most, as far as any outsider can see, to take their company from being just one of the pack to its present leadership position. The two were, of course, Tim Bell and Martin Sorrell. Very different characters but equally important in their different ways to the Saatchi story. Bell, the first-rate advertising front man with his easy-going charm; Sorrell, the brilliant financial wheeler and dealer, a North London Jew like the brothers themselves.

The whole group's fortunes were built on the advertising accounts (and cash) piled up during the dazzling period of growth of its main, Charlotte Street agency in the period of about seven years when Bell ran it. The brothers were again lucky (or was it clever man-management?) that Bell did not leave in the late 1970s when his influence at Charlotte Street was at its height, taking both clients and staff with him. Lucky also that Sorrell allowed his entrepreneurial instincts to be harnessed to the Saatchi chariot instead of his own for set the pattern of their acquisition strategy.

Dynamism and opportunism would not have been sufficient to confer success on the Saatchis if they had not happened to find themselves in a growth sector of the British economy. Advertising as a whole has done extremely well in the UK in recent years, especially by comparison with the many declining British industries; it has also won increasing public interest and approval. According to figures compiled by the Advertising Association, the undisputed authority on the subjct, advertising spending in Britain more than trebled in real (constant price) terms between 1956 and 1986. Over the same period it went up by about 69% as a proportion of gross domestic product. In 1985, the latest year for which comparative statistics are available, only Australia, Finland and the United States spent more on advertising than did the UK as a proportion of GDP.

The rise in ad expenditure has not been unbroken. There have been years, notably the mid-1970s during the economic crisis touched off by the Yom Kippur War and the leap in oil prices, when it fell in real terms. But since the late 1970s the upward trend has been marked. The following table shows it.

UK Ad Spending 1970–86

Year	At Current Prices (£m)	At Constant (1980) Prices	GDP (%)
1970	554	2,001	1.26
1971	591	1,948	1.18
1972	708	2,178	1.27
1973	874	2,464	1.34
1974	900	2,186	1.19
1975	967	1,892	1.01
1976	1,188	1,996	1.04
1977	1,499	2,174	1.16

1978	1,834	2,456	1.23
1979	2,137	2,519	1.25
1980	2,555	2,555	1.28
1981	2,818	2,516	1.29
1982	3,126	2,574	1.33
1983	3,579	2,819	1.39
1984	4,059	3,041	1.48
1985	4,441	3,139	1.47
1986	5,117	3,495	1.61

Source: Advertising Association

Despite its ups and downs advertising has been a good business to be in for most of the time the Saatchi brothers have been in it. But, if Adland has been good for them, they in turn have been, as pointed out earlier in this narrative, good for Adland. It was their company's success that opened the gates of the City of London to advertising agencies and allowed them to raise money in a manner and to an extent previously never contemplated. By winning over the investment community, Saatchi & Saatchi was able to launch its campaign of global expansion, acquiring the world's biggest advertising agency network on the way to becoming, as the brothers quite certainly hope, the world's biggest business services group.

Charles Saatchi says in private that his aim is to make the company one that will last a hundred years. How bright do the prospects look in 1987 for Saatchi & Saatchi? Can those enormous ambitions be fulfilled? Or is corporate pride riding for a fall? No definite answer can be given to those questions except by the actions of, and reactions to, the company itself in the coming years. What one can do is point to certain strengths and weaknesses that are likely to influence its future performance.

The group's first and most obvious strength is sheer size. By the standards of any of the fields in which it operates it is either big or very big. Whatever problems crop up, it is highly unlikely that the whole caboodle will collapse. It is worth saying that since it answers the question (in some cases the envious hope) of various people at various times of when the Saatchi bubble is going to burst. It is not a bubble but an extensive range of business operations with a large number of clients, including some of the world's biggest corporations, and it is not going to burst. Size in itself gives protection against many problems, since whatever goes wrong or fails to come right in one place will be balanced by success in another. This applies with particular force to a group such as Saatchis, which is not a single operating company like, say, IBM but a collection of really very diverse units with diverse qualities.

There is, therefore, strength in that diversity, but there is also weakness. While there are now several Saatchi-owned advertising agencies around the world that do excellent work and enjoy high reputations, no other has the same standing in its own market as that enjoyed by the Charlotte Street agency in London. Charlotte Street is both big and, by general consent, highly creative, even if it is reputationally not as pre-eminent as it once was. By contrast, Saatchi & Saatchi Compton in New York – larger in absolute terms of the amount of business handled even if smaller in proportion to its own marketplace – was unable to brighten up its image very much despite strenuous efforts. Whether the merger with DFS will help remains to be seen.

Though now only one piece of a much larger whole, the success of Charlotte Street has in the past been pivotal to the group's position on the London Stock Exchange as well as in Adland generally. Any setback to that one agency would, therefore, have dangerous consequences. Fortunately it appears to be in capable hands both managerially and creatively. However, it is struggling to stay at the top of the billings table against formidable competition from both J. Walter Thompson (JWT's London office is in far better shape than most of that group) and Charlotte Street's sister agency Dorlands. There is no guarantee that it will keep its number one label, but losing it will not do too much harm provided that the agency continues to perform well – which it is sure to do in the immediate future – and that its performance is not overshadowed by bad news from the rest of the Saatchi advertising empire.

Bad news would be if the attempts to rationalise the structure of the empire by merging some of the American ad agencies, thereby achieving cost economies, led to a serious haemorrhage of staff or clients or both. There is, it must be said, already a great deal of resentment among American ad agency folk about what is perceived to have been the destructive effect of the Saatchi takeover of Ted Bates on jobs in the industry. Much of that resentment is focused on the William Esty agency, the Bates subsidiary which has taken such a battering from departing clients, though account conflicts resulting from the Saatchi takeover are by no means the only factor in Esty's decline. Esty suffered from critical remarks about it made by Bob Jacoby, the former boss of Bates, after the latter bought it. Joe O'Donnell, who arrived at Esty late in the day, now has his work cut out to restore its fortunes.

It would also be bad news for the Saatchi group, especially in the eyes of investors, if the loss of billings by Bates itself turned out at the end of the full 1986–7 financial year to be greater than revealed by the interim results to March 1987. Since advertising accounts, when lost, are not usually yanked out immediately the clients' decisions are announced but may go on being handled by the incumbent agencies for quite a time before the money starts to flow through the agencies picked to replace them, there are suspicions in some quarters that the final, grisly truth about the fall-out from the Bates deal has yet to be learned.

The financial analysts have since 1986 become far more critical of the Saatchis. Some at least of them are suspicious about what has recently been going on in the Hay Group, where management changes, including the promotion of Milton Rock's son Bob to run the company in place of Charles Fiero and the appointment of Claudio Belli as European supremo, have led to the departure of several valuable employees. They are suspicious, too, about the level of the Hay contribution to group profits. The 1986 contribution of the whole Consulting division was stated in the annual report to be £14 million, up from £11.7 million the year before. What was not pointed out was that the 1985 figure included only nine months' Hay membership of the Saatchi group. Since the 1986 figure covered twelve months of Hay profits, as well as of Yankelovich Clancy Shulman's, there may have been an actual, though unadmitted, decline in Hay's financial performance. The 1987 annual report will be carefully scrutinised to see what has happened on that front.

Certain analysts are unhappy about what they see as a decline in the quality of information they get from Saatchi's top financial people these days. Finance director David Newlands, Andrew Woods, who is in charge of financial operations in the US, and other members of their department inspire less respect than did Martin Sorrell. For a company that talks in terms of continued acquisition this sea change in City sentiment could prove quite a handicap. Cash-rich Saatchi & Saatchi may be, but City support would still be desirable for a really major deal, such as buying one of the leading accountancy firms, though Victor Millar recently appeared to rule out that particular option.

Millar, as head of the Consulting division, is the man who at present appears to inspire the most confidence in the investment community, a confidence based on his track record at Arthur Andersen rather than anything he has yet achieved at Saatchi & Saatchi. However, since his Saatchi job is expected to be in a sense a re-run of his previous job, that is building up a management consultancy network, the confidence is logical.

On the other hand, some doubt hangs over the future success of Anthony Simonds-Gooding. He has a pretty good track record of his own as a marketing man but is now, as head of the Communications division, with particular responsibility for re-casting the group's ad agencies in the US, doing a job that is new to him. Likewise the men recently put in charge of the Saatchi & Saatchi Compton International network – Terry Bannister, Roy Warman, Alban Lloyd and Jeremy Sinclair – have yet to prove, despite their great combined experience, what kind of a fist they can make of that new job.

The main board of the Saatchi holding company consists of nine people – Millar, Simonds-Gooding, Newlands, Woods, Simon Mellor, company secretary David Perring, retired chairman (now president) Kenneth Gill and the two brothers. As already recounted, the Saatchi brothers now own between them less than 3% of the company but they, and Charles in particular, still call the shots. They are also still young men, both in their early forties. They doubtless have it in them to go on running the show for a long time and will do so unless something goes badly wrong. In the immediate future at least the group is bound to stay primarily interested in advertising. Its eventual aim is that the Consulting division should make as much money as Communications. If it were to do so, then Victor Millar or someone like him might become a candidate to be chairman in place of Maurice. One cannot imagine, though, that Charles would ever give up his unofficial position as boss without a struggle.

It is possible, though difficult to imagine, that if the share price were to tumble further as a result of investor suspicions, the boss might be induced to abandon his policy of taciturnity and attempt to influence opinion directly instead of indirectly. The mystique of unapproachability may have served Charles well for many years, but there is something rather tiresome about a man who buys up companies all over the world, sticks his name on half of them, then refuses to answer questions on the record about what he's up to. Purple passages in the company annual report about global marketing and how 'it is good to be big, it is better to be good, but it is best to be both,' are no substitute for straight talk about precise goals.

Despite the impressive Saatchi financial and managerial record, 1986 and 1987 produced enough unpleasant, as well as admirable, surprises about this public company to make Charles's ivory tower seclusion somewhat inappropriate. The ivory tower is the one in which he sits writing copy for British Airways and other favoured clients and planning corporate actions liable to affect the lives of a fair number of other people.

Size, we said before, is Saatchi & Saatchi's most obvious strength. It may also be a weakness, to the extent that the group is now seen by some, including some whose good will it needs to retain, as being in danger of becoming sluggish, bureaucratic and complacent, like the big agencies at which the young Saatchi brothers cocked a snook in 1970 when, with inspired impudence, they proclaimed they had come to offer 'a new kind of advertising'.

A new kind of advertising was in the end not what they had to offer at all, which is not to deny that some of their ads were very clever. What they really came up with was a new kind of advertising conglomerate – or, to be precise, an old kind with a few new twists. One of the twists is that a London-based company derives the greater part of its revenue from the United States. Already Americans own 20% of Saatchi & Saatchi, and one can imagine that, if they get over their qualms about the company, their stake could rise to more than 50%. What has become essentially a British-owned American company could be turned into an American-owned one. Then, at least, when New York agencies were merged and people lost their jobs, it would not be an occasion for anti-British xenophobia.

An equally stimulating thought is that Charles Saatchi, who with his American wife owns a house on Long Island, could move to the States himself. A rumour that he intended to do so to keep an eye on the group's American interests appeared in the US advertising trade press in 1986, but nothing came of it. Mind you, at least three members of the nine-member Saatchi main board spend most of their time in the US anyway. Since America is the heartland of all the industries in which the Saatchi group is active, and since most of its own work arises there, it is perhaps only a matter of time before its administrative centre shifts to where its centre of gravity already is. But it may be a long time.

No doubt Charles and Maurice will long before then have grabbed a good few more opportunities and surprised a lot more people. Their story has still a long way to go.

Epilogue

The annual general meeting of the Saatchi & Saatchi Company, which took place in London's Park Lane Hotel in March 1988, was a relaxed and cheerful affair. Shareholders attending it were each given a piece of the company's 18th birthday cake, in honour of its coming of age. The chairman, Maurice Saatchi, younger of the two brothers who founded a small advertising agency in 1970, boasted that profits had risen from £24,000 in that agency's first year to £124 million in the 1986–7 year of what was now a multinational conglomerate and the undisputed number one of the world ad industry.

That was not all he had to boast about. Saatchi & Saatchi had been the first British company, to enter the American advertising market in a big way. Now 20% of television advertising time in the United States was, he claimed, bought by Saatchi subsidiaries. The group derived 85% of its profits from its operations outside the United Kingdom, 55% in the form of dollars; 20% of its equity was held by US shareholders.

Saatchi success was not simply financial. The company, declared the chairman, had revolutionised the art of political propaganda. It had expanded into sixteen areas of expertise, in all of which it sought to become a market leader. He did not dwell on the fact that the group's flagship agency, Saatchi & Saatchi Advertising of London (its name recently changed from Saatchi & Saatchi Compton) had given up working for the British Conservative Party, formerly its most famous client. Nor was he eager to talk about the rebuffs suffered some months previously from two British banking concerns – Midland Bank and Hill Samuel – Saatchi & Saatchi had been interested in taking over.

Maurice dealt deftly and amiably with questions. Asked about reports that, as a consequence of the stock market crash of late 1987, the company had been considering going private, he reassured shareholders that there was nothing to worry about. While such a course could not be ruled out in all foreseeable circumstances, the company was dedicated to its public status.

Another question concerned the value of works of art owned by the company. The questioner was told that these accounted for a major part of an item labelled in the annual report as 'other fixed asset investments' and valued at £12.9 million. The works of art were housed in various museums around the world. No direct reference was made to the large private art gallery set up by Charles Saatchi and his wife Doris. Purchasing power has made Saatchi as important a name in the art world as in that of advertising, and some of the purchasing power behind the private Saatchi Collection comes from the public Saatchi & Saatchi Company. According to one authority, possibly a fifth of the works displayed in the Saatchi gallery belongs to the company, though the bulk of the money behind it is Charles's own, part of it raised from a 1981 sale of some of his Saatchi & Saatchi shares.

Most of the assembled shareholders in 1988 appeared uninterested in such matters, however, and there were no follow-up questions about art. The only slight note of discontent sounded at the meeting was when Maurice was pressed by two of those present to say why Charles was not among them and whether he could be prevailed upon to attend next year's AGM. Maurice's reply to the first question was that his brother was 'minding the shop', to the second that he would ask him to do so.

In fact, Charles Saatchi makes a habit of not attending annual general meetings of the company of which, though not the chairman, he is the driving force. Some at least of the shareholders present at the 1988 AGM felt that it was high time he gave up a little of his famous reclusiveness so that they might have an opportunity of meeting once a year the man principally responsible for the fate of their investment. In his absence, however, they were able to chat over a post-AGM glass of wine and slice of birthday cake with all the other principal Saatchi directors, including Victor Millar, the American who had recently been put in operational command of both divisions of the group (Saatchi & Saatchi Communications and Saatchi & Saatchi Consulting).

Millar's promotion to the role, if not the title, of chief operating officer of Saatchi & Saatchi is one of the important events to have occurred within the group since this book was completed in early 1987. He was originally hired to run only the Consulting division but was also given responsibility for Communications after that division's previous head, Anthony Simonds-Gooding, left the group in late 1987 to become chairman of a new company, British Satellite Broadcasting. The place thus left vacant on the main board was filled by Jeremy Sinclair, the only member of the original tiny Saatchi & Saatchi team, apart from the brothers, to have stayed with the company up to the present day. Sinclair and another director, Andrew Woods, were appointed group deputy chairmen.

Simonds-Gooding's decision to leave the Saatchis may have been influenced not only by the positive attractions of an exciting new job but by a measure of fatigue after many months spent in New York coaxing and bullying various Saatchi-owned agencies into mergers. These may have made economic sense but resulted in the loss of many jobs and much anti-Saatchi bitterness in the city that has become the group's centre of gravity even if its corporate headquarters remain in London.

Millar, as the group's new big cheese, appears to have introduced a new era of *glasnost* in its corporate style. Soon after taking on his enlarged responsibilities he gave an interview to a British television programme (Channel Four's *Business Programme*) in which he made it clear that in the immediate future there would be no more hasty attempts to get into the financial services field. In the wake of the Midland Bank's public rejection of takeover advances by Saatchi & Saatchi, which had earned the latter a great deal of unaccustomed ridicule – the idea of advertising agents running a major bank did not go down well with most UK financial commentators – this was a necessary piece of publicity damage limitation. The group's ambitions to get into the financial services field were redefined as long-term.

Perhaps more important than the content of the interview was the mere fact that it took place at all. Hitherto Saatchi & Saatchi had gained a reputation for clever public relations combined paradoxically with a refusal by the company's leading lights, the Saatchi brothers, to give journalists on-the-record interviews. No director of the company had ever previously appeared on TV to talk about its policy.

Millar was not asked to comment on the other Saatchi upset of the autumn, namely the resignation by the group's flagship London ad agency of the Conservative Party account after a decade in which its political advertising had made it and the group world famous. The strains that led up to that parting of the ways are described in Chapter Three of this book. Many people at the time saw the split as a defeat for the Saatchis, but from the business point of view it was probably a happy development. They had got as much mileage out of working for the Conservatives as they could ever hope to do, and there are dangers for a diversified business services group in being too closely identified with a political party. In any case it is far better to resign an account before one is fired.

Other changes to have taken place since this book was put together include the virtual elimination of the Compton name from the list of advertising agencies owned by the group. After years during which Saatchi & Saatchi had been the official name only of a holding company, while its main ad agency network had been called Saatchi & Saatchi Compton, it was decided to follow popular usage and drop the word Compton.

The move had considerable symbolic significance. For one thing it did away with a constant verbal reminder that the original Saatchi agency had got into the big league not through taking over, but through being taken over by Compton UK Partners and that international expansion had first come about through acquisition of the large but unexciting Compton Advertising of the US.

Secondly, the name change signalled a corporate will to perpetuate the identification – some would say the deliberate confusion – of the Saatchi advertising agency network with the holding company. This policy applies with particular force to the agency in London's Charlotte Street. With or without the Conservative Party, this is still the office that gets the group its most valuable publicity, partly because of the excellence of its creative

output – winning more major awards than any other UK agency –
and partly because it has managed to stay since 1979 at the top of
British Adland's turnover tree.

No effort has been spared to keep its billings high. For example,
in 1987, when the £31 million Dixons/Currys account moved from
one Saatchi subsidiary agency in the UK, Dorlands, to another,
Ted Bates, the responsibility for media-buying on the account was
given not to Bates but to Acme Media, yet another Saatchi subsidiary, billings of which were counted in by the company with
Saatchi & Saatchi Charlotte Street. The Charlotte Street agency
took number one position yet again in the 1987 billings table compiled by the magazine *Campaign* with a figure of £257 million,
ahead of J. Walter Thompson, with £222 million and Dorlands,
with £210 million.

Those were the figures supplied to *Campaign* by the agencies
themselves. Another set of 1987 billings figures, compiled by the
Media Register company and based on monitored expenditure on
press and TV advertising expenditure, put JWT ahead by a whis-
ker, with £163.18 million against £163.06 million for Saatchi &
Saatchi Advertising. By the autumn of 1988, however, it appeared
that the Saatchi agency was pulling well ahead, with, according to
Campaign, net new billings for the year to mid-September of
about £90 million, compared with only £25 million for JWT. One
of Charlotte Street's juicy new accounts was Dixons/Currys, completely transferred to Saatchi & Saatchi Advertising when the
London offices of Bates and Dorlands were merged in the spring to
form BSB Dorland.

The Charlotte Street agency's success has indeed been such that
it can weather a few mishaps such as the troubles with the Tories
or the loss in late 1987 of its joint chairman, Jennifer Laing, who
went off to be boss of another London agency, Aspect Hill Holli-
day. This left the Australian-born Bill Muirhead in sole charge as
chairman of Saatchi & Saatchi Advertising London.

Internationally the Saatchi & Saatchi Advertising network ended
1987 in second place to Young & Rubicam. Worldwide billings,
according to figures published by *Advertising Age*, were $4,906
million for Y & R against $4,609 million for Saatchi. Behind them
came BBDO (part of the Omnicom group), Ogilvy & Mather,
McCann-Erickson (part of Interpublic) and, in sixth place, the

Saatchi-owned Backer Spielvogel Bates Worldwide (the London arm of which is the aforementioned BSB Dorland). JWT was seventh. The total billings of all Saatchi-owned ad agencies amounted to more than $9,000 million, putting them well ahead of the field as the advertising industry's largest group.

In May 1988 a fresh round of managerial changes took place on the international coordination side of the Saatchi & Saatchi Advertising network. While Alban Lloyd stayed as chairman of Saatchi & Saatchi Advertising International, the joint chief executives, Roy Warman and Terry Bannister, left to join the holding company board. Their place was taken by Richard Humphreys, who moved over from running the Saatchi subsidiary KHBB in London. Muirhead was made deputy chairman of International while continuing as boss of Charlotte Street.

Warman and Bannister, meanwhile, were to continue as a double act, this time as joint directors of operations for all companies within the Communications division of the Saatchi group. To the reported suggestion that this represented an encroachment on the authority of Victor Millar, chairman of both the Communications and Consulting divisions, the latter replied that he was grateful for the extra help. Another view was that the move was intended to take some of the pressure off Millar so that he could get on with his original task of building up Consulting.

At the 1988 AGM Chairman Maurice had reaffirmed the company's intention to press ahead with more acquisitions, but with the emphasis more on the Consulting than on the Communications side. Approaches had reportedly been made, though without success, to Arthur Andersen to buy its management consultancy division, built up by Millar himself. As for market research, where efforts to expand the Saatchi presence had borne comparatively little fruit, another informal approach to AGB by Maurice Saatchi in 1987 had met with a rebuff.

Several acquisitions were, however, made in 1988. The most important was that of the Gartner Group, a publicly quoted American supplier of market research and consultancy services on information technology. Gartner, with turnover of $40 million, was bought for $77 million after negotiations between its founder and chief executive, Gideon Gartner, and Victor Millar. After the deal the sharp-tongued Gartner, a self-confessed cynic, was quoted by the *Financial Times* as saying 'I've not spoken to the Saatchi brothers ... If everything I read is true I may never meet them.'

The Gartner deal was accompanied by yet another Saatchi rights issue, this time of £176.5 million-worth of 6.75% redeemable convertible preference shares, designed to appeal to Euro-market investors. The proceeds were to be used partly to finance acquisitions, including Gartner, partly to pay off debt. The offer document repeated that Saatchi aimed to achieve leading positions in sixteen service lines, eleven of them on the Consulting side.

About 65% of the share issue was taken up by existing shareholders, the rest being placed with institutions. This was regarded as quite a success, given that the price of Saatchi ordinary shares had languished – and continued to languish – through most of 1988.

By now the City's love affair with the company was well and truly over. Even good results for the first half of the 1987–8 financial year, with pre-tax profits up 12% to £63.1 million, had done nothing to revive the share price. Earlier in the year financial commentators had pointed out sourly that a £200,000 pay rise for Charles and Maurice, taking the salary of each of the brothers to £500,000, far outstripped the annual rise in earnings per share.

Maurice replied to the critics in an interview with the *Sunday Times*, whose business editor, Ivan Fallon, has been a consistent fan of the Saatchis. The young chairman pointed out that Saatchi was one of only twenty-four British companies that had an unbroken ten-year record of growth in earnings per share. He repeated his faith in the benefits of having a group able to offer a whole variety of different services to its clients.

Saatchi & Saatchi claims that a fifth of all its new business comes from cross-referral, that is from clients of one of its subsidiaries hiring another to do a different job. And that despite the fact that many client companies are known to be sceptical about the advantages of putting all their eggs in one supplier basket. ('One-stop shopping' is still far from being, as John Jay, City editor of the *Sunday Times*, would have it, 'conventional wisdom' among advertisers.) The Consulting division has established in Washington D.C. a Centre for Competitive Advantage where Saatchi clients and others 'can meet to review issues, learn from each other and sharpen their own competitiveness'. And, the

Saatchis no doubt hope, to be influenced into giving their group yet more business.

Despite the tougher attitude of the stock market towards the company and the generally less starry-eyed coverage it nowadays gets in the press, Saatchi & Saatchi's is still a success story. Moreover, the group can still cause more of a stir with its initiatives than any other in Adland. Thus it was with its formation in mid-1988 of a centralised UK media-buying operation, named Zenith, capable of placing advertising worth up to £700 million a year on behalf of all Saatchi-owned agencies. The move filled media-owners and rival agencies with fear and admiration, a mixture which no doubt smelled sweet in the ambitious brothers' nostrils.

Philip Kleinman
December 1988

Select Bibliography

There are literally hundreds of books about advertising, many of them very good. They are concerned with different aspects of the industry, including its economic justification, the way ads are created, the use of advertising as one element in the marketing mix and personal reminiscences by successful practitioners. Very few try to present a comparative picture of different advertising agencies and how well they are doing in their struggles with each other. This subject is, on the other hand, exhaustively examined on a weekly basis by the advertising trade press, notably *Advertising Age* and *Adweek* in the US and *Campaign* and *Marketing Week* in the UK. Because of the speed with which things change in the industry, their articles soon get out of date. The same is true of the books, but they remain of interest to anyone curious about the industry's history. Among them are the following:

Kleinman, Philip, *Advertising Inside Out* (W. H. Allen, 1977)
Mayer, Martin, *Madison Avenue U.S.A.* (Penguin, 1958)
Pearson, John, and Turner, Graham, *The Persuasion Industry*
  (Eyre & Spottiswoode, 1965)

Other books more or less directly relevant to the story told in this one are the following:

Buxton, Edward, *Promise Them Anything* (Stein & Day, New York, 1972)
Della Femina, Jerry, *From Those Wonderful Folks Who Gave You Pearl Harbour*
  (Pitman, 1971)
Fletcher, Winston, *Advertising* (Hodder & Stoughton, 1978)
Honomichl, Jack, *Honomichl on Marketing Research*
  NTC Business Books, Lincolnwood, Illinois, 1986)
King, Stephen, *Developing New Brands* (Pitman, 1973)
Kleinman, Philip, *Market Research – Head Counting Becomes Big Business*
  (Comedia, 1985)
Kleinman, Philip, *World Advertising Review*
  (the three latest editions contain many Saatchi ads, Cassell, 1985, 1986, 1987)

Levitt, Theodore, *The Marketing Imagination* (The Free Press, New York, 1983)

Nevett, T. R., *Advertising in Britain* (Heinemann, 1982)

Ogilvy, David, *Confessions of an Advertising Man* (Longman, 1964)

Reeves, Rosser, *Reality in Advertising* (Alfred Knopf, New York, 1961)

Tyler, Rodney, *Campaign! The Selling of the Prime Minister* (Grafton, 1987)

Wight, Robin, *The Day the Pigs Refused to be Driven to Market*
  (Hart Davis, MacGibbon, 1972)

Books about non-advertising marketing services are almost entirely devoted to how to do them, not who makes money out of them. That applies to the fields of direct marketing, market research (with the exception of the titles mentioned above), public relations and sales promotion. But the trade press, notably *Direct Marketing* monthly in the US and *PR Week* in the UK, gives some idea of which firms are winning and losing.

Index

Abbott, David, 58, 140–2
Abbott Mead Vickers, 58, 129, 140–2
AC & R Advertising, 104
Access, 145
Ad Weekly, 7–8
Addison Consultancy, 144
Adweek, 17
AGB Research, 90, 117–18
Alas, 104
Alexon, 58
Allardyce, 43
Allen, Matthew, 161
Allen, Rod, 135
Allen Brady & Marsh, 10, 25, 135–6
Alliance, 142
Allied Breweries, 24, 39
Allied-Lyon, 59
American Motors, 80, 111
American West Coast PR, 125
Ammirati & Puris, 132
Andersen, Arthur, 115, 116, 168
Angotti Thomas Hedge, 132
Arbitron, 119
Arden, Paul, 61, 91
Arellano Ted Bates, 104
Argyll Group, 60, 108
Asahi Advertising, 103
Association of Canadian Advertisers, 121

Association of National Advertisers, 77
Ata Univers, 101
Atherton, Bill, 12, 15
Audley, Sir Bernard, 117
Austin Rover, 80, 97–8, 109, 110, 111
Ayer, N. W., 101

B & Q, 106
Backer, Bill, 68
Backer & Spielvogel, 67–9, 77, 79, 80, 82, 104
Backer Spielvogel Bates Worldwide, 104–5
Bain & Co., 115
Bainsfair, Paul, 91
Ball, Michael, 139
Ball Partnership, 139
Bank of Ireland, 102
Banks, John, 145
Bannister, Terry, 57, 61, 63, 89, 168
Barker, Charles, Group, 124
Barker, David, 53
Barkey, Len, 61, 64
Barraclough, David, 53
Bartle Bogle Hegarty, 6
Bates, Ted, 24, 58, 70
Bates New York, 73, 74

Bates Worldwide, 69–73, 77–9, 80, 81, 87, 95, 98–101, 103, 104, 107, 111–12, 139, 161, 166–7
Baulk, Michael, 142
BBC, 127
BBDO, 75, 101
BBDO International, 72–3
BBDO Worldwide, 95
BDDP, 100
Becker, 139
Bélier, 99, 100
Bell, Arthur, & Sons, 60
Bell, Tim, 11, 20, 21, 25–7, 31, 34, 51, 56–7, 62, 63, 90, 129, 131, 133–4, 136, 151, 163–4
Bellamy, Bob, 21
Belli, Claudio, 167
Benson, S.H., 3, 19, 127
Benson & Hedges, 4, 59
Bentley, John, 3, 38, 127
Benton & Bowles, 4, 6, 42, 70, 82, 132, 149
Bernbach, Bill, 2, 4, 72, 93, 137, 140
Bernstein, David, 5
Birmingham Crematorium, 17
Biss Lancaster, 124, 138
Black & Decker, 24, 58, 87
Blackett-Sample-Hummert, 67, 70
Blair, Andrew, 5
Blaupunkt, 102
Blue Nun, 109
BMW, 80, 132, 138
BMZ, 98
Boase, Martin, 129, 130, 132, 140
Boase Massimi Pollitt, 17, 34, 60–1, 129–32, 135
Booz Allen, 115
Bounty, 78, 79
Brand Character Index, 86
Breene, Tim, 139
Brentford Nylons, 43
British Airports Authority, 146
British Airways, 32, 58, 59, 88, 91, 105, 141

British Caledonian, 141
British Gas, 63, 145
British Leyland, 13, 24, 39, 58
British Market Research Bureau, 62, 1
British Petroleum, 24, 39, 59
British Printing Corporation, 7–8
British Rail, 39, 47, 135
British Telecom, 53
Brockie Haslam, 39
Brogan Developers, 16
Broulet Dru Dupuy Petit, 99
Buckley, Paul, 153
Bull, Stuart, 53
Bullmore, Jeremy, 146
Bungey, Michael, 46, 66, 108, 109, 1
Burdus, Ann, 23, 90
Burgess, Mark, 34
Burnett, Leo, 24, 59, 91
Burson-Marsteller, 54, 81, 122, 123, 124
Business Design Group, 143

Cadbury Schweppes, 59
Callaghan, Jim, 30
Cameron, Stuart, 58
Campaign, 7–9, 11, 16–17, 18, 153
Campaign Advertising, 50
Campaign Palace, 103
Campbell-Ewald, 133
Campbell-Mithun, 71, 79
Campbell's Soups, 39
Canard, 101
Carling Black Label, 138
Carlton Communication, 125
Carter Organization, 125
Castlemaine, 59
Castrol, 111
CFRP, 100
Chevrolet, 111
Citibank, 144
Citrus Marketing Board of Israel, 7
City & Commercial, 124
City of London Take-over Panel, 60
Clancy, Kevin, 119

Index

Clancy Shulman & Associates, 54
Cleveland Consulting Agencies, 117
Coal Board, 57, 134
Coca-Cola, 68, 84
Cochrane Chase Livingstone, 46
Cole, George, 141
Colgate, 70, 145
Colgate-Palmolive, 78
Collett Dickenson Pearce, 4–5, 25, 37–8, 59, 60–1, 132, 136–7, 151
Collings, John, 5, 6
Collins, 129
Collins, Ron, 12, 136
Colman Prentis & Varley, 3, 27, 35
Compar, 100
Compton Advertising of New York, 17, 21–2, 41
Compton Communications, 40–1, 49
Compton Group, 41
Compton International, 41
Compton UK Partners, 17–21, 41, 44, 127, 163
Conrad, Michael, & Leo Burnett, 98
Conservative Party, viii–ix, 3, 24, 25, 27–35, 62, 136, 145
Coopers & Lybrand, 115
Cope, Richard, 5, 6
Cornish, Alan, 134
Countrywide Communications, 124
Cramer, Ross, 4, 5–7
Cramer Saatchi, 5–7, 130
Crawford, W.S., 3
Crawford Hall Harrison Cowley, 46
Crawfords, 39, 42
Creamer Dickson Basford, 123, 138
Creative Business, 5
Creative Solutions, 131
Crisco, 79
Croisedale-Appleby, David, 135
Crossbow Films, 139
Cunningham & Walsh, 40
Currys, 106

Daage, Didier Colmet, 99

Dadda, Maurizio, 101
Dalton, Tony, 112
Damour, Pierre, 36–7
Dancer Fitzgerald Sample, 47, 66–7, 76, 77
D'Arcy, 68
D'Arcy MacManus & Masius, 82
D'Arcy Masius Benton & Bowles, 17, 82, 95, 98, 99, 101
Davidson Pearce, 28
Davis Wilkins, 132
Dawes, E.G., 16, 36
Day, Barry, 23, 28
DDB Needham Worldwide, 95
Deighton Mullen, 19–20
Delano, Les, 133
Della Femina, Jerry, 139
Della Femina, Travisano & Partners, 138–9
Deloitte Haskins & Sells, 115
Delvico, 104
Dentsu, 6, 81
Dentsu Young & Rubicam, 81
Department of Health and Social Security, 109
Designers and Art Directors Association, 15
Dewe Rogerson, 124
DFS Direct, 121
DFS Dorland, 63, 78, 80, 82, 96, 106, 108–11, 122
DFS Dorland Worldwide, 66–7
Diamonstein, Barbaralee, 68
Dickinson, Anne, 55
Diener/Hauser/Bates, 104
Direct Marketing Symposium, 122
Distillers Company, 60, 108, 134
Dixons, 106–7, 111, 112
Dobbs, Michael, 33, 61–2
Doping, 101
Doremus Porter Novelli, 123
Dorland, John, 67
Dorland Advertising, 3, 38, 39, 44, 46, 51, 66–7, 107–12, 127, 156

Dorland Direct, 122
Dorland Financial Services, 39
Doyle Dane Bernbach, 2, 40, 71–3, 75, 81, 87, 93, 98, 100, 140
Dun & Bradstreet, 118
Duncan, Stuart, 46
Dunlop, 13, 24, 25, 39, 58
Dupuy, Jean-Pierre, 99
Dupuy, Marie-Catherine, 99, 100
Dupuy Saatchi & Saatchi Compton, 99, 100
Duracell, 111

Ecom Univas, 99, 100
Edelman, Daniel J., 123, 124
Edge, Walter, 67
Eggert, R. W., 98
El Al, 6
Elrick & Lavidge, 119
Ernst & Whinney, 115
Esty, William, 71, 79, 104, 111, 166–7
Euro Advertising, 137
Eurocom, 81, 99
Everett, Mike, 136

Face Ronchetti, 136
Fairfax, 121
Fairfax Advertising, 41
FCA, 100
Fianna Fail, 102
Fiero, Charles, 167
Fleishman Hillard, 123
Foley, Paul, 68
Foote Cone & Belding, 40, 64, 100, 101
Foote Cone & Belding Communications, 95
Ford, 5, 144–5
Franklin, Mike, 51
French, Richard, 140
French Gold Abbott, 140
Futurs, 100

Gallaher, 58, 89
Gamma International, 116

Garland, S. T., Advertising Service, 18
Garland, Sidney, 18
Garland-Compton, 18–21
Garland Stewart & Roache, 139
Garrett, James, and Partners, 28
Garrott, Eric, 38–9, 44
Garrott Dorland Crawford Holdings, 38, 9
Geers Gross, 11, 53, 63, 93
Geier, Phil, 23, 46, 51, 68, 76
General Mills, 79
General Universal Stores, 122
Geraghty, Michael, 67
GFK, 118
GGK, 98
Gill, Kenneth, 21, 22, 52, 56, 65, 158
Goerke, Werner, 97
Gold, Michael, 140
Gold Greenlees Trott, 140, 142, 161
Goldstein, Robert, 79
Golin Harris, 123
Good, Tony, 55, 134
Good Relations, 55, 134
Good Relations City, 134
Goodall Alexander O'Hare, 139
Gordan, Norman, 154
Gossett, Milton, 40, 41, 42, 57, 93, 9
Gough Waterhouse, 46, 103
Graduate Appointments, 153
Granard, 54
Granard Communications, 124
Granby Marketing Services, 131
Grandfield, Nigel, 23, 51–2, 90
Grandfield Rork Collins, 51–2, 63
Grandfield Rork Collins Financial, 12
Grayling Group, 124
Great Clewes Warehouse, 16
Great Universal Stores, 13
Greater London Council, 34, 130
Grey Advertising, 95, 98
Guinness, 60, 108, 134, 135
Guinness Morison International, 44
Gulliver, James, 21, 60, 142
GUS, 59

Haines, Bruce, 141
Halifax Building Society, 109
Hall Advertising, 37
Halstead, Mike, 122
Hambros, 38
Hamlet cigars, 4
Hanson Trust, 134
Harp, 108
Harper, Marion, 45–6, 67, 68, 76, 111
Harrison Cowley, 46
Harrison Cowley PR, 124
Hart, Josephine, 153
Hart, Josephine, Productions, 153
Harvard Capital Group, 143
Havas, 99
Havas Conseil Marsteller, 81, 98, 99
Hay, Edward, 49
Hay Group, 48–50, 65, 114, 115, 122, 126, 167
Hayhurst, 50
Haymarket, 7, 11, 153
HBM/Creamer, 138
HCM, 81, 98, 99, 100
Health Education Council, 6, 7, 13, 15, 25, 140
Heath, Edward, 29
Heath, Len, 42, 43, 44
Hedger, Richard, 61, 62, 91
Hedger Mitchell Stark, 47, 62, 135
Hegarty, John, 6, 11
Heineken, 132–3
Heller, Robert, 12
Herzbrun, David, 93
Heseltine, Michael, 7–8, 11, 153
Hewitt Associates, 115
Heye Needham, 98
HH & S, 122
Hill, Emma, 155
Hill & Knowlton, 54, 123–4
Hines, Duncan, 79
Holsten, 142
Honomichl, 119
Honsinger, John, 122
Hovis, 4

Howard Rubenstein Associates, 123
Howard-Spink, Geoff, 133, 136
Hoyne, John, 73–4
Hudson, Hugh, 33
Huggins Financial Services, 116
Human Resource Management, 115
Humphreys, Richard, 52–3
Humphreys Bull & Barker, 52
Hunter Advertising, 46, 102
Hyundai, 80, 111

IBM, 24, 39, 59, 80
ICM Group, 55
Imperial Tobacco, 109
IMS International, 118, 119
Independent, 122
Independent Television Companies Association, 13
Infocom Group, 55
Information Resources, 119
Infratest, 118
Institute of Practioners in Advertising, 2, 5, 146
Interpublic, 45–6, 67–8, 72, 73, 76, 111, 112
Interpublic Spielvogel, 68
Irv Koons, 41

Jackson, Michael, 8, 9
Jacoby, Bob, 69–74, 81, 82, 147, 167
Jaffa, 7, 13
Jaguar, 80, 111
Jean, Gerard, 99
Jeep Commanche, 93
John Smith Yorkshire Bitter, 130
Johnson & Higgins, 115
Johnson & Johnson, 79
Johnston, Don, 104, 144
JWT Group, 73, 75, 104, 118, 122–4, 143–4

Kalms, Stanley, 107
Kaye, Michael, 51, 107
Kelloggs, 146

Kennedy, Robert E., 67
Kenyon & Eckhardt, 40, 140
Kersten, Matthias, 97
Ketchum PR, 123
Kettle, George, 67
KHBB, 110
Kimper, 43–5
King, Lord, 32, 58
King, Stephen, 146
Kingsley, Dave, 42, 43, 44
Kingsley Manton & Palmer, 42
Kingsway Public Relations, 55, 124
Kinnock, Neil, 33
Kirkwood, Ronnie, 19–20, 23, 44, 163
Kirkwood Company, 19, 163
Kleid, 54, 121
Klemtner Advertising, 41
KMP, 42–4, 53
KMP Humphreys Bull & Barker, 53
KMPH, 43
Kobs & Brady, 121
Kodak, 145
Kraft, 77

Labour Party, 29–35, 278
Laing, Jennifer, 61, 89, 90–1
Larkin, Martin, 102
Leagas, Ron, 26, 129, 141
Leagas Delaney, 129, 141
Leeds Building Society, 141
Levenson, Bob, 93
Levi jeans, 84
Levitt, Theodore, 84–5, 88
LHSBrompton, 136
Light, Larry, 73–4, 112
Lintas, 46, 100, 135
Liraghi Ogilvy & Mather, 101
Little, Arthur D., 115
Livesavers, 79
Lloyd, Alban, 89–90, 91, 168
Logue, Christopher, 92
London's Dockland, 142
Lopex, 19
Lord, Cyril, 135

Lowe, Frank, 35, 38, 57, 60, 132–3, 134, 136
Lowe & Howard-Spink, 60–1, 132–3
Lowe Bell Communications, 134
Lowe Bell Financial, 134
Lowe Howard-Spink & Bell, 12, 34, 129, 134
Lowe Howard-Spink Campbell-Ewald, 133
Lowe Howard-Spink Marschalk, 133–4
Lowe-Marschalk, 133
Lowther, James, 91
Lunn, Dyer, 139
Luvs, 78, 79

M/A/R/C/, 119
MAC, 101
McBer & Co., 48, 116
McCaffrey & McCall, 46, 80, 81, 94, 97, 104, 121
McCall, David, 97
McCann-Erickson, 19, 21, 23, 28, 45–6, 51, 64, 68, 90, 95, 98, 100, 101, 106–7
McCann-Erickson Worldwide, 76
McClure, Neil, 161
McCormack, Mark, 142
McDonalds, 58, 110
McGregor, Ian, 57, 134
McKinsey, 115
McSpadden, Peter, 67
Mail on Sunday, 58
Maile, John, 122
Management Selection Ltd, 49
Manning Selvage & Lee, 123
Manton, Michael, 42, 43, 44
Marcantonio, Alfredo, 133, 139
Maritz, 119
Market Facts, 119
Marketing Solutions, 131
Marlboro Marketing, 54
Marplan, 128
Mars, 74, 80, 112
Mars, Forrest, 74
Mars, John, 74

Marschalk, 133
Marschalk Cambell-Ewald, 76
Marsh, Peter, 10, 135–6
Martin, Chris, 12
Martini, 23
Masius Wynne-Williams, 17, 23
Massimi, Gabe, 129
Masters, Lindsay, 8, 11
Mather, Ron, 103
Mather & Crowther, 147
Matthews, Roger, 139
Mayo Infurna, 41
Mead, Peter, 142
MEAL, 106, 109–10
Medcalf, Gordon, 19
Media Department, 43
Mellor, Simon, 168
Mercedes, 80
Mercedes Benz, 111
Mercer-Meidinger, 115
Mercury, 122
Mercury House, 8
Midland Bank, 135
MIL Research Group, 117, 144
Milano & Grey, 101
Millar, Victor, 115, 116–17, 120, 126, 154, 168
Miller Brewing, 68
Millward, Colin, 4, 152
Mitchell, Stu, 21–2
Monitor, 119
Montmarin, Hubert de, 99
Morris, Philip, Miller Brewing, 68
MRB Group, 118, 119, 128
MSL, 116
Muirhead, Bill, 61, 62, 89, 91
Murdoch, Rupert, 52
Murphy, Brian, 28
Murray Parry, 17
MVL, 101

National Coal Board, 134
National Society for the Prevention of Cruelty to Children, 59, 132

Needham Harper, 75, 81
Needham Harper Worldwide, 72–3
Newlands, David, 65, 167–8
News International, 52
Newspaper Publishers Association, 13
NFO Research, 118, 119
Nichols, John, 73, 74
Nicholson, Keith, 21
Nielsen, A.C., 118, 119
Nissan, 105, 111
NMC, 154
Notley Advertising, 16, 64
NPD Group, 119

Oakley Young & Associates, 143
OASIS, 116
ODG, 101
O'Donnell, Joe, 104, 144, 167
Office of Fair Trading, 13
Ogilvy, David, 3, 10, 70, 146–7, 148
Ogilvy, Francis, 147
Ogilvy & Mather, 3, 10, 24, 28, 61, 62, 63, 95, 98, 100, 127, 134, 147
Ogilvy & Mather PR, 102, 123
Ogilvy Group, 73, 75, 118, 122
O'Kennedy-Brindley, 37, 102
O'Leary, Tom, 19
Olivetti, 80
Omnicom, 72, 75, 77, 81, 82, 95, 99
Opta Dragon, 36–7
Osband, Gillian, 153
Oxo, 146

Palmer, Brian, 42, 43, 44
Pampers, 86
Panasonic, 139
'Panorama', 35
Paragon Communications, 124
Parker, Michael, 61, 62
Parker Pens, 134
Pascoe, Alan, & Associates, 138
Patrick, Margaret, 151–2
Patterson, George, 103
Pearce, John, 4, 38, 132

Peat Marwick, 115
Perring, David, 56, 168
Perriss, John, 61
Persil, 146
Peters, Michael, 130
Pilkington Glass, 59
Pirella Gottsche, 101
Pollitt, Stanley, 129, 146
Powell, Chris, 131
Presto, 109
Price Waterhouse, 115
Prichard Wood, 129
Procter & Gamble, 18, 24, 25, 39, 40,
    54, 59, 66, 78–9, 86, 92, 93–4, 152
Proudfoot, Alexander, 115
Publicis Intermarco-Farner, 98
Publinter Ayer, 101
Publis, 100
Puttnam, David, 151

Quadrant, 37
Quaker Oats, 79
Qualcast, 138
Quant, Mary, 11

Rabl, Preston, 142, 143
Racal, 122
RCP Saatchi & Saatchi Compton, 102
Reece, Gordon, 32
Reeves, Rosser, 70–1, 87
Reeves, Trevor, 21
Références, 100
Regis McKenna, 123
Reliance, 48
Renault, 101, 111
Research International, 118, 122, 128
Rhys-Jones, Griff, 142
Riches, George, 43
Ridley, Richard, 161
Rimmer, Ron, 2, 21
RJA, 46, 102
RJR Nabisco, 77, 78, 79, 81
Robertshaw, Stephen, 21
Rock, Bob, 167

Rock, Milton, 49, 65, 115
Roe, Graeme, 52, 53
Roe, Downton, 53
Roe, Humphreys, 28, 52–3
Roff, Harry, 49
Rogale, Michel, 99
Rogers & Cowan, 123, 125
Rork, Andy, 51, 91
Rose, Stephen, 104
Rosenshine, Allen, 72
Rosenwald, Peter, 121–2
Rothermere, 58
Rowland, Herbert, 54, 122–4
Rowland Company, 54, 122, 125
Rowland International, 123
Rowntree, 18, 39, 80
Royal Automobile Club, 122
RSCG, 100, 101
RSVP Direct, 101
Rubins, Jack, 51, 67, 88, 107–9, 112–
    13
Ruder Finn & Rotman, 123
Rumrill-Hoyt, 41, 94, 97
Rutherford, Andrew, 129, 136

Saab, 111
Saatchi, Charles, 4, 148–54, *et passim*
Saatchi, David, 149
Saatchi, Doris, 149
Saatchi, Maurice, 4, 7, 153–4, *et passim*
Saatchi, Phil, 149
Saatchi & Saatchi Advertising
    Worldwide, 96
Saatchi & Saatchi Communications, 65,
    88, 114, 158
Saatchi & Saatchi Company, 47–8
Saatchi & Saatchi Compton, 21–2, 28,
    76–7, 96
Saatchi & Saatchi Compton Amsterdam,
    102
Saatchi & Saatchi Compton Australia,
    103
Saatchi & Saatchi Compton Frankfurt,
    80

Saatchi & Saatchi Compton London, 22, 42
Saatchi & Saatchi Compton New York, 80
Saatchi & Saatchi Compton Worldwide, 41, 57
Saatchi & Saatchi Consulting, 65, 88, 114, 158
Saatchi & Saatchi Direct, 121
Saatchi & Saatchi DFS Compton, 96, 105
Saatchi & Saatchi Garland-Compton, 22, 24–5, 41
Saatchi & Saatchi International, 51
Saatchi & Saatchi MLV, 101
Saatchi Damour, 16, 37
Saatchi Dawes, 16
Sainsbury, 52, 58, 141
Salem, 79
Sales Promotion Agency, 48, 122
Salvation Army, 42
SAMI/Burke, 119
Sampson Tyrell, 143
Samuel Montagu, 144
Saunders, 138
Saunders, Ernest, 60, 135
Sawdon & Bess, 104
Schnabel, Julian, 149
Scholz & Friends, 80, 98, 99
Schweppes, 39
Scott, Peter, 139
Seiko, 84
Seymour, Geoff, 60, 150
Shandwick Group, 124, 125
Sharkey, John, 34, 91
Sharps Advertising, 51, 107, 109
Sheth, Jagdish, 88
Shulman, Robert, 54, 120
Sidjakov Berman Gomez & Partners, 143
Siebert/Head, 138
Siegel & Gale, 54
Silk Cut, 59, 89
Simonds-Gooding, Anthony, 66, 74, 82, 96, 97, 108, 113, 121, 132, 154, 160, 168

Sinclair, Jeremy, 6, 12, 15, 21, 25, 57, 61, 89, 168
Skelly, Florence, 48, 54
Smash, 130
Smith, George J., 16
Smith, Maureen, 55, 134
Smith, Paul, 136
Smith, Rick, 122
Sorrell, Martin, 21, 37, 56, 57, 65, 82, 142–4, 154–5, 161, 163–4
Souhami, Mark, 107
Spielvogel, Carl, 67–8, 104
Spratling, John, 61, 62
SSC & B: Lintas, 46, 98, 101
Stark, Jeff, 47, 61, 91, 150
Stayfree Silhouette, 79
Steinberg, Saul, 48
Stella Artois, 136
Stewart-Hunter, David, 103
Streets Financial Strategy, 124
Sudler & Hennessey, 81
Sullivan Stauffer Colwell & Bayles, 46
Susnjara, Gary, 67, 96
Synergie Kenyon & Eckhardt, 100

Tatham-Laird & Kudner, 69
TBWA, 100, 101
Team/BBDO, 98
Tebbitt, Norman, vii, 34, 62
Tesco, 51, 52
Testa, Armando, 101
Thatcher, Margaret, 29, 30, 34
Thomas, Tim, 53
Thompson, J. Walter, 2, 14, 23, 24, 2 60, 62, 81, 95, 98, 100, 101, 104 110, 135, 145–6
Tilby, Alan, 12
Toshiba, 142
Touche Ross, 65, 115
Towers Perrin Foster & Crosby, 1
Toyota, 80, 111
Treasure, John, 61, 62–3, 15c
Trott, Dave, 142
Tylenol, 92–3

Index

Unilever, 46, 118, 122
United Biscuits, 24, 39, 80
Univas, 130
Upson, Stuart, 66, 96
US Steel, 50

Valin Pollen, 124, 125, 144
VAP, 143
Vickery, William, 67
Video Research, 118
Volkswagen, 2, 87
Volvo, 141

Walker Group/CNI, 143
Walker Research, 119
Warhol, Andy, 149
Warman, Roy, 21, 57, 61, 63, 89, 110, 168
Warner-Lambert, 79, 81, 145
Wasey Campbell-Ewald, 133
Wax, Ed, 90, 93, 96
WCRS, 136-9
WCRS Matthews Marcantonio, 139
Webster, John, 130, 131
Weiner, John, 77
Weisman, George, 68
Wells Rich Greene, 40, 93
Wertheim & Company, 155
Westat, 119
Whitbread, 66, 132
White, Arthur, 48

White Horse, 42
Wight, Ian, 136
Wight, Robin, 137
Wight Collins, 138-9
Wight Collins Rutherford Scott, 12, 129
Wight Company, 136
Wilkins Ayer, 98
Wilson, Harold, 29
Wilson, J. Tylee, 77
Wire & Plastics Products, 142
Wong Lam, 50
Woods, Andrew, 167-8
Woollams, Chris, 112
Woolworths, 106-7, 112, 135
WPP, 142-3, 145, 161
Wrangler, 99
Wunderman, 121, 122
Wyatt, 115
Wynne-Williams, Jack, 17

Yankovich, Daniel, 48
Yankelovich Clancy Shulman, 54, 65, 114, 119-20
Yankelovich Skelly & White, 48, 54, 116
Young & Rubicam, 24, 34, 38, 42, 63, 73, 76, 81, 94-5, 98, 99, 100, 101, 102, 144-6
Young, Arthur, 115

Zuckert, Donald, 73, 74, 104

Ivan Fallon and James Srodes
Takeovers £4.99
The truth behind the headlines

The penetrating analysis of the hottest subject in business today

Takeovers is an investigation of the high-risk, high-gain games that have rocked The City and Wall Street to their foundations.

Ivan Fallon and James Srodes go behind the scenes to reveal the truth as never before: the untold story of the colourful Harrods takeover; the struggle over Westland that split the government; the bitter recriminations of the Guinness affair.

Takeovers is packed with detail and information. It explains the jargon, identifies the 'spear carriers' — law firms, PR men and those who actually wage the takeover trench warfare, and investigates the people involved: Tiny Rowland, Rupert Murdoch, Ivan Boesky and many more.

Written with specialist knowledge and with information from unique sources, *Takeovers* is the compelling insider's book, and a timely, informative investigation of the hottest subject in business today.

Nancy Goldstone
Trading Up £4.99
One woman's story of survival in the Wall Street jungle

With only six weeks' experience in options trading, Nancy Goldstone was catapulted into a key role in a crazy world of colossal financial risks and astronomical earnings.

As head of department in a powerful Wall Street bank, she had to overcome deep-set prejudices in a male-dominated business – against a backdrop of mounting responsibility, where a second's hesitation could result in the loss of millions.

As she reveals, 'The only difference between the trading room of a major commercial bank and a Las Vegas gambling casino is that in Las Vegas, you can't lose more than you bet.'

When she took on the job, Nancy Goldstone freely admits she didn't know a Deutsch mark from a bench mark: three months later, she was the bank's youngest vice-president.

'A first-person account of a young woman's antic two year trip in one of Wall Street's faster lanes that is as notable for its unsparing self-appraisal as for its sardonic good humour' KIRKUS REVIEWS

'No doubt about it. Nancy Goldstone has written a very funny book' *NEW YORK TIMES* BOOK REVIEW

Forte £3.95
The autobiography of Charles Forte

'One of the most lively business biographies ever . . . it brilliantly depicts the character, the limitations and triumphs of the man'
MANAGEMENT TODAY

'It is a thrilling story . . . a story of triumph written by a man who does not flinch from examining the causes of failure as well as those of success. If anyone wants to know how to win they should read this book' LORD THORNEYCROFT

It took Charles Forte a little over thirty years to progress from owning a milk bar in Regent Street to heading one of the world's greatest hotel and catering complexes. Today he is one of Britain's most successful and respected businessmen, a man with a wonderfully encouraging story to tell.

Starting with his early life in Italy and Scotland, Lord Forte chronicles his rise to fame and fortune frankly and engagingly: the expansion of the milk bar business in London and Brighton; his love-at-first-sight marriage and wartime internment; the purchases, takeovers, sales and leasebacks that went into the consolidation of the business.

His spectacular ventures are well known to the world. Now, for the first time, he reveals the inside story of many of them, including the dramatic boardroom struggles that went on after the merger with Trust Houses, the bitter fight to stave off the takeover bid by Allied Breweries, and the cointinuing struggle to purchase outright ownership of the Savoy Group.

Peppered throughout with lively anecdotes, not only about business life, but about many of the fascinating figures whom he has encountered during his career, Lord Forte's autobiography proves that the story of building a business can not only be a dramatic one, but also inspiring, and even romantic.

All Pan books are available at your local bookshop or newsagent, or can be ordered direct from the publisher. Indicate the number of copies required and fill in the form below.

Send to: **CS Department, Pan Books Ltd., P.O. Box 40, Basingstoke, Hants. RG21 2YT.**

or phone: 0256 469551 (Ansaphone), quoting title, author and Credit Card number.

Please enclose a remittance* to the value of the cover price plus: 60p for the first book plus 30p per copy for each additional book ordered to a maximum charge of £2.40 to cover postage and packing.

*Payment may be made in sterling by UK personal cheque, postal order, sterling draft or international money order, made payable to Pan Books Ltd.

Alternatively by Barclaycard/Access:

Card No. ⬚⬚⬚⬚⬚⬚⬚⬚⬚⬚⬚⬚⬚⬚⬚⬚⬚⬚⬚

Signature:

Applicable only in the UK and Republic of Ireland.

While every effort is made to keep prices low, it is sometimes necessary to increase prices at short notice. Pan Books reserve the right to show on covers and charge new retail prices which may differ from those advertised in the text or elsewhere.

NAME AND ADDRESS IN BLOCK LETTERS PLEASE:

....

Name ————————————————————————

Address ———————————————————————

————————————————————————

————————————————————————

————————————————————————

3/87